GESTAPO HUNTER

GESTAPO HUNTER

The Remarkable Wartime Career of
Mosquito Navigator and Leader
TED SISMORE
DSO DFC** AFC

Sean Feast

SEAN FEAST

GRUB STREET • LONDON

Published by
Grub Street
4 Rainham Close
London SW11 6SS

Copyright © Grub Street 2024
Copyright text © Sean Feast 2024

A CIP record for this title is available from the British Library

ISBN-13: 978-1-911714-11-8

All rights reserved. No part of this publication may be reproduced, stored in a retrieval system, or transmitted in any form or by any means electronic, mechanical, photocopying, recording or otherwise, without the prior permission of the copyright owner.

Design by Myriam Bell Design, UK
Printed and bound by Finidr, Czechia

CONTENTS

ACKNOWLEDGEMENTS	6
CHAPTER ONE – FINDING HIS WINGS	8
CHAPTER TWO – ISLAND INTERLUDE	35
CHAPTER THREE – MOSQUITOES!	47
CHAPTER FOUR – RADIO DAYS	63
CHAPTER FIVE – OPTICAL ILLUSIONS	76
CHAPTER SIX – A CHANGE IN DIRECTION	85
CHAPTER SEVEN – PRISON BREAK	98
CHAPTER EIGHT – PREPARING FOR D-DAY	107
CHAPTER NINE – GESTAPO HUNTING	115
CHAPTER TEN – BREAKING RECORDS	137
CHAPTER ELEVEN – BACK TO BOMBERS	164
CHAPTER TWELVE – COMMERCIAL ENTERPRISE	179
SOURCES	192
ENDNOTES	196
INDEX	205

ACKNOWLEDGEMENTS

THE PRINCIPAL BUILDING BLOCKS OF this book stem from the excellent work of Colin Higgs and Bruce Vigar in recording two days of interviews with Ted in January and April 2010. Throughout the book this is the source of Ted's words unless otherwise noted in the endnotes. It was on Colin's suggestion that I looked deeper into Ted's story and knew that while much was known of his time on Mosquitoes, his flying career prior to that was little more than a footnote and his post-war career similarly summarised in a few lines in an obituary. Hopefully between us we have given the reader a wider appreciation of Ted's life, character and achievements.

To that end, Ted's son Martin has been incredibly helpful throughout, and his scrapbook of memories (diligently kept by Martin's wife Katherine) a veritable feast of information and insight – including Ted's written recollections of particular events – which have added to the book significantly. I am also grateful to Ted's daughter, Fiona Rogers, for providing her parent's wedding date! For general background on RAF service life, I'd like to thank once again my friend Group Captain Min Larkin CBE for putting me straight on a few things, and for Ted's post-war career at Marconi Radar Systems Limited I must thank Ian Gillis and his small army of enthusiastic and incredibly supportive 'MOGS' – most notably David Emery – who helped add to my knowledge of Skywave and Surface Wave and Ted's role in UKADGE. Having represented various GEC Marconi businesses myself on the agency side in the 1990s, it was a fascinating step back in time. My thanks also go to fellow author Steve Bond for answering my questions so adroitly on the Javelin, and Nick Dexter, a most excellent researcher at The National Archives who stepped up in my hour of need when a broken leg threatened to derail my ability to meet a pressing deadline.

My personal thanks go to John Davies and his first-class team at Grub Street in this, our eighth sortie together. John is still the finest luncheon companion any person could wish for and his support of my projects a constant wonder. We are both in a race to retirement which neither of us seems particularly keen to win. To my very best friends at work, Iona Yadallee and Imogen K. Hart, who have now tolerated my nonsense for 22 and 11 years respectively, I am once again in your debt. Work would be a far less fun place without you. And last but never least, my thanks and love to the genius that is my wife Elaine and our two boys Matt and James for giving me the space, time, and a second study to pursue my little hobby. I'm not done yet.

CHAPTER ONE
FINDING HIS WINGS

Edward Barnes Sismore – Ted to his friends and later 'Daisy' for his fresh-faced appearance – had always wanted to fly. Aircraft held a fascination for him from a very early age and he was an avid reader of aeroplane books, a sponge for tales of derring-do of the fighter pilots and other intrepid aviators from the First World War.

Born into a middle-class family in Kettering, Northamptonshire on June 23, 1921 to Claude and Doris Sismore, Ted's father worked for Timpsons, which was then a well-established retail boot and shoe business and one of the town's major employers.

Both father and son shared a passion for aircraft, Claude taking Ted to Wellingborough to see a barnstorming display by Alan Cobham's Flying Circus. The thrill of not only watching Cobham, a true aviation pioneer, and his merry band of similarly enthusiastic pilots throwing their flimsy biplanes all over the sky, but also giving young Ted his first experience of flying, cemented his interest. They also travelled down together to the south coast to watch the British and Italian flyers fight it out for the Schneider Trophy, more accurately the Coupe d'Aviation Maritime Jacques Schneider, awarded to the country (and the pilot) with the fastest seaplane flying around a fixed course. Such was the importance of the trophy to national prestige that the fascist dictator, Benito Mussolini, had instructed his aircraft industry to win the title 'at all costs'. Among Britain's winning designers was no less a man than Reginald Mitchell, who later went on to design the Spitfire, arguably the greatest fighter aircraft ever built, for Supermarine.

Ted was what might be considered a lucky child, having had two early scrapes with death. When only six months old, and in a pram parked outside his grandfather's pub by the side of the river, his grandfather tripped, grabbing at the pram as he fell and in doing so catapulting Ted into the water. A cousin immediately jumped in to save him. When he was 12, he fell into the water again, this time from a tree. Again, he was fortunate to escape soggy but unscathed. On a third occasion, when representing his town in a water polo match against a local police team in the river in Northampton, his head was forced under by an opposition player and he almost drowned. So exhausted was he at the end of the match that he couldn't make his way out of the water and had to be dragged out by a passer-by walking his dog.

At home, he enjoyed a happy family life. His mother was an excellent cook who ensured that Ted and his younger sister Eileen – who worshipped her older brother – were always well fed and looked after, creating superb dishes from the vegetables grown in their own kitchen garden. Ted was a bright boy who studied hard during his four years at Kettering Central School and was particularly drawn to mathematics and the understanding of how things worked. As well as aeroplanes, he was interested in anything fast, including motorbikes and speedway, and was as happy tinkering with an engine as he was splashing around in a pool. Don Sinclair, a contemporary who went on to fly Lysanders, always believed his friend was destined for high office[1].

On leaving school, Ted had little clear direction in terms of a future career. In the immediate term, he took a job at the local council as a clerk (his occupation on official records is sometimes noted as a tailor's cutter but that is thought to have been an error, mistaking his father's occupation for his own). With the war clouds gathering once more, it soon became clear that Ted would have to choose which of the armed forces to join. His father had been in the trenches in the First World War and the experience had changed him. A lance corporal in the Northamptonshire Regiment, he'd once seen a man shot dead while next to him in a marching line. Ted knew the story and the thought of fighting another war in the mud held little appeal. Neither did the navy. Since he had always wanted to fly, the RAF was the obvious choice:

> "I was 16 and we all knew that war was coming, perhaps even more so, I think, than people older than us. It was all we talked about at school. I was determined to join the Royal Air Force Volunteer Reserve [RAFVR] as soon as I was old enough and could persuade my father to sign the necessary papers."[2]

The RAFVR was created in August 1936 to give young men like Ted, between the ages of 18 and 25, a chance to become aircrew, either as a pilot or one of the other 'trades' – an observer or wireless operator/air gunner – while still in full-time employment. Although the RAF had an 'active' reserve, in the shape of the Royal Auxiliary Air Force, it recognised it needed a further pool of voluntary talent which it could call upon in the event of a war. In many regards it was similar to the Territorial Army and organised on a regional basis, with a ground training centre within a town or city and flying training conducted from a nearby aerodrome. These were often civilian flying schools, contracted to provide elementary instruction to volunteer personnel.[3]

Ted joined the RAFVR at the first opportunity, applying on his 18th birthday and being 'attested' (i.e. effectively 'sworn in') on August 1, 1939. Having received a telegram informing him that his training would commence on Saturday, September 2, it didn't work out quite as planned:

> "It was the Friday before the war broke out, and I was in the garden putting a hood on my motorcycle headlamp. I walked into the house and the radio was playing away by itself and the voice said: 'all RAF Volunteer Reservists to report immediately'. I rang up and asked whether this applied to me to which the man asked: 'have you been attested?' When I replied, 'yes', he said that it therefore did indeed apply to me and that I was to report for duty straight away."

Catching a bus to the reporting centre, Ted marched up to the desk and gave his name. He was then asked for his number:

"I told him I didn't have one and was handed a slip of paper with a number on it and told never to forget it (which of course I never did!). He then told me to come back the next morning, but since I had caught the last bus, and couldn't get home again, I camped out in the anteroom with one or two others, spending my first night in the RAF attempting to sleep in an uncomfortable armchair."

Ted's training followed the typical pattern of all fledgling aircrew in those days, each man distinguished by a white band in his forage cap. First stop was the seaside resort of Hastings, on the south coast, and eight weeks at an Initial Training Wing (ITW). Here he learned the rudiments of service life, how to wear a uniform properly, to march and salute. He also learned the importance of health and hygiene, of sport and exercise. In the classroom he was tested on his knowledge of mathematics, and acquired new skills in navigation, armaments, signals and aircraft recognition.

His initial ambition was to become a pilot, and he started with a few hours of dual instruction in a Miles Magister at Elementary Flying Training School (EFTS). More typically, perhaps, fledgling pilots began their ab initio training on the de Havilland DH82, the ubiquitous Tiger Moth. But whereas the Tiger Moth was a biplane, the Miles Magister was a monoplane, built to satisfy a need to better align the learning experience to the monoplanes they would later fly on operations. Of an all-wooden construction, the 'Maggie' – as she was affectionately known – became the first monoplane trainer to be used by the RAF on its introduction in September 1937. It was much faster than the Tiger Moth yet offered a modest landing speed of just 42mph. It was also fully certified for aerobatics and introduced pilots at an early stage to what was, for those days, the novelty of trailing edge split flaps.[4]

Sadly, Ted never got to experience any aerobatics; he barely got off the ground. Instructors gave their pupils around a dozen or so hours to learn the basics, after which they were expected to fly their first solo. Anything beyond 14 hours without going solo and they were likely to be 'scrubbed' – their flying training at an end. While Ted's instructor believed he might make it eventually, he had simply run out of patience – and hours. The trouble he had wasn't flying but landing:

"I tended to look at the ground too closely instead of keeping an eye on the horizon. The instructor said to me one day that I might make it, but needed extra tuition, and he just didn't have the time. There were also hundreds and hundreds of pilots being trained – there was always someone ready to take your place – whereas there was a very real shortage of observers."

Although bitterly disappointed at falling at the first hurdle, Ted vowed there and then that one day he would become a pilot. But for now, he immediately threw himself into his studies, first at Prestwick in the south-west of Scotland for basic navigation training with No. 1 Air Observers Navigation (1AONS) School and thence onwards to No. 9 Bombing and Gunnery School at Penrhos in Wales. Observers, at this stage in the war, were the original multi-taskers. They took on the role of principal navigator but were also expected to drop the bombs and work the guns if and when required.

The quality of air navigation at the start of the war left much to be desired. Pilots had been previously responsible for navigation and were reluctant to cede control to the observer. The observer, meanwhile, could only be trained on the techniques and technology then available, which were little short of woeful. Apart from map reading, the only aids to establishing an aircraft's position were W/T bearings taken from a loop aerial and Astro. Either of these would yield a single position line but it required at least two of these to construct a fix, and since the accuracy of neither line could be guaranteed, even a fix was of limited value.[5]

Astro navigation was especially difficult. The clue is in the title and relied upon the observer being able to see an identifiable star in the night sky. It also required the pilot to fly straight and level for the observer to obtain an accurate star shoot, something difficult enough in peacetime training over friendly shores, but rather more dangerous and unlikely over enemy territory. In a report in the midway point of the war, the average error of an astro fix by a Main Force navigator was more than 20 miles; it might be a useful tool to get you home but was wholly unsuitable as a means of accurately navigating your way to a target. The upshot was that very few observers were really capable of navigating an aeroplane with any confidence at night, in bad weather, or out of sight of land. This was to have a significant impact later on the targets chosen, the results obtained, and the losses incurred. One of the few who did excel at astro navigation was Ted. Partly it appealed to his intellectual nature; partly it may have had something to do with his love of Antoine de Saint-Exupéry, the pioneering aviator, poet and author, and whose book *Wind, Sand and Stars* was never far from his side.

John Mitchell, a distinguished navigator who flew Winston Churchill to many wartime conferences in Ascalon, the prime minister's personal aircraft, passed through 1AONS a few months before Ted. Their experiences would have been similar if not the same. They even trained in the same, antiquated aircraft, as John relates:

"The establishment of the AONS had been cleverly planned. They recruited a number of ex-master mariners from the world of the Merchant Navy, well-schooled in the art of dead reckoning, maps and charts, magnetism and compasses etc., albeit at a different speed. These men could, it was reasoned, provide the bulk of navigation experience at a cheap price. Just what value it might be to us, however, was more doubtful.

"For the purpose of air exercises, the school had acquired three second-hand Fokker FXXII and F36 airliners that had originally been built for KLM. They were great lumbering beasts powered by four Pratt & Whitney engines and could accommodate some 20 pupils and their instructors at any one time. The Fokkers were in turn supplemented by a handful of Avro Ansons (twin-engined training aircraft).

"We arrived at Prestwick station in the early hours of the morning and were soon marshalled outside the nearby Red Lion pub which became our town headquarters, or assembly point, for we were all billeted in the surrounding village and still wore our variety of civilian outfits. Our immediate mentors were two ex-army senior non-commissioned officers (SNCOs) dressed in snazzy warrant officer-style uniforms with the Scottish Aviation company's crest on their caps and buttons. They soon smartened us up and we were marched off to classes/duties in two platoons under the command of the two tallest students who had been 'promoted' to corporal.

"Classroom accommodation was good; textbooks, however, were few and far between, and indeed some among our number had even bought their own copies of *Martin's Air Navigation*, an accepted 'text' of the period written by an RAFO flight lieutenant of the same name. He turned out to be our instructor for met. Although the airfield was cold and under snow our billets were warm and my hostess gave us a big breakfast and high tea, as well as comfy beds – quite unlike my boarding school. It all seemed like great fun. There was no organised sport or PT, and with the exception of Morse code I found the syllabus relatively easy.

"I flew for the next six weeks on a series of map-reading and other navigational exercises. A brief record of each flight had to be recorded in ink in my observer's flying logbook that was to become my constant companion in the months and years ahead.

"My trips in the three Fokkers (along with G-AFZR were G-AFZP and G-AFXR) were interspersed with cross-countries in the station's Avro Ansons. With the completion of the first stage of my training I had recorded just short of 50 flying hours in total and had been rated 'above average' by the chief instructor."[6]

Ted too was rated 'above average' in the instructor's assessment of his newly acquired skills. Described as a 'very keen pupil', Leading Aircraftman (LAC) E. B. Sismore, as he had now become, qualified as an air observer and navigator on September 12, 1940, and as a bomb aimer and air gunner seven weeks later. He achieved high marks in all his exams, and was fortunate perhaps to survive his training, often in danger due to the over-exuberance of some of the school pilots. A large number were Polish, perhaps not yet trusted for an operational squadron but nonetheless a resource that could be put to good use. On one particular flight, Ted was in the rear, open cockpit of a Hawker Demon, a two-seater fighter derivative of the Hawker Hart light bomber and now employed on training duties. Ted was not properly strapped in but would have been had he known what his pilot intended. Without any warning, the Polish airman decided to fly inverted, and as he flicked the aircraft onto its back, Ted almost fell out and was left, quite literally, hanging on by his fingertips. More by luck than anything else, the pilot flicked the aircraft again, forcing Ted back into his seat, at which point he grabbed for his seat belt and strapped himself in tightly. Choice words were exchanged on the ground, although how much the Polish pilot actually understood is not known.

Now proudly sporting his observer's half wing brevet (known to all as 'the flying arsehole' because of its oval shape) above his left breast pocket, Ted proceeded to the final leg of his training at RAF Upwood, home to No. 17

Operational Training Unit (OTU). He was also promoted to sergeant, which was to be the minimum rank for new aircrew. Many seasoned non-commissioned officers with time served were understandably put out by those given three stripes within months rather than years of donning the blue serge uniform, but Ted experienced little in the way of hostility. Like others before and after him, he now felt a sense that his period of uncertain probation was over, and his real training was about to begin.

RAF Upwood had all the amenities a permanent station could afford, and after reporting to the guardroom, Ted was allocated his own room in which to unpack his kit. The privacy seemed to add dignity to his new situation, and he was excited about the prospect of being part of a crew. The purpose of an OTU was two-fold: firstly, to train aircrew on what life would be like on a front-line squadron; and secondly, to fly the aircraft they would crew on operations, to give them time on 'type' prior to being thrown into action. As such, it was not by chance that Ted found himself at a Blenheim OTU. When he was coming towards the end of his training, he'd been asked whether he wanted to fly light bombers, medium bombers or fly with Coastal Command. Ted wrote 'light bombers' because it seemed more interesting: "As it happens, I don't think it made the slightest difference as we all seemed to be posted to light-bomber squadrons. I went on to Blenheim training and crewed up with two Geordies."

'Crewing up', according to one contemporary, seemed a delightfully haphazard affair.[7] Personality and character compatibility appeared to be the most important issue for small groups of men who were to work, fly, fight – and possibly die – together, though the latter was furthest from their minds. Throughout the course, different crews were rostered to fly with one another, certainly in the first few weeks. In those weeks, and in the mess, assessments and friendships were made until one ventured whether another would like to take their life in their hands and fly together. It was no more or less complicated than that. Officialdom only intervened in cases when aircrew couldn't decide, and many successful combinations came about by sheer good luck.

Ted certainly got lucky with his crew. The two Geordies to whom he refers and with whom he struck up a close bond were Cyril Henry and William Pattinson. Cyril, his pilot, came from Tyne Dock in South Shields, a stone's throw from the shipyards at Jarrow, the glory days of which had ended with the Great Depression. Only a few short years before the war, around 200 'Jarrow Crusaders' had famously marched from north to south to confront the British government in London in a bid to shame them into doing something about the mass unemployment they faced resulting from the demise of the shipbuilding industry. Cyril was not yet 20, and like Ted wore the three stripes of a sergeant on his sleeve.

William Pattinson, the wireless operator/air gunner, was also a sergeant, and at 26 the 'old man' of the crew. He'd headed south from the pretty market town of Haltwhistle, on the banks of the River South Tyne which meets the River North Tyne near Hexham to form the main river on which so much of the local economy depended. He was soon to be married, having met and fallen in love with a pretty teenager from Durham. (Doreen Lewis was only 17 when they married).[8]

A lot of Ted's early instruction was on the ground in the classroom, repeating much of what he had learned before, while his pilot sought to master the controls of the 'new' aircraft. Until that point, dual instruction had been on Airspeed Oxfords at Flying Training School, a twin-engined workhorse used for all aspects of aircrew training. Now Cyril was converting to fly the Blenheim, a few hours of circuits and landings with an OTU staff pilot prior to the nervous excitement of going solo.

The Blenheim had come about as the result of a challenge by Lord Rothermere, the media magnate, for the British aviation industry to build the fastest commercial aeroplane in Europe. In doing so, Rothermere recognised how such an aircraft could also have military use. The Bristol Aeroplane Company took up the challenge with the Type 142 which flew for the first time in April 1935. Gratifying to Bristol, but perhaps of some concern to the RAF, was that the aircraft was faster than any British fighter then in service. Rothermere, who had stumped up half the cash to see the aircraft developed, was delighted, and ostentatiously presented 'Britain First' to the nation for formal evaluation as a potential bomber.

The Blenheim I entered service with 114 Squadron and proved immediately popular with its crews. It was fast, agile, easy to handle, had few vices, and its twin Bristol Mercury VIII air-cooled engines gave reliable and consistent performance, as well as a top speed in excess of 260mph. Even at cruising speed, for its time it could out-pace many of the world's fastest interceptors. As Tony Spooner, a contemporary pilot and navigator, wrote: 'Whatever may be said for or against the aircraft, all who flew it came to love its flying and handling qualities.'[9]

Within 18 months, production switched to the more advanced Blenheim IV, with more powerful engines (two Bristol Mercury XVs delivering an additional

80 horsepower). The aircraft was slightly faster, had a greater range (1,460 miles compared to 1,125 miles for the Mk I) and significantly greater endurance (8.65 hours compared to 5.65 hours). It was also better armed; the single Vickers 'K' in the dorsal turret was replaced by twin 0.303s and a further gun was added in a blister beneath the nose, and it could carry 320lbs of bombs externally, to add to the 1,000lbs of bombs within its bomb bay. Armour plating had also been added, and would be needed, many a pilot being grateful for its protective embrace. Of more significance, however, was the re-design of the nose. The Mk I was 'snub' nosed, pilot and observer sat side by side, giving Ted little room to work. The crew position left much to be desired, and some criticism had been voiced at squadron level.[10] The appropriately named 'long-nose' Mk IV addressed this concern and gave Ted and his fellow observers 'a proper station' to operate more effectively.[11]

As part of his new crew, Ted flew a series of training sorties of varying duration to practise bombing, gunnery and navigation, as well as flying in formation, a somewhat disconcerting experience but essential to the type of operations they would later be assigned. Given the time of year, several trips were cut short due to the weather. Air-to-air gunnery was particularly exciting, at least for the poor pilot obliged to tow the target drogue trailing off the back of a lumbering Miles Master. He felt he was being shot at not only by the air gunner in the dorsal turret, but also by the pilot using the Browning .303 mounted in the wing and Ted blasting away with the gun under the nose. It was not unheard of for the towing aircraft to be hit and returning gunners who recorded scores of less than one per cent of rounds fired were the rule, rather than the exception!

Although the Blenheim had been deployed primarily at low level in the initial stages of the war, and especially in France, they also had to learn the technique of high-level bombing at heights of around 10,000ft. To help him, Ted had a rather primitive course-setting bombsight. This had an ordinary magnetic compass as a base with two metal bars about a foot long sticking out ahead of it to which were attached 'drift' wires. Prior to approaching the target, Ted would set the aircraft's speed, height and the assumed drift. As the target came into view through the Perspex bomb-aiming panel, he gave Cyril changes in course direction so that it appeared to travel straight between the drift wires he could see. When the 'image' reached the ring sight, he pressed the button, releasing the bombs.

The equipment was not stabilized, which meant any sudden change in direction – from turbulence, flak, or pilot 'twitch' – rendered the set-up virtually useless. As one contemporary said: 'It seemed to me that it would be little short of a miracle if one could hit the right city, let alone a particular building within it!'[12]

Low-level bombing was more exciting, and more precise. For their practice runs they flew to a wrecked ship off the Norfolk coast, making their approach at wave-top height and then pulling up and away as they dropped their 6lb practice bombs. For these attacks responsibility fell to the pilot, who had a bomb-release button on his control column. 'Aiming' was purely a visual affair, one of personal judgement, intelligent guesswork and skill.

There were dangers in flying so low. More than one pilot misjudged their approach and hit the mast of the wreck they were trying to bomb. There were other dangers too, brought about by poor skill, poor judgement, or simply poor luck. On November 26, 1940, two Blenheims crashed in bad weather, all six men on board being killed. Earlier that month a pilot had survived, and saved his crew, after being stunned when a bird came through the windscreen and struck him squarely in the face. Bird strikes were to be a constant feature in Ted's service career, especially at low level. December proved a particularly deadly month. At least 12 men were killed and one injured in a series of accidents, one crew while practising flying in cloud, one flew into a hill, and a third hit high-tension cables. A further crew was lucky to get away without injury after their aircraft stalled shortly after take-off following a loss of power in at least one engine. Often that could prove fatal.

With the course completed, and Ted's logbook dutifully signed by the Officer Commanding 17 OTU, the crew awaited their posting. Some were being sent to 107 Squadron at Wattisham; others to 114 Squadron at Thornaby. Ted, Cyril and William were posted to Wattisham, a few miles north-west of Ipswich, which as well as hosting 107 was also home to 110 (Hyderabad) Squadron. The posting was effective March 2, 1941.

As a light-bomber unit, 110 (Hyderabad) Squadron could trace its history back to the winter of 1917 when it was formed at Rendcombe, a small airfield nestling in the peaceful beauty of the Cotswolds' countryside.

Any hopes of a quick posting to France, however, were dashed by lack of aircraft, and its flying crews spent the first eight months of the squadron's existence training on various types in Sedgeford, Norfolk, a stone's throw from the Royal Sandringham Estate, before at last receiving the first of their DH9s. The DH9 was the successor to the admirable DH4. Like the DH4, the DH9 was a single-engined bomber from the stable of the redoubtable Geoffrey de Havilland, the designer whose creations would later go on to play such a pivotal role in Ted's life, and indeed shared many parts including the wings and tail. The early variants, however, were disappointing and although used extensively, the aircraft gained a poor reputation. The air and ground crews of 110 Squadron embarked for the Western Front in September 1918 as part of the Independent Air Force and began a series of daylight raids on industrial targets in Germany, mainly in the Saar. It disbanded in August 1919, by which time it had been relegated, somewhat ignominiously and certainly ingloriously in some minds, to carrying mail.

With the heightening tensions in Europe in the 1930s, and the mad and somewhat late-in-the-day rush to re-arm, the squadron reformed in May 1937, resuming its initial purpose as a bombing squadron. Depending on their role (e.g. bomber, fighter, reconnaissance etc.), each squadron was placed into a 'Group', 110 Squadron being allocated to 2 Group in September 1939. Now equipped with the pacey and popular Bristol Blenheim, 110 Squadron gained the honour, along with 107 Squadron, of conducting the RAF's first bombing attack of the war when it struck enemy shipping in German waters. In April 1940 it moved from its base in Wattisham to Lossiemouth, on temporary detachment, to support British forces then fighting it out in Norway, principally in a reconnaissance role.

As the disquiet generated by the Phoney War was shattered with the invasion of the Low Countries in May 1940, 110 Squadron was immediately thrown into the battle, taking part in a series of attacks on enemy troop concentrations and communications, before switching its attentions to barges and shipping being assembled for Operation Sealion, the planned invasion of mainland Britain. With the defeat of the Luftwaffe and victory in the Battle of Britain for the famous 'few' of Fighter Command, the 'many' of Bomber Command stepped up their attacks on industrial targets and shipping, 110 Squadron playing its part and paying the price with heavy losses. The Blenheim, while popular to fly, was poorly armed and could now be easily caught by the new generation of fighters, the German Messerschmitt Bf 109s by day and Bf 110s by night; Germany's aircraft designers were more than a match for their British counterparts, and the early advantage of the Blenheim's speed had long-since been negated. The aircraft was also vulnerable to flak, especially at low level.

To this end, the planners struggled to find the right balance. When operating at height over land, the Blenheims could be easily intercepted, but at low level the light flak could be equally devastating. If the aircraft bunched together, for mutual protection, and put into practice the tight formation flying skills they had been taught at OTU, they made a splendid target the German gunners couldn't miss. Conversely, if they broke formation and gained height, they fell easy victim to the waiting fighters.[13]

In the crucial months of the Battle of Britain, Bomber Command lost a greater number of aircrew than Fighter Command. For every Blenheim shot down, three men were lost – some killed, others captured and taken prisoner, and some simply 'missing'. A Blenheim hit at low level gave the crew little if no chance to leave the aircraft, and if they did gain sufficient height to bale out, they did so over enemy territory.

As if losses from enemy action weren't enough to contend with, there were some who found the Blenheim 'hot' to fly. This, coupled with the inexperience of many of the crews, led to a high number of casualties. One source suggests that of 869 Blenheims delivered to squadrons over the course of a year, about 195 were written off in accidents. As another 395 were lost in action and others damaged, only 52 ever reached the stage where they could be struck off as being 'time expired'.[14] Lack of any meaningful landing aids meant few crews were prepared to fly in or above cloud. That meant low flying in bad weather, with all of the inherent problems that brought. And if the British weather wasn't bad enough, crews also had to contend with 'friendly' balloon barrages and trigger-happy Territorial Army gunners only too willing to mistake a Blenheim for a Junkers 88 and fire first and ask questions later.

Despite consistently losing crews to accidents and enemy action, morale remained steadfastly high, not surprising given the remarkable qualities of 110 Squadron's Commanding Officer (CO).[15] Philip Sutcliffe was above average in every sense: as a pilot; a squadron commander; and as a man.[16]

Not long after Ted's arrival, Sutcliffe led the squadron on a Main Force raid against Hamburg on the night of March 13/14, 1941, inflicting heavy damage on the Blohm & Voss shipyard and neighbouring facilities and causing significant loss of life. Ted's crew was stood down and did not take part. Although 'fully trained', they were still a 'sprog' crew in the eyes of the CO and there was still much to learn: "The squadron when I joined was on night operations but I'd never been in the air at night in any aeroplane so the first thing we had to do was a bit of night flying."

Ted had been at Wattisham only a few days when the squadron was obliged to move. Heavy rain had turned the grass field into a mud bath, and it was from Horsham St Faith (now Norwich Airport) that Ted began flying. He may have wondered why he bothered. On their very first night-training exercise, they landed heavily and broke the undercarriage. Neither the squadron commander, nor their flight commander, Squadron Leader Donovan 'Don' Gericke, was impressed. Then came their first radio-assisted 'blind' landing, known as a 'ZZ' landing (zero visibility/zero cloud base), at Mildenhall.

With a ZZ landing, the system depended on a ground controller positioned at the upwind end of the runway. He was equipped with RF Direction Finding (DF) to locate and 'guide' the aircraft over the field, having transmitted the QFE (the barometric pressure at airfield height) by Morse. The pilot would ensure a height of not less than 500ft, confirmed overhead by Morse by the operator on the ground below. The pilot would then perform a 180-degree turn plus 30 degrees and fly away from the active runway threshold using a stopwatch for a period of eight minutes before turning through 210 degrees and letting down gradually via a very shallow descent to final approach. Throughout the approach, the QDM (course to steer) was continually advised and revised if needed. Both pilot and operator had to have total trust in one another, but this was not often the case. The controller also had to physically 'see' the aircraft just before it touched down. If all was well to land, and the pilot had judged his approach accurately, the controller would send two dashes and two dots (dah-dah-dit-dit) twice, to symbolize 'ZZ' in Morse. If the controller judged the pilot needed to abort, he would send a dot and three dashes (dit-dah-dah-dah) twice – JJ.

On this particular occasion, William, the wireless operator/air gunner (WOp/Ag), made contact with the DF station and Cyril's earphones were soon filled with the familiar sounds of Morse. As each new bearing was relayed, Cyril altered course until he was sure he was over the field. Then he turned away and started his stopwatch. He then turned again and started his approach. The weather conditions were such that they could see nothing around them other than thick fog. Cyril stared fixedly at his instruments as the altimeter slowly wound down. Ted wasn't happy and addressed his pilot. He thought he was letting down too soon and so it proved: "The next thing I saw was a tree flashing past the wingtip and we hit the ground in the middle of a ploughed field."

Miraculously they didn't crash. Since the wheels were still retracted the belly of the Blenheim simply bounced off mother earth as the pilot slammed the throttles forwards and desperately yanked on the control column to make height. Much chastened by their experience, an uneasy silence pervaded the cockpit. Ted resisted saying 'I told you so'. The incident made for an interesting debriefing on their return to base.

On the morning of April 6, Ted breakfasted in the mess and reported to Don Gericke's office. His eyes were immediately drawn to the notice board where a single, type-written sheet was pinned comprising a series of names, crews and aircraft. Ted scanned quickly though the list of crews and was excited to find his name on this, a so-called Battle Order, for the first time for a raid planned for that night. Five other crews were also listed to attack a range of different targets including the airfield at Eindhoven, the oil tanks at Rotterdam, and a variety of targets in Brussels, Antwerp, and Grimbergen.

The crew busied themselves throughout the morning with what was to become routine for all subsequent operations. Richard Passmore, a WOp/Ag who flew Blenheim operations in 1940/1941 recalls:

"The first job was as ever to get the kites into full operational order. Pilots checked the F700s (to confirm the airworthiness of the aircraft) and if fussy ran up the engines themselves and checked mag drop with fitters, mildly miffed, drooping over their left shoulders; observers fussed around with bombsites, pulled open bomb doors and looked thoughtfully at the loads; operators checked radios and intercom with the aid of anyone working in the front end at the time. One way or another we idled the time away until we should be summoned for briefing. War was mostly waiting for something to happen and then disliking intensely whatever did happen."[17]

As Ted remembers, night-time raids were still very much in fashion within 2 Group at that time:

"The targets came up all over the place. My first successful attack was to Emden with an alternative of Rotterdam. We had many coastal targets because in those days you relied on your eyesight to find the target and, of course, those that were near the coast were better than those inland, because there's more chance of finding them."

In the late afternoon, the Tannoy sounded for a briefing which left much to be desired. John Mitchell, who before joining the crew of Ascalon (named after the spear used by St George to slay the dragon) completed a tour in an Armstrong Whitworth twin-engined Whitley squadron in the winter of 1940/41, recalls one night being briefed to attack an oil refinery at Reisholz, an industrial quarter in the south-west of Düsseldorf:

"The detail of the raid came not in the briefing, but in a folder from the Air Ministry with precise aiming points and intelligence that if they could hit this particular generator at this particular point, they could put the whole of the Reisholz oil refinery out of action. It was nonsense, of course; we knew that even a near miss would unlikely damage a target to the point it was destroyed, and we also knew, from talking to other observers, that they'd been scattering their bombs all over the place. Finding the city of Düsseldorf itself would be a challenge, let alone a particular target.

"After the briefing, I spent the next hour working out my route and trying to find Reisholz on the map. There was no station navigation officer to consult; we were all left to our own devices. The intelligence officer had suggested steering clear of the Frisian Islands but that was it. There was no such thing as the comfort of being in a 'stream', with all aircraft concentrated over the target to a set time to overwhelm the defences. That was a tactic that Bomber Command had yet to discover. Not at all. We had been given a time on target (ToT), but how we got there was down to me. The wireless operator was given the frequencies of known night-fighter defences by the signals officer (at least they had one of those) but since he never passed them on to the observer, they were less than useless. It would just be a dozen or so squadron aircraft meandering their way across Europe in the dark, hoping we didn't bump into one another along the way or worse, bump into an enemy fighter. Fortunately, there weren't that many of them about."[18]

Ted's experience was much the same:

"It's very interesting thinking back to how we started operations in those days. The very first operation we did we were given our target, a time on target, (usually a gap of about 20 minutes) and told to go away and work it out. Which way will you go? What height will you fly at? As a new crew, we had total freedom to choose how to do it, so we talked to everyone in the crew room. They might say 'don't go there as there's always heavy flak' or 'don't go there as they have a bank of searchlights' and so on. We did three operations in three consecutive nights on this sort of basis before we were considered a fully operational experienced crew."

On his first trip, they returned with the bombs still onboard, the target covered in 10/10ths cloud. On their second, they nearly managed to shoot themselves down, a problem with a runaway gun tearing great lumps out of the tail, leaving the elevator and their nerves in tatters. Their third trip was the most successful, dropping bombs and incendiaries to start fires in Bremerhaven.

Good results were often reported, but whether any of the bombers actually achieved the damage they claimed is doubtful. Typically, of a dozen or so Blenheims from 110 that set out each night, one might return home early with engine trouble or some other equipment failure, seven might find the primary target and bomb, and the remaining crews would get lost and attack alternative installations, some of limited military value. Flak and searchlights were beginning to cause difficulties, and the first regular encounters with night fighters were being reported, giving the air gunners plenty of target practice.

On one of their early operations, a squadron colleague was attacked by a Messerschmitt Bf 110, a heavily armed twin-engined fighter nicknamed 'The destroyer'; it had been built, quite literally, with the intention of destroying other aircraft, though its poor performance in daylight had seen Bf 110 squadrons converted to a night-fighting role. Happily, it was the German who came off second best, the Blenheim gunner scoring hits and claiming the aircraft as probably destroyed. The destroyer did not match up to its billing.

In the second week of April, the squadron was instructed to stand down from night operations and received orders that they would be operating by day in the near future. This could only mean one thing: shipping. Ted remembers Don Gericke rushing into the crew room one morning and shouting 'Great news, fellas, we're going onto daylight shipping': "I think 'great news' was somewhat over-optimistic; shipping was a rather dangerous operation."

Ted wasn't wrong, and Don Gericke, a thoroughly likeable 27-year-old South African from Graaff-Reinet in the Eastern Cape, might not have been quite so excited had he known what was to follow. The shift to attack shipping was part of a much wider strategy then being enacted. The Admiralty was convinced that the war was now going to be won or lost at sea, and in the Atlantic in particular. They had Churchill's ear, and the prime minister was listening. On March 6, 1941, he issued a directive that the Battle of the Atlantic was to have full priority, and Bomber Command was to concentrate its efforts on naval targets. It was the reason that Bremerhaven, Kiel and Hamburg were proving so popular. The Battle of the Atlantic would also benefit from a sea blockade of Germany, and so orders were given to 'halt the movement of all coastal shipping between the Brittany peninsula and Germany'. The AOC 2 Group, Air Vice-Marshal Donald Stevenson, was given a clear instruction that any enemy ships found in these waters were to be sunk. For the crews given the task of carrying out these orders, with the exception of Don Gericke there was little enthusiasm. France had been bad; far worse was now to hand.[19]

Highly decorated in the first war as a reconnaissance pilot on the Western Front, Stevenson pursued his instructions with some zeal, so much so that he was given the name 'Butcher' and 'Red Steve'. His refusal to curtail operations as the weeks progressed and the losses became unsustainable, earned him the universal dislike within his group and within the RAF generally.

In the Operations Order (No. 20) issued to all 2 Group Stations, Stevenson explained why attacks on enemy shipping were essential. These ships were carrying iron ore (dug in 'neutral' Sweden) from ports in Norway to Hamburg; oil was being shipped from neutral Spain past Ushant to France and then Germany; and perhaps most important of all, convoys from Hamburg were carrying almost all of the stores and provisions needed to sustain the occupying forces in the Netherlands, Belgium and France. 'The convoys offered tempting targets, but the ships would have to be sunk close inshore in the face of murderous fire from accompanying flak ships, shore batteries and defending fighters.'[20]

At a practical level, areas of attack were divided into 'Beats', and small numbers (usually up to six if conditions allowed) would patrol each 'Beat' hoping to chance upon an enemy vessel and press home their attack from very low level before the enemy had time to respond. Speed was essential and flying undetected for as long as possible similarly critical. Fifty feet was the prescribed flying height – lower if at all possible – to avoid radar detection. It took skill, it took luck, and it took guts, and the Blenheim crews were equal to it. Ted recalls usually being sent out in pairs with orders to fly parallel to the German-Dutch-French coast to look for shipping.

Occasionally they had intelligence that certain convoys were present but mostly it was just a case of 'go and take a look':

> "It was sheer luck whether you actually ran into a convoy or whether you came back saying there's nothing there. The worst one we had was when we chanced upon what we thought was a convoy, and actually it was one main vessel accompanied by seven flak ships. It was not very nice. We bombed it but we missed."

Flak ships were German patrol boats that cruised around coastal areas, often as escorts to larger vessels, and designed purely as a floating anti-aircraft artillery platform. Known as *Vorpostenboote*, the ships typically carried one or two medium-calibre guns (88mm) to shoot at higher-level aircraft and multiple smaller-calibre, rapid-firing guns of between 20–40cm which were deadly at low level. Many an unsuspecting pilot would fall victim to a flak ship during the war, the presence of which was seldom known until it was too late.

Don Gericke failed to return from the squadron's first shipping daylight sortie (April 12, 1941). He'd flown in the morning and attacked a small merchant vessel in an area known as 'Beat B', one mile off West Kapelle. He'd pressed home his attack from 100ft. Returning to base, he phoned station headquarters to relay the information regarding the vessel, and then jumped into another Blenheim for another go at the ship. He didn't make it back. A sweep was made by the squadron later that day, hoping to find his ditched aircraft, but nothing was found, nor any indication of a missing Blenheim.[21]

Ted remembers how low they flew and the dangers they faced in trying to place their four, 250lb semi-armour piercing bombs on the target:

> "We'd keep under the radar and then, if you found a ship, you'd go in full throttle. Bombing was done visually by the pilot which made good sense because he could literally aim the aircraft at the ship and with a bit of luck you hit it. We didn't try and bomb the deck; if you did your bombs would simply bounce off. We put our bombs in the side of the ship where they could do the most damage."

Some of the pilots took low flying to the extreme:

"We had one chap who'd gone out one night and after he came back and landed, one of his engines was burning. On closer inspection we could see a piece of timber against the cylinders, smouldering. We asked him what happened, and he said that he'd gone in to attack a ship and as he bombed it, he pulled up over the mast and dropped down the other side but as he did so there was a second ship that he hadn't seen and couldn't avoid. The mast had struck his aircraft and hit the engine, somehow missing the propeller, and a piece had snapped off and finished up burning against the cylinders."

The pilot in question was lucky; others weren't quite so fortunate. When operating at night, the loss rate had been relatively modest. Now with orders to attack shipping, the 'chop' rate began to increase considerably. In the period that Ted operated with 110, between March and July 1941, 2 Group could claim to have attacked more than 400 enemy vessels but lost 68 aircraft in the process. Before August was out, another 77 Blenheims had also managed to launch attacks on enemy ships but of these, 23 never came back – a loss rate of 30 per cent. The AOC 'Butcher' Stevenson was earning his nickname.

Experience and practice could only take a crew so far; they also needed a large slice of luck, for the Blenheim's engines were vulnerable to cannon and machine-gun fire from flak or fighters. The squadron began losing some of its most experienced crews. George Lings, a flight lieutenant who'd won the DFC in May 1940, was shot down and killed north of Texel on 26 April. Nothing had been seen or heard from his aircraft after taking off to patrol Beat 9. (It was later believed he had been the victim of Leutnant Otto Vinzent. Lings was lost along with his observer, Flight Sergeant Charles Martin and WOp/Ag Sergeant Stephen Peplar. Martin was a Dubliner; Peplar had survived being shot down earlier in the war while flying with 114 Squadron.) Two weeks later, Edward Steel, a 24-year-old New Zealander, was also lost attacking a convoy which included three destroyers. A transmission was heard that they would try and make it back to base but then silence. The sodden and battered body of his wireless operator, Joseph Bramhall, was later washed up on the German coast. (Remarkably he was still alive but died soon after in hospital.) 'Teddy' Steel had flown more than a dozen low-level operations.

The attacks on enemy shipping involved several squadrons and continued throughout the summer and autumn of 1941 and into the early winter. Success was limited, much like in the early night raids. Sinkings were claimed but not substantiated. The official history records that the Admiralty estimated that between March and September 1941, 101 ships were sunk or seriously damaged and another 70 were hit. The German records for the same period suggest the loss of only 29 ships with a further 21 seriously damaged. As such it concludes that 'claims bore little relation to the true results obtained'.[22]

Ted flew at least ten anti-shipping strikes in April/May, punctuated with attacks on the Frisian Islands of Borkum and Norderney off the north-west German coast. They suffered a burst tyre on take-off on April 24, being forced to abandon their operation before it had begun. A few days later, Ted claimed to have sunk a 50-ton vessel, but such successes were few and far between. Then on May 8, pilot and crew used up one of their nine lives with a return to night-time operations and a 'special' briefing to intercept an enemy vessel heading down the Kiel Canal – a man-made body of water that linked the North Sea at Brunsbüttel to the Baltic Sea at Kiel-Holtenau.

In the extended nose of his Mk IV Blenheim Ted mapped the route to the target as they headed out over the coast. He had the same sense of healthy fear that he always had as they left the safety of the English shoreline – that one day he may never return. He tended not to dwell on the theoretical possibilities, neither did he start rating each operation in terms of its risks or dangers. It was a job; he had chosen to do it, and he wanted to do it to the best of his ability.

Ted checked and re-checked his position, and with his charts suggesting they were close to the mouth of the canal, the pilot gently lost height in the hope they might see something below. Steadily he eased the control column forward keeping a close eye on the altimeter on the control panel to his front, the needle slowly unwinding on the dial. In the dark, finding the entrance to the canal was proving something of a problem and the surface of the water was shrouded in mist. Still the pilot edged the aircraft down. Then there was an almighty crash as the pilot misjudged his height, hit the water – and bounced: "Suddenly my compartment and half the cockpit were flooded with water. It was quite a shock."

Fortunately, the Blenheim had hit the water at a comparatively shallow angle and rebounded into the air like a bizarre game of mechanical ducks and drakes. For a brief, heart-stopping moment, both engines spluttered and stopped before they fired again and power was restored, and a much-chastened pilot managed to regain control of his aircraft and breathe again. He immediately jettisoned the bombs:

"Not surprisingly, the aircraft started vibrating badly and so we immediately set a course to steer for home. Coming along the top of the Frisian Islands, the Germans started shooting at us, however, and the flak became a little distracting, so we decided we would cut out into the North Sea and risk having to ditch."

It was a dangerous strategy. Ditching in daylight was difficult enough at the best of times and in ideal conditions, but ditching in the dark was another matter, especially with a potentially badly damaged aircraft. It required huge skill from the pilot and an even larger slice of luck. The task would be doubly difficult if the aircraft did not respond precisely to the pilot's controls. One wrong move and a telegram would be on its way to their next of kin the following day, posting them as 'Missing', another crew having failed to return, their fate unknown:

"I remember saying that if we can reach 100 miles from the coast and then ditch, we'll be OK. We'll be picked up in the morning by the air-sea rescue. Looking back on it, I think I was being rather optimistic."

The next 90 minutes were an agony of watching and waiting: watching the instruments for any hint of trouble; waiting until they were far enough out to sea and close enough to the English coast to put Ted's plan into action if needed. Mile after mile over the cold, dark water, Ted tracked their progress. He could scarcely believe his luck. The aircraft, flight controls and engines were holding together, albeit somewhat precariously. So were the crew. Cyril was a picture of concentration, focused on keeping the Blenheim straight and level, and on course for home. The minutes passed slowly until at last, Ted estimated that they should soon be in sight of land. Then he could see it, a dark smudge ahead, somehow darker than the sea before it. A silent cheer went up in Ted's mind and a short prayer of thanks. They had made landfall against the odds, and now had less than 40 miles to run. The aircraft began to vibrate, somewhat alarmingly, as they skirted Ipswich and approached Wattisham. The strange noises it was making made the airfield controller switch off all the lights, assuming the unfamiliar sounds to be coming from an enemy aircraft. The wireless op had some difficulty in raising the station and persuading them that their intentions were friendly.

In the event they landed safely, and in the morning went out to dispersal to inspect the damage. The cause of the strange noises was now more than apparent. One propeller blade was missing altogether, and the other five were all bent. The tailwheel was absent, and there was damage to the leading edges of the mainplanes. The air scoops for the engines were also missing and the under-gun turret torn off.

The stout station commander at Wattisham, Oswald Gayford, stared incredulously at the state of the aircraft. As a long-distance record-breaking pilot before the war, Gayford knew better than most how lucky the pilot had been, and reflected on the good fortune of the crew with the Senior Air Staff Officer (SASO) of 2 Group, Hugh Pughe Lloyd. Both agreed that the pilot was no doubt sadder but wiser from the experience.[23]

It was, on reflection, incredible that they had made it back at all, but with new propellers, a new tailwheel and repairs made to the rest of the aircraft and a quick air test, all seemed fine. But it wasn't:

"I went back into the crew room and said 'What do you think fellas? Do you think we should swing the compass?'[24] I know the propellers are not magnetic, but we had a little discussion and eventually decided we should. As I was approaching the aircraft there was an airman standing by the wingtip staring at our Blenheim. Now airmen don't stand looking at aeroplanes, it's not in their nature, so I went across and said to him 'What's wrong?' 'Well,' he said 'I keep looking at that engine and it doesn't look quite right.' I looked at it and thought 'No it doesn't'. We decided to take the cowlings off, and in doing so found that the top two engine bearers were broken. Had we tried to take off again I think it would have been disaster."

Ted had, in the modern parlance of today, got away with one. The question was whether his luck would hold. For now, RAF commanders had a new role for 2 Group and its Blenheim crews to take the fight to the Germans: Operation Circus. While the Nazis were still intent on carrying out their blitz on London and other major cities, Hitler and his generals now had their eyes on a much bigger prize: Russia. Troops, armour and aircraft were being moved east in huge numbers in preparation for the invasion planned for the summer. This coincided, intentionally, in an increased effort by the RAF to tie the Luftwaffe down in France, and a new phase of Circus operations that had first been trialled in January.

The purpose of a Circus operation was laudable. Having beaten off the efforts of the Luftwaffe during the Battle of Britain, the desire now was to take the fight to the Germans. Small groups of light bombers, escorted by larger numbers of Spitfire and Hurricane fighters, would attack German airfields and similar tactical targets in daylight, with the principal purpose of enticing the Luftwaffe up to fight. It was a war of attrition they were prepared to take on. Ted recognised that the role was a dangerous one:

"If the Germans saw that there were only fighters overhead, they wouldn't bother to fly because they couldn't do them any harm. That's why we were there to drop a few bombs, irritate them, and make them come up and fight!"

Such operations were flawed from the start and the RAF found themselves experiencing the same issues that had confronted the Germans in the summer of 1940. Indeed, in many ways it was a complete role reversal. British fighters had only limited endurance and were effectively defensive rather than offensive machines. An RAF fighter pilot shot down over enemy territory was *hors de combat* for the rest of the war; a Luftwaffe pilot could bale out in the morning and be back in the air that afternoon. Of the bombers, a dozen Blenheims dropping a total of 12,000lbs or so of bombs at best could expect to do very little real damage, and yet they faced fierce defences, especially over the German airfields.

The first Circus was flown on January 10, 1941. A further eight operations were flown between then and the middle of May when 110 Squadron joined the fight for Circus 10, a planned attack on a power station and Benzol oil refinery at Gosnay, a former coal-mining town near Béthune in the Pas-de-Calais. Only six crews were available to join 82 and 101 Squadrons at Watton for the attack, the three squadrons setting out in the late afternoon to rendezvous with their escort over Kenley.

Ted was in good company: within the six crews from Wattisham were the new squadron commander, Theodore Hunt – known to his friends as 'Joe' – and one of the flight commanders, Douglas Seale. Hunt, who looked much older than his 26 years, had taken over command of the squadron only a few days earlier from Ian Spencer who had been standing in since the departure of Philip Sutcliffe.[25] Pilot

Officer Michael Potier and Sergeants Jackson and Cawthen made up the rest of the squadron contingent.

The attack was a complicated affair involving a close escort of fighters and multiple offensive and defensive tiers of fighter squadrons. They were there to guess and second guess the German intentions and an expected counterpunch by the enemy to attack the returning fighters over their airfields when at their most vulnerable. In the event, no such attack was forthcoming, but soon after dropping their bombs the Blenheims came under attack from an aggressive bunch of Bf 109s, determined to hack them from the sky. British fighters were hotly engaged, the air full of streaming tracer rounds and swirling aircraft as they danced their deadly dance. Then one of the Blenheims was being singled out and fired upon by a gaggle of five Bf 109s, all with bright yellow noses, all having a go. Two in particular seemed more determined than most. The contest was one-sided, and despite the heroic efforts of the gunner, the Blenheim was soon in a spin from which it couldn't recover, enveloped in thick, black smoke.

The official report states that direct hits were scored on both objectives causing clouds of steam and smoke confirmed in subsequent photo reconnaissance. Certainly the 110 Squadron records (and appendices) similarly detail direct hits and explosions seen in the target area. Thirteen squadrons of fighters were engaged in escorting the bombers and covering their withdrawal and six fighters and one bomber were lost. Five enemy fighters were claimed as shot down and eight others damaged.[26] One of those damaged had been hit by one of the Blenheim's air gunners who later reported he had seen tracer enter the fuselage prompting the pilot to break suddenly away, trailing white smoke.

The Blenheim seen to be going down in smoke was flown by 20-year-old Maurice Jackson, one of the sergeant pilots from 110 Squadron. Later reports suggested that the port engine was on fire, the turret was ablaze, and one wing seemed to be shattered. Jackson and his two crew members – 20-year-old Joseph Donovan and Tudor Beattie, 27 – were not seen to bale out; all were posted as missing believed killed.[27]

Weeks of bad weather prevented the pace of Circus operations from being maintained. On June 14, nine aircraft from 110 Squadron joined three Blenheims from 107 Squadron at Swanton Morley for an early morning attack on the aerodrome at St Omer-Fort Rouge. Short of the enemy coast, two aircraft were obliged to return home, both with engine trouble, leaving only ten. The attack took the Germans by surprise, and they were late in joining battle. Two Bf 109s were shot down as they desperately tried to gain sufficient height to intercept the attacking force. Soon, however, they were in amongst them, bullying their way through the close-escort fighters to get at the bombers. Two Blenheims were claimed as shot down, though in reality only one was missing. One other landed away at Manston, having effectively lost an engine. The missing pilot was Peter Windram, a 28-year-old flight lieutenant who'd been one of Ted's contemporaries at OTU. Early in his flying career he had walked away from a forced landing in a field, the result of engine failure. This time there would be no happy return.

Ted was back on anti-shipping duties for his next couple of trips, flying morning and afternoon, before being on the Battle Order for further Circus operations in the last ten days of June, including those of the 21st (to Desvres aerodrome) and the oil refinery at Choques (on the 23rd). Circus 17, the attack on Desvres on the afternoon of the 21st, was a lively affair, the squadron giving as good as they got. Concentrated fire from the 110 Blenheims flying in tight box formations accounted for one Bf 109F as being probably destroyed and although Ted's Blenheim was hit in the starboard wing tip by cannon fire, no aircraft were lost. Similarly, all aircraft returned safely to base following the attack on Choques in the company of aircraft from 21 and 105 Squadrons. Two friendly fighters, however, were seen to collide on their way out to the target.

Surviving daylight Circus operations relied upon teamwork. For the pilot and observer this was easy, since they were close physically, and always aware of one another's actions. The air gunner was slightly more remote, and communication essential, especially when under attack:

"In a Blenheim, the air gunner couldn't fire directly astern because of the tail fin and rudder which got in the way. That meant that when attacked from the rear, I had to operate the rearward-firing gun from the nose.

"On the Circus operation of June 21, the German fighters had broken through the escort and a Bf109 was trying to get onto our tail. The gunner shouted 'he's coming in dead astern. I can't fire. Get on the gun.' I dropped onto the gun which was directly under my seat and looked into the mirror sight where I could see the 109 coming into attack. I aimed at him and fired. Of course, as soon as I opened up, the guns and the mirror started to vibrate, and you couldn't see a thing. The 109 also fired at us and I could see and feel his bullets hit our wing. Luckily, he can't have been a very good shot and as he broke away, we could see a Hurricane dive after him and follow him down. I lost sight of both of them so don't know what happened after that."

On June 25, Ted flew his last operation from Wattisham, a successful daylight attack on the marshalling yards at Hazebrouck. In his logbook he had recorded 18 daylight and eight night-time sorties – 26 operations in all.

Then orders were received that the squadron was to proceed on detachment to Malta, and a new and even more deadly game of low-level bombing.

CHAPTER TWO
ISLAND INTERLUDE

THE PEOPLE OF MALTA WERE no strangers to conflict or oppression. Resting in the central channel that connects the eastern and western basins of the Mediterranean Sea, Malta has held both a fascination and strategic importance throughout history, from the early Phoenicians to the Romans and the Arabs, before being invaded towards the end of the 11th century to become part of the Kingdom of Sicily. Given to the Order of St John in 1530, the island was subjected to the Great Siege of 1565 when a comparatively small, yet heroic band of knights at the head of a citizen army fought off the Ottoman horde of Suleiman the Magnificent and a legend was created. The island did finally succumb to an invasion by the French in 1798, but the unwelcome visitors were soon after repelled, and the island became a British Protectorate, and an important naval base for Britain's Mediterranean Fleet.

The British steadily turned Malta into a naval and military fortress, as a critical base linking Gibraltar with Alexandria in Egypt. With war looming, a decision was taken to move the headquarters of the Mediterranean Fleet from Malta to the safety of Alexandria, stripping the island of its naval protection. The smart money at the time determined that while the island was important, it could not be defended, and a period of conflicting actions ensued where on the one hand, the

British increased the island's defences, while on the other effectively offered Malta on a plate to Mussolini, the Italian Fascist dictator, by way of appeasement. For reasons that are still confusing, not least Churchill's role in the whole affair, the islands were still in British hands come Italy's entry into the war.

The first Italian bombers of the Regia Aeronautica appeared over the islands on June 11, 1940, heralding the start of a battle that waged through to the winter of 1942, before the siege-raising ships fought through to the island and the battle was effectively won. In those two and a half years, however, the balance of power ebbed and flowed, very much mirroring the Axis armies' fortunes in the region. The need to reinforce the Italians in North Africa led to the creation of the famous Afrika Korps under Erwin Rommel. To keep Rommel's troops supplied, however, meant hazardous trips across the Med, exposing Axis shipping to attacks from aircraft and submarines then based on Malta. Mussolini's failure to deal with Malta when he had the chance came back to haunt him, and the German Luftwaffe then threw their weight behind a renewed aerial bombardment intended to bring the island to its knees.

The history of the air battle for Malta has been told elsewhere many times, but despite enormous pressure, the Maltese and their Allied defenders held out, often against overwhelming odds. Notwithstanding their bravery – later acknowledged with the unprecedented award of a collective George Cross – the decision by Hitler to invade the Soviet Union in June led to the withdrawal of large numbers of German aircraft to support Operation Barbarossa. This in turn gave the defenders a brief respite, just at the point that a new Air Officer Commanding (AOC) Malta arrived in the shape of Hugh Pughe Lloyd – the man who only a few weeks before had marvelled at Ted's lucky escape from Kiel.

The pugnacious Lloyd was the right man at the right time, a fighting man among fighting men. In the trenches in the First World War, he'd been wounded on no fewer than three occasions before joining the Royal Flying Corps.

Lloyd was alarmed by what he found but determined to shift defence into attack. The RAF had fewer than 60 aircraft of all types, including fighters, bombers and reconnaissance aircraft, along with a handful of Fairey Swordfish from the Fleet Air Arm. Spares and replacement parts were in short supply, as were the tools needed to fit them, and the ground crews obliged to cannibalise other aircraft to scrounge what they could. What they did have was concentrated at one air base, Kalafrana, and dangerously exposed. Air refuelling was still conducted by hand from individual drums. Having served both in Bomber Command and in 2 Group, Lloyd was appalled: 'All manner of things that we had taken for granted in Bomber Command were missing.'[28]

Lloyd's orders from the Chief of the Air Staff, Sir Charles Portal, were to go on the offensive. 'Your main task,' Portal noted, 'is to sink Axis shipping sailing between Europe and Africa.'[29] If the Maryland reconnaissance aircraft, flown by the likes of the most important pilot in the RAF, Adrian Warburton, could find the convoys, the Blenheims and Swordfish would attack them with bombs and torpedoes, day and night.[30] The targets Lloyd liked best of all were those convoys heading south, 'packed to the brim with the sinews of war for Africa'.[31] The sinking of any one of them 'meant the loss to the enemy in the desert of at least ten tanks, two or three batteries of artillery, one hundred motor vehicles, and perhaps sufficient spares for one hundred or more aeroplanes, food for a month for one hundred thousand men and the ammunition for one hundred guns for battle'. Tankers were, of course, a particular favourite, since the sinking of one tanker might mean hundreds of tanks, half trucks or other vehicles sitting idle, starved of fuel. The aircraft would not only seek out ships in open sea, in convoy; they would also hunt them down in their harbours, and places of safe refuge. This brought new dangers to the attacking crews.

The first detachment thrown into the assault was from 21 Squadron under the command of Leslie 'Attie' Atkinson. From that moment on, 2 Group adopted a policy of sending its squadrons out to the island on rotation, usually for a period of four or five weeks, or till the rate of attrition called for more timely intervention. Atkinson returned to Malta as the commanding officer of 82 Squadron, which in turn passed the baton to 'Joe' Hunt of 110 who had himself held a long association with the squadron he was replacing. Joe had been awarded the DFC in June 1940, when his 82 Squadron Blenheim had been badly shot up over enemy territory, shattering the cockpit and the nose. Somehow he and his observer, Harold 'Bish' Bishop, managed to bring the crippled bomber home, despite 'Bish' losing all of his maps and charts.[32]

Ted's journey out to Malta started with a few days' overseas posting leave followed by a series of endurance tests with new machines adapted for use in desert conditions in preparation for the long haul to Gibraltar, a staging post prior to their onward flight to the island. To make Gibraltar, even with overload fuel tanks stowed in the bomb bay, would take the aircraft to the extreme limit of its range, especially since it meant keeping well clear of the Iberian Peninsula where long-range Luftwaffe fighters were known to lurk. Rather than setting off from Wattisham, the 110 Squadron detachment of 17 aircraft planned to fly first to Portreath, in Cornwall, on June 29, where they would wait for favourable conditions and a following wind. The influx of crews was more than the station could accommodate, and some of the crews found themselves temporarily billeted in bell tents which a contemporary described as making them feel like 'a group of convicts waiting to be deported'.[33] For his part, Ted was obliged to divert to St Eval on his flight down, and it was from St Eval that he took off the following afternoon for the first leg to Gib.

In planning his route, the full dangers of what lay ahead finally dawned. The flight was to be made without any radio aids, and navigation would be wholly dependent on dead reckoning and the pilot flying an accurate course. The journey out was to be at a steady speed of 140mph and an economical height of 10,000ft. Ted estimated the flight time to be around seven hours and 30 minutes. That gave him a 30-minute margin should something go wrong. If he was intercepted by an enemy fighter at any stage, for example, and obliged to make a run for it, they would not have sufficient fuel to make the mighty Rock.

It was with this at the back of his mind that Ted's pilot manoeuvred their aircraft into its take-off position. In the cockpit, the skipper had completed his usual pre-flight checks as though this was any other flight: HTMPFFG – hydraulics, trimming tabs (neutral), mixture (normal), propeller pitch (fine), fuel (check contents and cocks), flaps (20 degrees down) and gills closed on the engine cowlings. With the brakes on he pulled back on the control column and opened the throttles to half power. The skipper then switched off the magnetos in turn and checked for any drop in engine speed. All seemed well, as did all critical temperature and pressure readings. The power of the engines made the aircraft vibrate gently and rock on its undercarriage. A green light from the Aldis lamp in the control caravan was their signal to go, and with a hiss of escaping air, the pilot released the brakes and the Blenheim rolled forward, gaining speed as he pushed the throttles further forward to attain plus five inches of boost. He dabbed the left rudder to account for the crosswind swing as the aircraft began eating up the runway, slowly at first and then steadily accelerating.

Ted held his breath as the aircraft slowly, painfully, gathered speed, using much more of the runway than usual before his pilot pushed gently on the control column to lift the tail and then eased back on the column to bring the Blenheim into the air. With the weight of additional fuel, ammunition, and kit, it was amazing that the aircraft wanted to take off at all. Then, just as Ted thought the Blenheim was firmly rooted to the ground, the aircraft bounced once and then took flight, as the runway gave out and the grass perimeter came into play. The skipper reached to the right for the undercarriage selector, protected under a hinged metal flap, and the wheels came up slowly and nestled into the bottom of the engine nacelles. The Blenheim struggled for the first few moments of flight and as they crossed the coast it took all of the pilot's skill to stop the aircraft from plunging into the uninvitingly grey sea below. He held the aircraft straight until the airspeed increased sufficiently to attempt a climb. Then, and only then, did they begin to relax.

The flight to Gibraltar was long and arduous in such a tightly packed aircraft, with little or no room to move around. But then Ted was too busy concentrating to worry much about his discomfort, and too alive to the possibility of being intercepted by a long-range German Focke-Wulf Fw 200 Condor or Junkers 88 against which they stood very little chance if found. [34]

Five hours into the flight passed without incident. The aircraft was now much lighter from the fuel consumed and the pilot risked taking her above the clouds where the flying was less demanding. Soon they began to consider their descent toward Gibraltar, and soon after that they would discover whether Ted's navigation and the course flown by his pilot was accurate. They need not have worried. Land was in sight, and after a few more minutes flying they could pick out a harbour and dockyards and the mountains of Spain further east. Then they saw the mighty Rock itself and the pilot started his approach, easing back on the throttles and trimming the nose as he lowered the flaps and undercarriage for landing. The runway was short, and as they touched down they noticed an odd assortment of Hurricanes, Swordfish and a Hudson to their right, and what they hoped would be some of their own squadron Blenheims.

It was a happy reunion and a great sense of relief to see so many friendly faces after such an epic journey. They slept late into the next morning and then passed a pleasant day in the narrow streets of Gibraltar, marvelling at the food and delicacies on offer that were now virtually unheard of and unseen in the austerity of their native land. The heat was also unfamiliar, and they were pleased to don their tropical uniforms for the first time, somewhat self-conscious of their obviously white legs.

Ted and his crew were not on Gibraltar for long before they were briefed for the second and final leg to Malta. The brief was far from reassuring. They would fly most of the seven-hour hop at low level, and radio silence was essential, so it meant Ted couldn't get any bearings. Malta was described somewhat romantically as being like a leaf floating on the sea, and more prosaically as a tiny piece of rock that was going to be difficult to find. The crews also had to fly between enemy territory on both sides, very much running the gauntlet of Italian, German and Vichy French fighters.

Their first attempt at reaching the island on July 2 was abandoned because of bad weather. They tried again the next day. Taking off in 'vics' of three, all seemed well until 15 minutes and 10,000ft into the flight when an engine on Ted's Blenheim cut unexpectedly. Back on the ground, it took several days to locate the problem, and it was only at the third attempt – and with the engine still suspect – that Ted finally made Malta on the afternoon of July 8. The engine that had caused them so many problems beforehand continued to misfire, and a seven-hour trip with a suspect engine that could fail at any time made for an uncomfortable journey. Despite the French occupying Algeria, their fighters remained on the ground, and Ted arrived on Malta without encountering another aircraft. Ironically, the delay in their arrival might well have saved their lives:

> "When we got to Malta, the squadron had already had quite severe losses in the first few days. I can't remember how many but there was quite a number, especially attacking Tripoli harbour which was a notorious hotspot. I was lucky in many ways."

Ted was indeed fortunate, and the squadron did experience quite terrible losses in those first few days operating from the island. On their first operation on July 7, the day before Ted arrived, they returned without success, having failed to locate the convoy they had been detailed to attack. Two days later, on July 9, however, seven of their aircraft took off from Luqa, one of the principal airfields on the island, to attack shipping in the port of Tripoli. With great gallantry, the crews pressed home their attack, several 250lb and 500lb bombs being seen to explode in the harbour, hitting one 12,000-ton ship, two 10,000-ton ships, and a 7,000-ton merchant vessel, as well as destroying warehousing and other facilities. Hits were also registered on the Mole. But the success came at a terrible cost: four of their number failed to return, and only much later was the story pieced together about how so many came to be lost.

As the Blenheims approached their target, Italian Fiat G.50 Freccia (Arrow) and Fiat CR.42 Falco (Falcon) fighters were scrambled to intercept. The aircraft may not have been the best, and were comparatively poorly armed, but they were fast and manoeuvrable, and more than a match for the heavily laden Blenheims.

Maresciallo Aldo Buvoli from 378ª Squadriglia in a single-seat G.50 spotted a formation of four Blenheims, followed at a distance by a fifth. The two other Blenheims were nowhere to be seen, perhaps having already turned for home. Early returns were not uncommon. Swooping in for the kill, Buvoli singled out the leader of the formation and promptly shot it down over the harbour. He then pursued a second Blenheim as it sought to make good its escape, taking snap shots at the fleeing aircraft as it jinked in front of him, finally bringing it down after a long chase. Two other Blenheims were claimed by Maresciallo Paolo Montanari (of 366ª Squadriglia) and Sergente Ottorino Ambrosi in their CR.42 biplanes.[35]

Of the Blenheims that were lost, Douglas Seale's aircraft was seen to force land in the sea but the 24-year-old and his two crew were all killed[36]; Walter Lowe and his crew were similarly missing.[37] Sergeant William Twist and his crew were shot down a few miles north of the harbour and managed to make it out of their aircraft to become prisoners of war, so too did two of the crew of the Blenheim flown by Michael Potier.[38] Twelve men missing from the mess after their first taste of Mediterranean action led to a sombre mood in the squadron, made more miserable by the news that in actual fact, not a single ship had been sunk or even badly damaged. They would have to do it all again.

They had considerably better luck on the 13th, when four of their number were despatched to attack a convoy spotted off the coast at Tripoli. The convoy was believed to include a tanker, the most desirable of targets, though the golden rule was to sink every ship as every one counted, however small.[39] They intercepted the convoy in good time and unobserved, coming in at mast-top height, their bombs hitting the tanker and setting her on fire. Huge columns of thick, oily black smoke were seen billowing from the vessel, confirming her heritage, and rising to a great height. Soon after, an enormous explosion heralded its final demise, the tanker being claimed as completely destroyed. A three-masted schooner, packed to the gunnels with ammunition was also hit, again leading to a spectacular explosion as the vessel broke apart and began to sink. A further smaller vessel (estimated at 500 tons) was also struck and left burning. This time they had photographs to prove their claims were valid, and it was a much happier squadron that sat down to its spartan dinner later that evening.

Attacks on shipping were far from one-sided affairs, but it was the most important show in town. As Hugh Lloyd wrote: 'The battle of supply was key to the contest: no supplies, no Rommel; no Rommel, no campaign in Africa. The victory in Africa hinged on sinking ships.' The Axis navies began significantly beefing up their defences. While they attempted to route their convoys in such a way as to make them difficult to find, especially at night, and steer as far away from Malta as was practically possible, they also increased their escort. Now a handful of ships might be escorted by half a dozen or so destroyers, each with significant firepower to defend against attacking aircraft. John Broadway, a 26-year-old sergeant observer, was killed on July 15, for example, when his aircraft was hit by anti-aircraft fire while mounting a convoy attack.[40]

While ships were critical, and so too the destruction of their not-so-safe havens, they were not the only targets. On July 14, two aircraft attacked an aerodrome on the Libyan coast, scoring direct hits on the HQ buildings and machine-gunning transport aircraft with some success. One Junkers 52 transporter was set on fire. A further three bombers were detailed to patrol the long, featureless road between Tripoli and Benghazi, where troop columns and motorised transport stuck out like ants crawling across white paper. They also ventured further afield to bomb the port and the barracks at Misrata. All of the aircraft returned safely to base.

On July 20 came another target. Six Blenheims set out to attack a power station in Tripoli, the squadron CO, 'Joe' Hunt, leading the first section of three aircraft, the second section under the command of Kenneth Forsythe, a Canadian flight commander.

At some point in the journey, the second formation lost contact with the first, and returned to base. Undeterred, the first formation continued onwards, ultimately making landfall 15 miles east of the capital. The CO turned across the harbour with his two wingmen following behind him in loose formation. Then he saw it, slightly to the west, and started his bombing run, his mind and his whole body focused on the task in hand. When he was certain he couldn't miss, he released the bombs, and his observer Ken Tucker had the satisfaction of seeing them straddle the power station and explode, large chunks of masonry flying into the air, causing a huge pall of smoke. Now came the second aircraft, but its bombs fell wide, and the third was frustratingly obliged to abandon its bombing run due to technical failure. The three aircraft formed up as best they could and steered away from the target area.

By now the Italians were alive to the threat, and their fighters were already making their way into the sky to intercept. Turning for home only a few minutes after bombing and nine miles off the coast, Fred Thripp, the WOp/AG in 'Joe' Hunt's aircraft shouted as an Italian Fiat CR.42 biplane fighter appeared on the scene and took a chance shot at the fleeing Blenheims at long range. Although appearing to aim at the second aircraft in the formation, he hit the squadron CO, dealing his aircraft a fatal blow. Unable to control his aircraft, the Blenheim fell out of the sky and crashed into the sea, leaving the crew with no chance of survival. The fighter continued to pursue a second aircraft, but wasn't fast enough, and the Blenheim escaped.

Hunt had been a popular CO, and the squadron was distressed to hear from the pilot of the second Blenheim that it was unlikely any of the crew could have made it out alive. Forsythe assumed temporary command until the arrival a few days later of John Cree, an acting wing commander, to lead the squadron.

Over the next 48 hours, on the 22nd and 23rd of the month, the squadron enjoyed notable success in what Hugh Lloyd describes as 'a bright period'. On July 22, four Blenheims led by Kenneth Forsythe attacked a convoy of five merchant vessels escorted by a similar number of destroyers who put up a fierce barrage of anti-aircraft fire. Ignoring the dangers around them, the four bombers pressed home their attack, scoring direct hits on one 7,000-ton vessel evidenced by a huge sheet of flame and a column of black and white smoke. A tanker. Another smaller vessel (6,000 tons) was also hit and damaged, more smoke being seen, while a 5,000-ton vessel exploded when two 250lb bombs found their mark. Later reconnaissance confirmed that only three merchant vessels were left in the convoy, a fourth having sunk and a destroyer observed rescuing survivors. A fifth ship had only the stern showing above the water. What was left of the convoy was later finished off by Swordfish torpedo bombers, attacking at night.

The next day, four squadron Blenheims led by Pilot Officer Noel Cathles set out to attack MVs in Trapani harbour at the north-west end of Sicily. One aircraft returned early with engine trouble, but the remaining bombers pressed on to the objective and appeared to take the enemy completely by surprise, scoring hits on a 7,000-ton ship resulting in sheets of flame and smoke. Two direct hits were also recorded on a 3,000-ton vessel, also setting it on fire. Both ships were claimed as destroyed. One aircraft failed to attack its primary target and so turned its attentions instead to an aerodrome on the coast which its pilot observed was 'lined with torpedo aircraft'. It attacked 'with excellent effect'. No flak or fighters were reported.

The bare facts of this particular raid don't quite tell the whole story, however. Twice on the way to the target, Cathles' aircraft was seen to hit the water but despite giving his observer a soaking, they carried on to execute a successful attack. The pilot pushed his luck too far however, his Blenheim failing to return. It was later reported that his aircraft had crashed into the ground. All three crew members were killed.

The death of three more of their friends was a crushing blow. Since arriving on the island only two weeks earlier, the squadron had lost 18 of their number killed, wounded or captured, including its squadron commander and two flight commanders. It was a dreadful attrition rate and unsustainable if the squadron was to continue to operate effectively. Aircraft were also unavoidably being written off having returned with mechanical failure or battle damage.

A further death was reported when it was announced on July 25 that 27-year-old observer William Sargent had died of his wounds following an attack on Tripoli harbour where his Blenheim had been damaged by an Italian fighter.[41] His pilot, Laurence Ware, had also been badly injured in the attack but managed to return to Malta, despite his wounds. Not surprisingly, though perhaps of little consolation, some of the squadron pilots were recognised for their efforts with gallantry awards, Laurence Ware receiving the DFM and Kenneth Forsythe the DFC.[42]

Ted's own contribution to their tour of duty was not all he hoped. He flew just the one operation on July 18, an inconclusive trip to Tripoli cut short by a faulty gun turret. A day or so later he was taken seriously ill:

"I had a violent fever one night and went in to see the doctor the next morning. I remember it still. He asked me whether I had brought any kit. I said 'no' so he told me to come back the next day and to bring some kit with me so he could put me in the local hospital and find out what was wrong. At that I collapsed and fell onto the floor. I came to and found myself in an ambulance heading towards Mtarfa (a small town in the north of the island)."

Ted was distressed that he wasn't allowed any food. By the second day he was ravenous:

> "I had to get out of there but remember the sister saying that I was in a Dysentery Ward and would be quarantined for five weeks. It was very depressing. The next day they gave me some Bovril, which was a start. Then they tried me on a little bread and butter. I was asked how I was feeling to which I replied 'hungry'. The sister then asked if I was fit to travel. She told me to go to the laundry, collect my clothes and come back, and they'd get me onto a flying boat heading for Gibraltar that night."

Ted swung his legs out of bed and promptly fell over. Weak and debilitated, he found he didn't have the strength to stand. Eventually he got up and worked his way down the ward to recover his clothes:

> "A couple of airmen came in from the ambulance and I told them my problem. I didn't want to make it obvious that I couldn't walk, and so they'd have to help me which they did. They were very good. They helped me into the ambulance and got some sort of food inside me to build my strength. That night I left the island for the Rock, so my experience of Malta was somewhat limited."

Ted was flown to Gibraltar in a mighty Sunderland, a four-engined flying boat modelled on the long-range passenger aircraft operated by British Overseas Airways Corporation (BOAC) to serve routes to the east before the war. He arrived on the 27th. From the Rock, Ted was put onto the troopship the *Louis Pasteur*, a former French luxury liner. It was a new ship which had fortunately been filled up in Canada, so the food was excellent in every sense. They spent three weeks tied up to the outer harbour in Gibraltar and were only allowed ashore once. This, Ted says, was a little frustrating, as was the nightly taunt from Lord 'Haw Haw' (the nickname given to the traitor William Joyce) that he knew the *Louis Pasteur* was in Gibraltar and the Germans were going to sink her as soon as she started to make a move. It was not a happy thought:

"I presume they tried but we had a most marvellous escort. We had the battleship *Renown* (part of Force H, based in Gibraltar and assigned principally to escort duties) and four destroyers, and because the troopship was quite fast, we came back at 25 knots. We sailed halfway across the Atlantic before we turned north and eventually came in and docked in the Clyde."

Ted's Malta interlude was over. The squadron had been decimated, and only a few familiar faces were there to greet him on his return to Wattisham. He officially ceased to be attached overseas on August 15, and on the 26th was posted as a crew to 13 Operational Training Unit in Bicester.

CHAPTER THREE
MOSQUITOES!

TED DID NOT TAKE WELL to being an instructor. Neither did he particularly see eye to eye with the OTU's commanding officer, Wallace 'Digger' Kyle. Kyle was a no-nonsense, 31-year-old Australian who'd been commissioned into the RAF from Cranwell at the end of 1929, and later qualified as a flying instructor. At the beginning of the war, he'd been in command of 139 Squadron, so knew all about flying Blenheims and the dangers involved. He was nobody's fool. Indeed, he had been awarded the DFC for leading a very low-level attack on the Ijmuiden Iron and Steel Works in April 1941 in which he had not only dodged flak but also the attention of a patrol of Bf 109s. He'd arrived at 13 OTU shortly after as chief instructor, assuming command of RAF Bicester the month before Ted's arrival.

Ted's run-in with Kyle occurred when he was told he was being sent from Bicester to complete a bombing instructor's course. Ted didn't want to go and made no secret of the fact. So when the officer commanding the course asked who didn't want to be there, he told him:

> "We made a deal. He said that if after the first half of the course I still felt the same way, that he would send me back. So halfway through the course I went back to him, and he said, 'a deal's a deal' and I returned to Bicester."

On his return he was immediately sent for by his boss. Kyle was not best pleased and felt Ted needed putting in his place:

"He said 'who do you think you are, and didn't I know there was a war on' etc. I wanted to point out that the whole purpose of avoiding training was that I wanted to get back to the war but thought better of it. I went to the satellite airfield for a while and flew in the Anson Flight there, until I learned that two navigators were being sought to go to 24 OTU at Honeybourne and I was selected."

Honeybourne, on the eastern fringes of the county of Worcestershire, officially opened for business on March 15, 1942, steadily building its strength under the watchful eye of the station commander Group Captain Eric Barnes, a qualified flying instructor who had spent much of his service career in charge of flying schools and other training units. He was joined in his endeavours by the chief flying instructor, Wing Commander Peter Heath.

Part of 7 Group Bomber Command, 24 OTU was established to train night-bomber crews using the workhorse Whitley. The Whitley had been one of the RAF's principal bombers at the start of the war, alongside the Vickers Wellington and Handley Page Hampden. It was a Whitley that became the first to visit Berlin while conducting a leaflet raid, and a Whitley that first attacked targets in Italy. Now, however, the Whitley was steadily being relegated to training duties or redeployed to bolster a depleted Coastal Command. The Mk V with which the OTU was equipped, was the main production variant. Rather than the Armstrong Siddeley Tiger engines that powered the earlier marks, the Mk V had Rolls-Royce Merlins with significantly more horsepower. Nominally it made it 30mph faster and increased its initial climb. Ted – who was one of more than 40 NCO instructors – remembers simply that they flew quite well but slowly. He also recalls that they were neither built for comfort nor for speed: the navigator was obliged to sit on a small, fold-out wooden seat.

Ted's time at Honeybourne coincided with seismic changes occurring in Bomber Command. Until that point, the command had struggled; poor leadership, as well as poor tactics, poor training and poor luck had led some to doubt whether its very existence was worth the investment in resource. Losses had been troublesome, and its strength constantly depleted to serve the needs of Coastal Command (fighting the Battle of the Atlantic) and to equip squadrons in the Middle East. The arrival in February 1942 of Sir Arthur Harris as its new commander-in-chief changed all that. He brought with him a fresh dynamism and the fire in his belly that his predecessor lacked. But as with Napoleon in his generals, he was also lucky; whereas the overall strength of Bomber Command had remained reasonably static throughout 1941, the types of aircraft under his command were improving. And that was fortunate. Twin engines were steadily being superseded by four, as the Short Stirling and Handley Page Halifax heavy bombers began to appear in numbers. The Avro Lancaster, without doubt the most famous RAF bomber of all, also began feeding through to the front-line squadrons, replacing the disappointing twin-engined Manchester (which had preceded it), and eventually the doughty Hampdens. So while Bomber Command's overall strength would not increase in 1942, its bomb-carrying capacity would.[43]

Harris was also lucky because his force now had 'Gee', a navigational aid that was little short of revolutionary for its day. A Gee 'Box' in the aircraft received pulse signals from three Gee stations, widely dispersed across England. The magic box computed the difference between receipt of these signals to give the navigator an instant 'fix'. The magic had its limitations; it was a 'line of sight' device and as such its accuracy was limited by an aircraft's height and range, but it was a step change from what had been available till then.

With his new aircraft and equipment, Harris also addressed tactics. The strategy – which included the now controversial 'area bombing' directive – had been set by others, namely the Air Ministry. Tactics, however, were left to the air chief marshal. Rather than penny-packet forces attacking multiple targets, or at least attempting to, Harris preferred to concentrate a larger number of bombers on a single objective. Early success was difficult to come by, and the future of Bomber Command still remained in doubt, an easy target for inter-service rivalries. But Harris had a bold stroke up his sleeve, an attack involving 1,000 bombers, which if successful would silence his critics once and for all and deliver a welcome shot in the arm for his beleaguered force. It might also cause some damage to German industry to boot.

In theory, Harris didn't have the resources to mount such an attack; he had only 400 or so aircraft and crews at his disposal. There were several hundred more aircraft, however, in various conversion units and OTUs which could be called upon at a push, and aircraft could also be borrowed from both Coastal and Flying Training Commands. Although Harris was eventually denied use of Coastal Command aircraft, he still managed to scrape together the magic number needed, and on the night of May 30/31, 1942, 1,047 aircraft set out to attack Cologne. A third of that number comprised aircraft from OTUs, some – but by no means all – flown by experienced captains and staff (i.e. instructors) with a tour of operations already under their belts. Other aircraft were flown by crews who had not yet crossed the enemy coast, even in training. Harris was taking a frightful gamble, but it paid off; a significant tonnage of bombs and incendiaries were dropped, and an impressive list of industry and property damaged or destroyed. On the debit side, 41 bombers were lost, less than half the 100 aircraft Churchill was prepared to lose.[44]

An innovation introduced into the planning was the bomber stream. Crews were given a common route to fly and a constant speed to and from the target. They were also given an allocated height and a time on target to minimise the risk of collisions. Concentrating an attack in this manner was designed to be safer for the crews taking part and deliver more meaningful results. It was also designed to swamp the enemy defences by a sheer weight of numbers and undermine the morale (a specific component of the Air Ministry's directive) of the average German citizen who had been promised foolishly by Hermann Göring, the Luftwaffe chief, that no enemy plane would ever fly over Reich territory.

Ted missed the first of the 1,000 bomber raids as the OTU was not then in a position to contribute. The Whitleys had been slow to arrive. He did, however, take part in a raid on the night of June 25/26, 1942, when the 'Thousand Force' was re-assembled to attack Bremen.

It had been a troublesome few weeks for the unit. It suffered, as every OTU suffered, from poor serviceability of its aircraft. Forced landings due to engine failures were commonplace, and on June 17 a fatal crash had occurred when a Whitley stalled just as it was coming into land, killing five of those on board.[45] For the night of June 25/26, the unit mustered some 16 aircraft: ten of those aircraft were to be flown by 'screened' instructors, and the balance by pupil crews who, while senior, were yet to fly on operations. Ted was part of a scratch crew of experienced men led by one of the staff pilots, Pilot Officer Lionel Mason, who had previously flown Halifaxes with 35 Squadron before being screened.[46]

While Ted had flown as part of Main Force before, he had never been involved in an attack of such scale. Even with 1,000 bombers in the sky all at the same time, however, for all the time in the air he still didn't see another aircraft: "It was almost as though you were all on your own," he said afterwards. Ted understood the necessity of arriving at their specified bombing time, but it was far from easy:

> "It was important to get us arriving at the target altogether. But this was difficult in a Whitley. If you were late, you didn't have much scope for a change of speed. And bombing at 10,000ft at 120mph when you know the rest of the Main Force is above you at 17,000ft is not a happy thought."

The slow speed and limited performance of the Whitley gave Ted a good insight into what his night-bombing colleagues in Bomber Command had been contending with while he had been flying low-level operations in daylight. Both had their challenges, and their risks. Out of an attacking force that night of 1,067 bombers of mixed type, performance and heritage, a record number were lost for the time. More than 50 failed to return, the heaviest casualties being born by the OTUs. It may have been for the reasons Ted infers; training units were usually equipped with ageing aircraft at the end of their useful working lives, and the round trip to Bremen was a good 200 miles further than the Cologne and Essen raids that had started the Thousand Plan. From Honeybourne, three aircraft were lost and 15 aircrew missing. This included one Whitley crewed by four instructors. Their aircraft had sent out a distress signal but was beyond the reach of air-sea rescue. Ted's aircraft returned with some of its incendiary load still on board having suffered what was known as a 'hang up'.[47]

A month after Bremen, the 1,000 directive was re-enacted for a planned return to Hamburg, though in the event the aircraft were recalled. For the night of July 31, the unit was instructed by Group to provide a dozen aircraft to attack Düsseldorf. On this occasion, Ted flew in a different aircraft with a different crew, captained by a former 58 Squadron Australian pilot, Cecil Parsons.[48]

The raid on Düsseldorf comprised a modest 630 aircraft, but casualties were again heavy. More than ten per cent of OTU aircraft taking part were lost. Of the 12 aircraft that set out from Honeybourne, three returned early (one with engine trouble, one through an inability to gain height, and the third because of a faulty rear turret) and two were missing, although one of the pilots survived to become a prisoner of war (only later to be shot) and three others evaded captivity eventually to make it home.

One of the biggest difficulties in night bombing for those that did get through the flak belts, searchlights and fighter defences was being able to see the target. That night, somebody dropped a stick of incendiaries on the bridge over the Rhine which lit up the target area, enabling Ted to see the aiming point very clearly:

"It was the easiest target I ever dealt with. Heading home, however, we were into a westerly wind, and we were only doing 120mph (a Whitley's cruising speed was 185mph). The wind was something like 50kts, so we agreed this wouldn't do and rather than flying above 10,000ft we came down to where the wind was less and flew home across Holland at something like 1,000ft, hoping to confuse the German defences."

It worked, the crew landing safely at 0539 hrs after a trip of nearly six hours.

The experience convinced Ted that he was not cut out for Main Force operations. It did not allow him the flexibility afforded by his earlier tour on Blenheims. He discussed it often with the B Flight commander, Lewis Hodges, with whom he flew on a number of occasions. Hodges was a remarkable man, who not only held the DFC & Bar but also a Military Cross for a successful escape from occupied France earlier in the war.

By now Ted was also aware of a new and more remarkable aircraft with which his name would become synonymous: the de Havilland Mosquito. He had first heard of this aircraft while on *Louis Pasteur* in Gibraltar harbour and the rumours that it was made of wood and stuck together with glue. While he'd flown wooden aircraft before, all modern aircraft were metal, and it was only when he got back to the UK that he discovered the rumours were true: "However, when I saw my first Mosquito and was so impressed with its speed and manoeuvrability I knew that's the aircraft I wanted to fly. That became my aim – to fly on a Mosquito squadron."

The history of the Mosquito has already been written, and its achievements are legendary. It ranks along with the Spitfire and the Lancaster as one of the most outstandingly successful products of the British aircraft industry in the Second World War.[49] The manufacturers, de Havilland, had first planned the Mosquito, powered by twin Merlin engines, as a private venture in the winter of 1938. Of all wooden construction, to address the increasing shortage of aluminium, the bomber would rely purely on its speed for safety, for it carried no defensive armament.

Officialdom showed little interest, but Sir Wilfred Freeman, Member for Research, Development and Production on the Air Council thought differently, as he often did,[50] and de Havilland was sanctioned to commence detail design work against a general requirement for a light bomber capable of carrying 1,000lbs of bombs a distance of 1,500 miles. Work began on December 29, 1939, and on March 1, 1940 an official order was placed for 50 bombers in accordance with specification B.1/40.

The first prototype was readied in 11 months and made its maiden flight in Hatfield on November 25, 1940, with Geoffrey de Havilland Jr at the controls. Official guests were astounded by the aircraft's performance as the all yellow-painted phenomenon proceeded to flash across the airfield with the agility of a fighter and performed upward rolls with one airscrew feathered. By February 1941, official trials were in hand, and within months, large-scale production had started. The Mk IV was the first light bomber version to enter service, capable of carrying twice the bombload that had originally been specified. It was powered by two, 1,250hp Merlin XXI engines. The first squadron (though not the first *unit*) to take delivery of the aircraft was 105 Squadron at Swanton Morley, and fast became the envy of all other squadrons in 2 Group. The first operational sortie was made on May 31, 1942, when four aircraft made a lightning daylight attack on Cologne, just hours after the first of the 1,000 bomber raids the previous night – an important footnote to the 1,000 Plan story that is often overlooked. Establishing its new base at Marham, 105 Squadron was soon after joined by 139 Squadron in October 1942, beginning a new era in low-level bombing attacks.

Ted's desire to fly the new aircraft was matched only by his keenness to fly with a particular pilot and fellow instructor at Honeybourne, Reg Reynolds. Reg looked a little older than his 23 years, and with his round, almost cherubic face, did not necessarily conform to the poster-boy image of a dashing RAF pilot. There was no doubting his flying ability, however. He was a very different character to Ted in some ways, but similar in others. Both were keen to fly Mosquitoes:

"Reg had flown two tours in Bomber Command and had apparently been told he could go wherever he chose if he went back for the third one. He chose to go to 105 with the Mosquito and I managed to suggest to him gently that maybe I should go with him. He agreed, thank goodness, and after a phone call to Personnel, and having satisfied themselves that I had already completed a tour with 2 Group, we went off together to Marham."

Reg was a pre-war regular whose journey to the front seat of the Mosquito began in August 1937 when he started his flying training in Perth. Quickly progressing from the Tiger Moth to the Hawker Hart and Audax at 9 Flying Training School (FTS), he soon after qualified and following a period at the School of Air Navigation he was posted to 144 Squadron at RAF Hemswell in Lincolnshire. The squadron was initially equipped with the Blenheim but soon after swapped its Blenheims for Handley Page Hampdens with which it went to war.

Throughout the winter of 1939/1940, Reg was mainly employed dropping leaflets and phosphorus discs, about the size of an aspirin, and North Sea sweeps in search of the German navy. Following the invasion of France, attention was focused on the bombing of the invasion barges in the Channel ports and the occasional attack on Germany itself. Mine laying in the Dortmund–Ems canal proved a popular choice with the planners – though not with the crews – as did the attacks on the synthetic oil plant at Leuna. Both of these latter targets required very low-level flying, requiring considerable skill and placing the crews in significant danger from light flak. Despite these dangers, Reg came through his first tour of operations by the autumn of 1940 unscathed and received the DFC into the bargain, having recorded 34 successful trips. The citation, strongly endorsed by Arthur Harris (at the time the AOC of 5 Group) specifically mentions Reg's 'resolution and determination' when carrying out raids 'from very low altitudes'. It was a skill that would be very much in demand with the Mosquito.

Posted to 207 Squadron in April 1941, Reg was one of the pilots responsible for introducing the ill-fated Avro Manchester into service, but soon after returned to flying Hampdens as a flight commander with 455 Squadron, the first Australian bomber squadron to be formed in Britain. With 455 RAAF, operating from Swinderby, he carried out two strikes against Berlin, as well as trips to Cologne, Kiel and Hamburg before the year was out.

Tour expired by the end of 1941, Reg spent almost a year in the OTU systems teaching novice crews about the realities of operational life (and also taking part in two of the showpiece 1,000-bomber raids) before at last agreeing to take Ted with him to Marham, where he was to assume a flight commander's role in the rank of squadron leader.

Ted and Reg were formally posted to Marham on November 6, 1942 and arrived in the morning to find a squadron much buoyed by its early success. They reported first to the station commander, none other than 'Digger' Kyle, with whom Ted had enjoyed a somewhat scratchy relationship at Bicester and who was now in charge at Marham. Happily for Ted, 'Digger' seemed more intent in venting his frustrations at Reg: "I remember him saying, 'Reynolds, I choose my crews and I didn't choose you, so you get one chance, and you get one chance only. Good day!'"

They received a warmer welcome from Hughie Edwards, the 28-year-old Australian wing commander, who'd been in command of the squadron since the summer. Edwards was a man who led from the front, and beneath the pilot's wings on his tunic he wore the ribbon of the Victoria Cross which he'd been awarded a year earlier for his part in an attack in daylight on the port of Bremen during which his aircraft was hit more than 20 times. Tall and good looking, he was an impressive character in every sense. So too were the flight commanders:

"Hughie Edwards was a well-known 2 Group character from the Blenheim days, and the two flight commanders at the time were George Parry and Roy Ralston. They were similarly experienced 2 Group pilots who both had experienced 2 Group navigators and so the basis of the squadron was very sound. Upon our arrival, Reg took over from George. The squadron was very well established, if a little short of aeroplanes."

Ted knew George Parry well from his own Blenheim days, as both had served with 110 Squadron earlier in the war when George had been his first flight commander. As a child, George had been inspired by the daring exploits of the First World War fighter pilots. As an adult, with his fine moustache and film-star looks, he was the epitome of a dashing RAF hero, and was both a distinguished and popular member of the squadron. He was also incredibly brave. Just a few weeks before Ted's arrival at Marham, George had led four aircraft to attack the headquarters of the German secret state police, the Gestapo (from the German *Geheime Staatspolizei*), in Oslo, causing significant damage. It was also one of the first raids to establish the Mosquito's credentials for destroying pinpoint targets, often in heavily built-up areas. George was vacating A Flight for Reg to take over.

Roy Ralston, in charge of B Flight, was less familiar but no less experienced. For Roy, the RAF was his life, and had been since he was a teenager. Although the same age as George, his dark features and angular nose made him look older. He'd joined at the age of 15 as an apprentice, one of the famous 'Trenchard Brats' at RAF Halton, and qualified as a metal rigger. He'd initially served as ground crew with 54 Squadron, helping to keep Bristol Bulldog biplane fighters in the air with their complicated struts and wires, and then won a coveted spot to train as a pilot. He gained his 'wings' in December 1937, and as a newly fledged sergeant pilot joined 108 Bomber Squadron at Bassingbourn. After the Munich Crisis, the squadron re-equipped with Blenheims, and on the outbreak of war he was posted to 107 Squadron at Wattisham, shortly after its CO was shot down. It was at Wattisham that Roy first became acquainted with Syd Clayton, his observer, and the beginning of a new legend was formed.

Roy and Syd took part in a very low-level attack on Heligoland on May 21, 1941 when at 50ft over the target, one of the leading Blenheims, piloted by Ken Wolstenholme (later a famous BBC commentator), suffered a direct hit in the nose, killing 'Polly' Wilson, his navigator outright. Ken managed to maintain control and spotted two other Blenheims making for home and so joined them. One of the pair almost immediately nose-dived into the sea and the second, with Roy at the controls, and himself slightly wounded with his instrument panel shot away, climbed to 1,500ft to send a plain language signal giving the ditched Blenheim's location. It was a considerable risk, for he left himself wide open to attack by any marauding German fighters. Happily his luck held and his bravery was rewarded with a Distinguished Flying Medal (DFM).[51]

Commissioned in the winter of 1941, and with a logbook filled with 50 operations, Roy spent some time on instructional duties before joining 105 Squadron in May 1942 to convert to the Mosquito. He led a series of attacks in the first few months of operations, and was steadily promoted, his efforts being recognised with a Distinguished Service Order (DSO) for his 'outstanding leadership and determination'. He took over B Flight on November 7 on promotion to squadron leader and celebrated by leading six Mosquitoes on an attack on German shipping in the Gironde Estuary.

Ted was delighted to be surrounded by men with such proven experience and eager to get into the fray. Reg had a number of duties to fulfil as flight commander, and immediately set about getting to know the men under his command, their individual strengths and their routines. Ted, who had been commissioned over the summer and now had the single thin stripe of a pilot officer on his battledress shoulder, assisted where he could. He was very much aware, however, that there were other navigators on the squadron and in his flight with comparable if not more experience than his own, and each had their own way of doing things:

> "I'm not sure what makes a good navigator. Clear thinking and attention to detail helped, but everyone had a slightly different way of doing things. Syd Clayton, for example, was a brilliant low-level navigator and worked in a completely different way to me. Some people had a flair for navigation and others found it almost impossible. I could never put my finger on why one man could do it and another could not. You couldn't generalise."

No operational flying was possible until Reg and Ted had converted to the Mosquito, and within short order of their arrival the two were attached to 1655 Mosquito Training Unit to begin their conversion. Mosquitoes were still in short supply, every aircraft being required for operations against the enemy which meant some of the initial familiarisation and navigation training was conducted on twin-engined Bisleys, a development of the Blenheim with which Ted was well acquainted. A contemporary, Edward Sniders, with whom Ted flew on a training exercise, recalls:

> "In the training unit we used Bisleys for pupil navigators. In them we flew distances, day after day in all weathers but bad fog, over great stretches of England, Wales and parts of the sea, mostly at two to five thousand feet and with plenty of low level in specified areas to accustom our pupils to map reading in what would soon be their frequent medium. Each of these flights was about half as long as the average operational sorties but were twice as frequent. Flying the Bisley was enjoyable work: beautiful green shores, mountains, moorlands, coastlines huge below, the endless change of the cloud scenery around us, the heady excitement of low flying which, outside of operations, was rarely allowed. But of course nothing could compare with flying the Mosquito on operations."[52]

Reg went first, not surprisingly as conversion was mainly for Reg's benefit and included the rudiments of taxiing, stalling, single-engine flying, and steep turns and circuits. He also learned how to land the aeroplane with a single engine feathered (turning the blades of the propeller to be parallel to the airflow to reduce drag following an engine failure in flight) and with/without flaps, and the procedure for overshooting the runway and action in the event of a fire. Little did he know how soon this knowledge and these skills would be put to the test.

After an hour and a half dual instruction with one of the more experienced squadron pilots, Reg went solo for half an hour of circuits and bumps. Ted flew in a Mosquito for the first time on November 8, 1942, with Terry Dodwell at the controls.[53] He then joined Reg flying Bisleys on November 15 before the pair of them were finally allowed to fly a Mosquito together on the 23rd.

The benefit to Ted was to familiarise himself with the wireless (he qualified as a wireless operator on November 30) and navigational aids, as well as the safety procedures, not least how to get out of a Mosquito in an emergency. While there was an escape hatch above their heads, they were advised never to use it while still in the air; it was not likely to end well. If they had to bale out, they should leave the aircraft the same way they came in, via the small hatch to Ted's right, pulling the emergency door release. If they could feather the starboard propeller beforehand, so much the better.

As a crew new to the Mosquito, Ted and Reg had much to learn, but learned it quickly, and within a few hours both were checked out by the OC 1655 MTU, Peter Channer.[54] Further training ensued with practice low-level bombing – again with flying split between the Mosquito and the Bisley – dropping dummy bombs on the Gooderstone range as well as conducting mock attacks on a water tower at Hunstanton. Ted remembers the excitement of flying the Mosquito for the first time: "She was very fast and manoeuvrable, and the first twin-engined aeroplane where you could fly on one engine with real confidence. It was a joy."

Notable in their training were two very distinct modes of attack now being perfected within 105 and 139 Squadrons: one was the familiar 'low-level' attack; the other was what was known as 'the shallow dive'. In a low-level attack, the aircraft would drop bombs at *c.*50ft with a time delay (abbreviated to 'TD' in operations record books) of 11 seconds, so as to give the bomber suitable time to have left the target before the bombs exploded. In a shallow dive, the Mosquitoes would climb to around 2,000ft and then peel off and dive onto the target dropping bombs that were fused for instantaneous explosion upon hitting the ground. With a low-level attack, only a small number of Mosquitoes could be brought to bear on any single target, such were the risks; shallow-dive attacks, however, allowed for a much larger number of Mosquitoes to be engaged. Both were to become familiar to Ted and Reg in the months to come. In the Blenheim Ted had not only been the navigator, but also the bomb aimer and an air gunner; in a Mosquito he was the navigator, bomb aimer and wireless operator:

> "On a low attack, Reg would drop the bombs; in a shallow dive or high-level attack, I would do it. You were close together in the cockpit of a Mosquito, and that made you close in your thinking. I think that's why Mosquito crews formed such a special bond; this closeness was important."

Such proximity was not to everyone's liking. While Ted felt at home in the cockpit of the Mosquito from the start, the love affair wasn't universal. Observers who had flown a full tour in heavy bombers found the cockpit claustrophobic. Charles Whitehead, who joined 139 Squadron in the summer of 1944 after tours with 44, 97 and 635 Squadrons (75 ops in 'heavies' – all equipped with the Lancaster) said that he 'hated' the Mosquito: "My partner and I were like two sardines in a tin so that if anything had happened, we had no chance of evicting!"[55]

Attacks at any level of 1,500ft or less were not simply being made to ensure accuracy. On the Channel Front, the RAF had been caught completely unawares by the Luftwaffe's introduction of a new, radial-engined fighter from Focke-Wulf Flugzeugbau AG. Imagined by the brilliant aircraft designer Kurt Tank, the fighter was the best they had, and for a time dominated the battles over Northern France. While the RAF eventually achieved parity, it was not until after a number of their best pilots had been lost, and the Fw 190 presented a formidable challenge to the unarmed Mosquitoes now seeking out targets over Western Europe. Without the means with which to fight back, the bomber version of the Mosquito relied on its speed for defence. At height, and in a straight dive, the German pilots had the advantage; lower down, the Mosquito was faster, and with those few precious additional miles per hour could steadily outrun its attacker, justifying its claim to be the fastest day bomber in the world.[56] Another advantage in flying low was that they would come upon flak posts in a flash, and more often than not catch the flak gunners unawares. Even if the Germans were waiting for them, by the time they had arrived they were gone, and the Germans had little time to bring their weapons to bear.

Returning from attachment, Ted was pleased to see the squadron had been busy. Other crews who had been waiting to fly the Mosquito now had their chance as new aircraft arrived to swell their numbers. The crew room that had often been full with bored and impatient aircrew was now empty, as men had found better ways of spending time rather than playing darts or cards.[57]

As the flight commander, it was down to Reg to determine who flew and when. Reg put himself and Ted on the Battle Order for an attack on the Gare Maritime marshalling yards at Ghent on December 14, 1942 which passed off without incident and with little to show for it. Their bombs failed to release on the first pass. With 'Digger' Kyle watching their every move, it was not the perfect start they were looking for:

> "We went in on a shallow dive, and whereas in a Blenheim you could put your head forward in the nose and actually see the bombs come out and falling, its wasn't the same in a Mosquito. Our bombs got stuck, so I instructed Reg to go down onto the deck, turn 180 degrees, and come back around again while I tried to find out what the problem was."

Reg made a circuit and in the meantime Ted discovered that the bomb-release plug had come loose. Having fixed it, Reg climbed, turned, and went in to make a second run. Whereas on the first run there had been no opposition, on the second attack the guns opened up:

> "The first thing Hughie Edwards said to us on our return is that no matter what happens, the first rule of low attack is that you go in once, and if you miss or there is a problem, you come home. You never go around again."

While their first 'test' was something of a failure the same could not be said, however, for an attack six days later in which the benefits of their new-found training bore fruit. The plan was to seek out and attack railway assets in north-west Germany, especially in the area of Oldenburg–Bremen. The weather was such that an early morning take-off was preferred, and Reg was detailed to lead not only six aircraft from 105 Squadron but also six from 139 (although in the event one failed to take off).

Ted and Reg were in good company. As they raced towards the target area, Reg spotted a gas installation on the port side, just the sort of thing they were looking for, and peeled off to attack. Ted lined up and dropped the four, 500lb general-purpose (GP) bombs right on target and as they climbed away, he took a quick look back over his shoulder to see a succession of explosions and the gasholders on fire. Zooming skywards, their aircraft was almost immediately hit, and a series of 40mm flak shells struck home on the port wing. Reg glanced at the temperature gauges and didn't like what he saw. The radiator for the port engine had clearly been hit for coolant was beginning to leak freely, the temperature was now through the roof and the cockpit began filling with smoke.

Clipping on their oxygen masks, Reg quickly throttled back and switched off the useless engine, feathering the propeller first by depressing the feathering button long enough to ensure that it stayed in by itself, and then releasing it so that it could spring out once the process was complete. With one engine down he re-trimmed the aircraft for single-engined flight, as he had been taught, keeping a close eye on the temperature on the remaining 'good' engine and opening the radiator flap to allow for the increase in power required. Satisfied that there was no terminal damage, he headed for home, struggling to keep the aircraft in the air due to the instability caused by the damaged radiator. The whole episode had lasted just a few seconds, but they were not out of the woods yet.

Ted worked out a course to steer for Marham, prepared to divert if the one remaining engine gave any cause for concern. In an act of solidarity and defiance, one of the other pilots in his Flight, Warrant Officer Arthur Noseda, drew up alongside and gave a cheerful wave. Ted waved back, and together the two Mosquitoes re-crossed the enemy coast at Wilhelmshaven Bay. Even if they did have to ditch now, Noseda would be able to transmit their position accurately and there was a good chance they would be rescued.

Predictably, the enemy coastal batteries opened up on them and were almost immediately joined by a German warship, the heavier calibre shells of which exploded beneath the aircraft sending huge plumes of salty spray into the air, drenching the plywood airframes. Even at a reduced flying speed of around 200mph, Reg was quickly through it and away, and eventually out of range.

Both pilot and navigator continued to keep an eye on the dials during the long flight home. Ted sent out an SOS on the wireless transmitter (W/T) just in case. The oil pressure on the good engine began to fall from 90 to 45psi, causing some anxious glances between pilot and navigator, but after an hour and 45 minutes the

English coast came into view and Reg steadily began to lose what little height they had remaining to make his approach.

Reg kept glancing at his airspeed indicator. A stall now would be fatal. He took the decision, therefore, not to lower the undercarriage, fearing that the increased drag might lead to loss of control. As such he was coming in for a landing at a much higher speed than he fancied. Knowing that he had but the one chance of making it down in one piece, Reg fully committed to the task and pulled off a textbook belly landing. Fire trucks and the blood wagon (ambulance) were quickly alongside. The escape hatch above the crew's heads had jammed, and it took a firefighter with an axe to chop them free.[58]

Ted had little time to dwell on it. What he remembers most about the operation was the trouble he was in for failing to cancel his SOS message once he crossed the English coast. Doubtless he had other things on his mind.

The attack had been only partially successful and cost the lives of one of the 139 Squadron crews. Squadron Leader Jack Houlston DFC, AFC and his observer, Warrant Officer James Armitage failed to return. Arthur Noseda returned safely to the grateful thanks of his flight commander but did not have long to live himself. A few weeks later he was shot down and killed whilst attacking railway yards at Rouen. It was a comparatively easy target to some of those he had faced in a near suicidal six weeks in Malta just a few months before. Such were the odds.

The new year promised happier tidings.

CHAPTER FOUR
RADIO DAYS

WHILE JOSEPH GOEBBELS DID NOT invent propaganda, he took it to a new art form. No opportunity was wasted, no anniversary forgotten. Like the anniversary to celebrate Hitler's appointment as chancellor of Germany on January 30, 1933. Ten years on, and Goebbels had two major events planned: Hermann Göring, chief of the Luftwaffe, was to address a mass rally at the Berlin air ministry in the morning, an occasion that would be broadcast live to the German people; and Goebbels himself would speak to the nation from the Berlin Schoneberg Sportpalast, later in the afternoon. His speech was also to be broadcast.

The timing was awkward. The once mighty German Wehrmacht had suffered a number of major reversals in fortune. The Allies were winning in North Africa, having captured Tripoli, and in Russia, the 6th Army of Friedrich Paulus was on the point of collapse, having been refused permission by the Führer to withdraw from Stalingrad.[59] The leaders of the three Allied superpowers, America, Russia and Great Britain had met at Casablanca, and agreed that nothing short of total, unconditional surrender by Hitler and his cronies would suffice. The German people, of course, knew little of the truth, save what their leaders told them. Only the troops returning from the front line on leave, and the mounting casualty lists printed in local newspapers and posted on *Rathaus* notice boards, suggested anything of the calamity that would soon overwhelm them.

For the aircrew at Marham, the first few weeks of the year had been busy. Reg and Ted had flown on the 3rd, a low-level attack on the engine sheds at Amiens, and ten days later on the 13th, another low-level sortie to Laon. Elsewhere, others had attacked Tergnier, Aulnoye and Hengelo, often returning with holes in the fuselage, wings or tailplane, or belly landing on one engine. One of their number, Leonard Skinner and his navigator Fred Saunders, went missing on a raid near Oldenburg, and were never seen or heard of again. A further crew, James Dawson and Ronald Cox, hit high tension cables over Denmark a few days later, and smashed into the ground. On the same trip, Richard Clare and Edward Doyle died after their aircraft hit a barrage balloon and crashed after its starboard engine failed.

In the context of what the station commander, 'Digger' Kyle, described as 'a very heavy week' both 105 and 139 Squadrons were stood down.[60] While Kyle conceded that his squadrons operated largely in heavily defended areas, their losses were generally relatively light. To lose three crews in almost as many days was unusual, and he felt that his men deserved a break.

Independent of the main bombing force, Kyle's squadrons had been given a general operational directive, but beyond that, the detailed planning, including the selection of specific targets and the timing of the raids, was left to the Australian and his two squadron commanders. It was a surprise, therefore, that on the Friday afternoon of the 29th, he received a phone call from the group captain operations at Bomber Command, Charles Elworthy, and told that he was to mount an attack on Berlin the following morning at 1100 hrs precisely. 'The timing would restrict our tactical freedom of action,' he later wrote, 'and meant we would be exposed to fighter attack both during penetration and, again, on withdrawal when the advantage of surprise was gone. I said we would be lucky to get away with it without severe casualties.'

Elworthy agreed with Kyle's assessment. He had commanded 82 Squadron earlier in the war and flown daylight operations in Blenheims, being awarded the DSO. 'He knew the operational form well enough,' Kyle added, 'and offered to represent this to the C-in-C.'

Not long after putting down the receiver, the black Bakelite phone rang again. He listened quietly but with mounting disbelief. Despite Kyle's understandable reluctance, he was being overruled. Worse, Harris wanted 'Digger's' men to go back and attack Berlin later that same afternoon! The conversation that followed, in typical Aussie style, was 'short and pithy', but there was nothing for it but to get the squadron commanders together as quickly as he could and work out a detailed operational plan. Peter Shand, the OC 139 Squadron, had gone on leave just a few days earlier and Squadron Leader Donald Darling had assumed temporary command in his absence. Darling had been a night-fighter pilot with 151 Squadron earlier in the war and was inclined to wear his best uniform with his top button undone, an affectation of the fighter community. It was odd now to be flying bombers, and stranger still to be flying unarmed. He listened as Kyle outlined the gist of the conversation with Elworthy. The only decision to be made now was who went in the morning, and who flew later in the day. 'Digger' tossed a coin; Reg and Ted would be up first.

Ted knew nothing of what lay in store until later when he was advised to get to bed and told he would be operating early the next day:

"We'd had a quiet day in the squadron and having been told that there were no operations scheduled for the following day we gathered in the mess after dinner to discuss our plans for the remainder of the evening. Before we reached a decision Reggie was called to the telephone and came back to say that new plans were developing, and we should after all remain on the station."

Ted was called at five in the morning and quickly washed, dressed, and made his way to the mess for breakfast. It was, he recalls, a horrible morning. There was a strong wind, low, oppressive clouds and the rain was lashing against the windowpanes. It was the kind of morning where aircrew joked that even the birds were walking. Ted had little appetite; he seldom did before an op. The same couldn't be said of Tony Wickham, sitting with his navigator Bill Makin. Tony, who had been briefly a farmer before the war, was positively ravenous and polished off six fried eggs washed down with three tins of orange juice, something of a station record.

Ted, Tony, Bill and two other aircrew, John 'Flash' Gordon and Ralph Hayes then clambered into the flight van that would take them to the briefing room with Reg at the wheel. Ted was already having his doubts: "I wondered what on earth was going on and where we were going because we tended to operate at dusk whenever possible. This was obviously going to be a daylight raid."

Reg remained unusually quiet, other than to say that rather than a low-level op, this time it would be 'different' and they would climb once they crossed the Elbe. Ted knew very well where the Elbe was, since it meandered its way across central Europe south of the German capital and was a useful navigation reference. But why would they be so close to the Elbe? As he sat in the van, he began to wonder: what did Reg mean by 'different'?

All became clear as they entered the ops room and took their seats at the trestle tables that had been arranged for the briefing. On the map on the wall was a familiar stretch of red tape. As his eyes followed the tape from its starting point at Marham, fixed on with a brass drawing pin, he noticed first that the route to target was comparatively straight, without the usual diversions to throw the German defenders off the scent. Then he noticed where the ribbon ended, and the second drawing pin was fixed. Berlin:

> "Everybody immediately thought and said the same thing: do we have enough fuel? We were told that somebody had done the calculations and there would be just enough. We were to go in low level, cross the Elbe south of Hamburg, then climb to 25,000ft."

The route chosen was indeed pretty well direct, and by flying at low level the three aircraft would be able to stay under radar cover as far as Hanover. Flying in daylight was dangerous, even on the deck, but Kyle and his planning staff reckoned they would have the sufficient element of surprise to catch the Germans unaware, and by attacking at 25,000ft, they could then use their height advantage to dive away at maximum speed and head for home before the Luftwaffe could react. 'Withdrawal was to head to Norway,' Digger recalls, 'without too much regard for Swedish airspace, and then directly back to base. This was about the limit of endurance for the Mk IV Mosquito in the low-high-low profile.'[61]

Ted was still sceptical. Endurance depended on a number of variables, not least 100 per cent accuracy of navigation, and the weather was not on their side. Although the Met men who predicted the weather expected few problems en route or at base, one glance skywards suggested otherwise. It was with some anxiety that the three crews made for their aircraft and headed off into the gloom, their take-off time being logged in chalk at Flying Control at 0849 hrs.

The two-hour, 500-mile flight out was long and uncomfortable, Ted and Reg exchanging only a few words and then only to give and acknowledge an alternation in course. Reg flew low and slow to conserve fuel. Flying low required intense concentration from pilot and navigator alike; flying over water could be mesmerising, and in low cloud and poor visibility it was easy to become quickly disorientated at a time when even the slightest misjudgement could be fatal. Ted had only the most primitive navigational aids to help him, plotting his course on a map balanced on his lap and taking into account forecasted winds and temperatures.

They crossed the coast two miles south of track at Eierland on the northern tip of Texel and three minutes later left the town of Sneek about a mile to port, low enough to see the Dutch flag flapping above the town hall.[62] Despite the rain, Ted had little trouble in picking out the various church spires that told him he was on track.

They crossed the Dutch–German border and immediately noticed the red and white striped sentry boxes that marked the frontier. The weather started to improve. The wind dropped and the clouds lifted. Navigation was easy. There was little movement on German roads, save for an incongruous red bus and a large number of rather more familiar cyclists. The three Mosquitoes roared over open fields as workers looked up in astonishment and terror. A ploughman was out in the field with his drays and fell flat on his face in the mud. Ted laughed. Another labourer was seen to pull his hat down tightly over his head, fall down onto his knees and start to pray. Lucky for him that his prayers were answered.

All went well until they reached the Elbe and began climbing through the thick cloud. Now they were only a few minutes flying time from the target, and very keen to upset the Reichsmarschall's big day. Their specific target was *Haus des Rundfunks,* the headquarters of the German state broadcasting company. Destroying the radio station would render Göring, quite literally, speechless, and ruin the day of thousands of loyal Nazis gathered around their wireless sets or out on the streets celebrating with their Swastika banners and flags flying:

> "We went through cloud at about 14,000ft and as we came out of the top, all we could see was solid cloud everywhere around us. I knew that our estimated time of arrival (ETA) was fast approaching but I still couldn't see anything."

Ted clambered through into the nose, a difficult enough feat at any time but particularly so with a full flying suit and gear. He still couldn't see anything. They had levelled off and were at their most vulnerable. A Mosquito could not outrun an Fw 190 at this height and they had to keep a sharp lookout for trouble. If any fighters had been scrambled, then they were bound to have seen them in the climb.

> "We were on a steady course for Berlin with nothing for me to do but fuse the bombs and wait for the cloud to break. As we flew eastwards in bright sunshine with very good visibility it soon became apparent that the Met was not going to be quite right. The bank of cloud below us seemed to stretch on for hundreds of miles."

Then just as Ted was about to tell Reg that they would have to bomb on an estimated time and hope for the best, a small and somewhat provident hole appeared in the clouds directly ahead of them:

> "I looked through and could clearly see the lakes to the west of Berlin and from there could identify the location of the radio station. With the bombsight we had in those days to hit anything from 25,000ft was rather hopeful but at least I could see the target and the radio station itself. I pressed the bomb release and felt the aircraft lift slightly as the bombs fell away."

Ted was not able to observe the results, for Reg was already diving away and heading for the Norwegian coast. They had been troubled neither by flak nor fighters, but Reg had no intention of hanging around and inviting trouble. "Until we dropped the bombs, I don't even think they knew we were there," Ted said later. He was right; they didn't. The air raid sirens did not start nor the first puffs of exploding flak shells appear until after their bombs had already fallen and the Mosquitoes were leaving the scene. Reg hid himself in thick cloud which persisted all the way to the German coast. They crossed at Schleswig, near the Danish frontier, and headed out over the North Sea, letting down to sea level and comparative safety. Once well clear of the coast Ted knew their chances of reaching base successfully had improved significantly.

Behind Reg and Ted, 'Flash' Gordon was obliged to bomb on ETA, having earlier also been able to see the lakes glistening below, and Tony Wickham dropped a stick of bombs on a railway junction to the north before turning for home.

'Flash' found himself off course and over Bremen, where the German defences opened up. His fault for being there, he admitted later. Tony was the last to land, recorded at 1352 hrs.

Twenty minutes earlier, the three crews in the second formation of 139 Squadron Mosquitoes led by Donald Darling had taken off for their encore performance. Sadly, Kyle's concerns had proven well-founded. By now the Germans were alive to the threat and whereas they may have been caught out once, they were not going to be humiliated again:

"We were apprehensive about the afternoon because the defences had obviously been stirred up. We certainly didn't think we should follow the same penetration and withdrawal routes. After a lot of discussion with the crews we decided on the simple solution of reversing the routes."[63]

Digger calculated that by reversing the routes, the crews should enjoy optimum surprise, especially since they would be skirting the fringes of Swedish airspace. He also hoped they would be protected on the way home, since by then, dusk would be falling over Germany and the Netherlands to cover their retreat.

The station commander may well have believed in his plan. But it didn't work. The three aircraft flew low level over the North Sea to a point north of Heligoland and onto Lübeck, and then began climbing as they headed inland. The skies were clear, and the timing of the attack was once again accurate – or near enough. As Goebbels stepped up to the lectern to make his speech, the Mosquitoes arrived over Berlin. The noise of explosions, screaming engines and bursting shells filled the air as the three aircraft sped through a corridor of heavy flak, each one jinking to avoid being hit. Pete McGeehan and Reg Morris spotted a couple of fighters climbing to intercept, but McGeehan dodged into the clouds and wasn't seen. 'Lofty' Fletcher, navigator to Joe Massey also noticed a Focke-Wulf Fw 190 just as they were leaving the city, and used cloud cover to make good their escape. The two Mosquitoes landed back at Marham shortly before half past six in the evening. Of the third Mosquito, the one flown by the raid commander Donald Darling, there was no news. Later it was confirmed he had been shot down in the vicinity of Altengrabow, about 100km west of Berlin, and both he and his navigator Bill Wright had been killed. Peter Shand, the 139 Squadron commander returned from leave that evening and had the sad duty of writing to their next of kin.

In the bar that evening, and notwithstanding Darling's loss, the two squadrons were in the mood to celebrate. A recording was played of Göring's address, and just before he was due to speak, the unmistakable sound of exploding bombs could be heard faintly in the background, along with an air raid siren blaring over the airwaves and several people shouting. This was followed by silence, and the sound of the funeral Adagio movement from Bruckner's Seventh Symphony while Göring regained his composure. A similar recording was played that suggested the second raid had been equally disruptive.

The two attacks did little material damage, but much like the American raid on Tokyo by James Doolittle and his men flying off the USS *Hornet* the previous year, it made the city dwellers feel vulnerable, and nailed the fanciful lie made by Göring at the start of the war. It was, in Kyle's words, the 'impudence of the whole affair' that made an obviously hazardous operation 'exciting and stimulating' and one that resulted in 'great jubilation' for the aircrew at Marham.[64]

As a stunt, the attack on Berlin was a propaganda coup for the British, the RAF and the Mosquito. Tony Wickham was shortly after whisked away to give an account of the raid, which was broadcast after the nine o'clock news, and on the morning of February 1 the ten surviving crew members proceeded to London to be feted by the press and officially congratulated by the Chief of the Air Staff. Several photographs were taken and appeared in the newspapers as 'the crews who took part on the Berlin Raid'. The story became a headline writer's dream; the crews – Ted included – enjoyed their night out on the town once their official duties had been dispensed with.

Perhaps not surprisingly, there were medals for all of those who took part. As the lead pilot, Reg Reynolds was awarded an immediate DSO (his record shows that he was originally recommended for a Bar to his DFC but this was upgraded) and Ted his first DFC. The citation that appeared in the *London Gazette* (February 16, 1943) stated that the success of the attack was a 'high tribute to the calm courage, resolution and endurance' of the crews who took part. Ted was of course delighted to have had his part in the raid recognised with a medal but was always saddened by the loss of the 139 Squadron crew. He thought that with the morning raid, they had made their point:

"We'd scored a propaganda victory – which was all it was really – so I'm never quite convinced we should have gone back there again. I should imagine that the top brass at Bomber Command headquarters felt pleased with it. The Mosquito had been to Berlin before, but this was the first time we had dropped any bombs."

It would not be the last.

The raid on Berlin had not only just been a propaganda success. Lessons had also been learned about the Mosquito's fuel consumption and future fighting ability. Now it was proven that a Mosquito could easily reach Berlin or a similarly distant target with a full load of bombs and fuel, and this was essential knowledge for the planning of future raids for which the Mosquito would be tasked.

After the excitement of the attack on Berlin – the only high-level bombing sortie Ted completed in a Mosquito – the squadron returned to 'business as usual', including a visit by the Secretary of State for Air, Sir Archibald Sinclair on February 13. Two days later, the squadron embarked on another attack on the engine sheds at Tours in a period that came to be known as 'The Great Tours Derby' when both 105 and 139 Squadrons were tasked with destroying specific rail infrastructure targets in the town.

Reg and Ted led one of these attacks on February 15 with two distinct targets: the repair shops; and what was known as the round house. The repair shops were to be hit at low level; the round house in a shallow dive. Reg and Ted were to lead the former; a doughty and much-admired Australian, Bill Blessing, and his navigator the latter.

The weather for once was on their side but the wind was up which made for a bumpy trip out. As the two formations reached the River Loire, they divided, Blessing taking his section up to 3,000ft while Reg and Ted carried straight on. Reg spotted what he took to be the target and let the bombs go, convinced he had scored a direct hit. Only later, when the photographs from the raid had been developed, could they see that he had not hit the repair shops, but rather the goods depot, complete with a signal box with the word 'Tours' clearly visible in large black letters on a white board. Blessing had rather more luck; five out of his six aircraft bombed the primary target. Two days later, the largest formation of Mosquitoes yet to be assembled hit the engine sheds again, this time all-but finishing the job. One of their number, William Sutherland, was lucky to make it home when he ran into another danger with low flying: sea birds. Running into a flock of birds over the coast, one shattered the bomb aimer's Perspex panel while another holed the starboard mainplane, and a third was protruding from the port mainplane. The observer's eye was cut by flying shards of Perspex:

> "Sea birds, which became known as 'Quisling Ducks', presented us with a severe problem. They achieved far more success at interception than did German fighters. Bulletproof windscreens appeared to be the only solution."[65]

With March came the most extensive month's work undertaken by both squadrons, and Reg and Ted were in the thick of it. There had also been a change in leadership. Hughie Edwards was promoted group captain in early February and left to take up a post at HQ Bomber Command prior to becoming station master at RAF Binbrook. His place was taken by Geoffrey Longfield, a 33-year-old regular officer and former first-class cricketer, but Longfield was only in harness a few days before he was killed in a collision over Rennes. Owing to a navigational error he had turned sharply, colliding with the second Mosquito in his formation. His place was taken by John Deacon, a 35-year-old observer, but he and his pilot were killed the next day when their aircraft fell out of the sky, the result of structural failure. The squadron's run of ill-luck was ended with the appointment of John Wooldridge, affectionately known as 'Dim', but who was anything but. Not only was he a skilful and lucky pilot, but he was also a gifted composer and academic, having studied under Jean Sibelius.

Throughout March, Ted chalked off a series of targets that reflected 2 Group's campaign against the railways including Le Mans, Tergnier, and the John Cockerill Works at Liège where he had the satisfaction of seeing their bombs bursting among blast furnaces, power station and engine works. There was a certain irony in having to bomb a facility originally founded by an Englishman and now turning out war materiel in the services of the Axis cause.[66]

Ted's logbook (and subsequent memories of his flying career) underplays his role in the raid's success. The briefing, which had lasted two and half hours, had been meticulous in its detail, and the attacking force made landfall precisely where it needed to be, thanks to Ted's superb navigation. As they flashed over the coast, almost line abreast and far too fast for any of the defences to react, one of their number – Flying Officer R. B. Smith RAAF – nearly took the roof off a hotel in all the excitement, frightening himself half to death in the process. Describing the moment as 'terrifically exhilarating', and the flight across country as 'just like a steeplechase', he later recalled:

> "As we got nearer to our target, we again tightened up formation. When we were within a minute or so of our target, I could see no sign of Liège and the light was suddenly failing. I thought maybe we had missed it, when suddenly we passed over the brow of a fairly steep hill and there below us lay the town, with our target easily discernible close to the River Meuse. The bombing run was perfect. Squadron Leader Reynolds took us across in such a way that each of us could line up on our own particular section of the works. The target came up at such a speed that it was all over in a matter of seconds. Immediately after bombing, the formation split up and we set course for home. The raid was a great success, thanks to Squadron Leader Reynolds and 'Sis' [nickname for Ted], who led our formation."[67]

On March 16, the two Marham squadrons were tasked with a deep penetration raid to the engine sheds in Paderborn, Germany. One aircraft failed to return and another crash-landed near base. Ted remembers a similar patrol in the area on the evening of March 24 and attacking a train, executing what the records describe as 'a roving commission'. Unusually bad navigation on Ted's part took them too close to Osnabrück, and an enemy flak position:[68]

> "As we ran in to do a dive-bombing attack, we were hit, probably by something quite small. The result was we lost all our hydraulics, so we'd still got the bombs onboard and the bomb doors open. It also meant we had no flaps and no undercarriage. When we came back, we successfully landed on the grass (Marham was fortunately still a grass airfield in those days) and skidded along on the open bomb doors hoping and praying that the bombs didn't come loose.
>
> "The only way out, of course, of a Mk IV Mosquito, because the door was in the floor (and we're now sitting on the floor), was to pull the lever and open the escape hatch in the roof. The trouble was that the escape hatch was operated by a handle and a cable, and the cable pulled a series of catches and by some error, that we could never obviously trace, the catches had never been attached to the cable. That meant that despite pulling the cable, the

escape hatch wouldn't come off. I tried to hit it with the escape axe, but from within the aeroplane I couldn't get enough leverage to break it."

Fortunately, the fire engine arrived with the squadron doctor who seized the fire axe, clambered onto the roof of the Mosquito and began hacking at the canopy while Ted cowered on the floor, praying he wouldn't chop his head off!

Such was the ruggedness of the Mosquito that the next day, they popped the aeroplane onto a pair of jacks to fix what had been broken. In flushing new hydraulics into the system, they were able to pump open and close the bomb-bay doors without any further repairs being needed. As Ted remarked afterwards: "You'd never have done that with a metal aeroplane."

A period of leave followed at the beginning of April, squadron commanders being very wary of over-stretching their aircrew and the authorities issuing a regular pattern of temporary respite to keep their crews fresh and giving them something to live for – quite literally. Reg and Ted tended to take their leave at the same time, Ted heading home to spend time with his parents. While they were away the squadron continued to operate, their CO using up one of his nine lives on one sortie when his aircraft was hit by intense and accurate light flak over the target and returned on one engine. Flak was not their only concern. Increasingly, crews were returning having been intercepted by German fighters, and the Fw 190 in particular was becoming something of a nuisance. On one occasion, the squadron opted to abandon its sortie having been targeted over the Channel and deciding to leg it back to base rather than push their luck unnecessarily.

Ted and Reg were back in the cockpit on the afternoon of May 1, preparing for a low-level attack on the Phillips Works at Eindhoven. It was a popular target for the planners and 2 Group in particular, who had mounted a significant raid on the works five months earlier, achieving considerable success, albeit at a heavy cost.[69] Ted's logbook simply states that the formation was recalled less than 20 minutes after take-off. That word 'recalled' hides a greater tragedy, for as they were forming up, one of their number appeared to drop out of formation and into a spin from which it failed to recover. Both the Kiwi pilot and his navigator were killed and the operation aborted. Later it was discovered that the aircraft had suffered an engine failure, and the pilot feathered the airscrew on the one remaining 'good' engine by mistake.[70]

On May 2, Ted was briefed for an attack on Thionville, a pretty historic city in the north-east French department of Moselle, famed for its wine. Of greater interest to the military planners was its steel production capabilities. A late evening operation was laid on, seven Mosquitoes from 105 Squadron taking part, Reg and Ted leading. For Ted, it proved to be a near-perfect sortie, or so he thought:

> "The raid on Thionville was fairly deep penetration and I didn't have to make corrections in course or speed or anything. I just flew the flight plan. It was perfect. If a track line on the map went over a crossroads, so the crossroads came up in the bombing window. It was just one of those raids."

Perhaps because he was concentrating so hard on his navigation during the near four-hour round trip, Ted didn't see a gun firing or a fighter in the sky. When he jumped back down onto the grass on landing, he told his ground crew that the trip had been 'absolutely marvellous'. It was only then that he realised they had been hit: "The boys came up and said: 'You've got a bullet hole in the tailplane'. They were right. We had. It meant someone had been firing at us all along, and I hadn't seen them!"

It was a worthy trip for Ted to end his first association with the men of 105 Squadron, the ORB describing the attack as 'extremely successful'.[71] On May 4, Reg was promoted to fill the wing commander's post at 139 Squadron and succeed Peter Shand. Shand had been killed a few days earlier on operations over the Netherlands. He had only recently been awarded the DFC (and his navigator the DFM) for their part in the Great Tours Derby. Theirs were big boots to fill, and to do so Reg was taking Ted as the new squadron navigation officer. It meant promotion for Ted too; he was now acting flight lieutenant.

If Ted's time at 105 Squadron had been exciting, things were just about to step up another level.

CHAPTER FIVE
OPTICAL ILLUSIONS

MOVING SQUADRONS, IN THIS CASE, meant very little disruption, as they shared the same base and facilities. But whereas Ted had always until now had to answer to others, as navigation officer he would be the one issuing the orders, and with ultimate responsibility for the navigational performance of the men under his command.

On the morning of May 27, Ted was called early to the ops room to meet with the senior station staff. They congratulated him first on the award of his DFC, for just a few days prior, Ted had gone to Buckingham Palace with Reg to receive his medal from King George VI. With the pleasantries over they settled down to business and Ted was shown the proposed targets for the day's operation. There were two: The Schott Glass Works and the Zeiss Optical Instrument Works. Both were located at Jena, about 45 miles from Leipzig.

Instantly, Ted was excited; this was to be no normal operation and no normal target. Earlier in the month he'd gone with Reg to Berlin on the first of what was to become known as a 'siren raid' to keep the sirens sounding over Berlin and play havoc with the enemy's nerves. While 'different' it had all been rather routine. The raid he was now hearing about was different in a more exciting way and put into context the long hours of low-flying training they had recently been doing.

Deep penetration raids were Ted's favourites. They were usually the most successful, and from the moment the briefing began, it was clear that the planning staff had spent considerable time in determining the route in – and out – so as to encounter the minimum of flak and avoid local fighter defences. It also took into account the difficulties of low-level navigation. The intelligence officer had managed to magic up several good photographs of the target which they viewed through an epidiascope to get a better idea of how it may look like on the approach to the bombing run. The briefing proved a lengthy affair. The group captain went into considerable detail about the plan of the attack until everyone was certain they knew their own part, from their take-off time to the planned getaway and return home.

Reg and Ted were to lead the whole attack formation which was split into two sections. The first section, comprising six aircraft of 139 Squadron, would attack Schott; the second section, comprising eight aircraft from 105 Squadron and led by Bill Blessing, would attack Zeiss. The Met officer was confident about the weather; it seemed perfect. Ted was promised low cloud and poor visibility in the area where German fighters were expected, meaning they should have a clear run into the target. With the customary 'Good Luck' from the station commander, the briefing drew to a close, and Ted headed for the crew room, chatting with the others as they collected their parachutes and other essential flying items and deposited any personal effects that could be of use to the enemy in their named lockers. They didn't bother locking them.

It was a pleasant evening as Ted and Reg walked out to their waiting aircraft. Others went with them and took the chance of a quick cigarette, flicking away the last of the glowing butt before climbing aboard and settling themselves as comfortably as they could in preparation for the long flight ahead. Ted too cupped a Player's Navy Cut in his hands for one last drag, savouring the moment. He'd always smoked Player's – untipped; one of his few vices.

Across the station, actions were being repeated in other aircraft as the minutes ticked by and the time came to start engines. Within moments the roar of a dozen Merlin engines created a deafening wall of sound to be accompanied by more than a dozen more soon after. Then they started their slow taxi out to their take-off positions, six aircraft leaving the ground at the appointed hour followed into the sky by eight more. Above the airfield, Reg allowed the others in his section to form up while below them the ground crews continued to watch as the noise began to fade slowly in the distance as the Mosquitoes set course for the Dutch coast.

Ted glanced both left and right to see the others behind him, a formidable force ready to catch the Germans napping. They flew low over the English countryside, fields and farms racing by in the blink of an eye until they crossed the coast, the cool blue sea looking incongruously inviting, gently glinting beneath them as the watery sun began to fade on the horizon.

The route across the North Sea was comparatively short and flown at wavetop height, the salt spray again frosting the windshield. The flat coast of the Netherlands appeared ahead as the formation closed up and increased speed for the quick dash across, Reg reaching with his left hand to ease the throttle levers forward. This was always a tense and dangerous moment. This was where the flak defences could get you, assuming they were alive to your presence, or you could get hit by a bird. Reg always referred to them as the enemy of low-flying aircraft, and the kinetic force of a bird strike could do serious damage, especially to flying furniture.

Ted could see the beach clearly and the sea wall, at first a blur and then becoming more distinct, and then, right in front of them, three wireless masts about a mile apart appeared as if from nowhere. Had they been marked on Ted's charts? Were they crossing the coast at the right point? It was too late to lead the formation around and the only option was to fly between them. It was a risk, but they were lucky, for there were no connecting wires which would have spelled disaster. Ted could only imagine the result of hitting a steel cable at 350mph in a wooden aeroplane, and it didn't bear thinking about. A single flak gun opened up but its shots fell wide. Reg looked beneath him as a cyclist leaped off his bicycle to wave and children began running along unmade roads in a race they couldn't possibly win, unheard laughter and shouting below. Cars and vehicles didn't exist, not unless they were German. Startled horses bolted and terrified farm animals scattered in every direction.

For a few minutes all was calm. Ahead lay the Zuider Zee, a still body of water upon which a large fleet of some 200 fishing boats were innocently going about their daily business, their skippers very much taken unawares by the aircraft that zoomed low between their masts, causing the sails to flap and the boats to rock. The Mosquitoes continued on their journey, across the reclaimed and deserted Polder, and the old coastline of the Netherlands. The weather was still clear, and the little houses beneath them with their fairy-tale red roofs suggested a peace and calm that the Dutch people had not experienced for three years under the Nazi jackboot.

The two sections crossed the German frontier, turning south after the River Ems and flying over undulating countryside, dotted with dense woods. Visibility was still good, and Ted found navigating easy as he picked out instantly identifiable landmarks including the spires and chimneys of Münster a dozen or so miles off to the west. The weather was supposed to be good with some rain or cloud cover over the Ruhr and the mountainous area behind Kassel, clearing at the target. But it was the other way around. Cloud began to build up ahead in the place Ted hoped it would break.

The Mosquitoes flew between the Mohne and Eder dams which had only two weeks before been attacked by Guy Gibson and his crews from 617 Squadron, and evidence of the devastating damage caused by the extensive flooding was everywhere to see in the surrounding countryside. After the raid, the Germans had moved significantly more flak units into the area and now one opened up, causing one of the Mosquito pilots instinctively to take avoiding action, only to hit another Mosquito in the formation. There was a sickening crash as both aircraft hung momentarily in the sky before plunging into the hillside giving neither crew a chance to bale out. Ted noted their position and how it looked a nasty mess. Twenty-seven-year-old Harold Sutton, something of a celebrity football player in his hometown of Edmonton before joining the Royal Canadian Air Force, was one of those killed.

Now their small force comprised only 12 aircraft, the four in the first section pressing ahead and gaining height to clear the hilltops until they were in quite mountainous territory in poor flying conditions. The aircraft began to bob up and down to follow the contours as though prescribing a heartbeat, a dangerous occupation at the best of times but potentially fatal in poor light and when attempting to fly in formation. The aircraft raced through the valleys where they could, rising only to clear a peak before dropping back down as low as they could go to avoid trouble. At one point they were flying so low that they were beneath a house built on a small cone-shaped hill and as Ted shot by, he caught a clear glimpse of a man walking out of his front door, his mouth open in awe. A little further on and they passed a German observation point, a man clearly tracking their progress through binoculars. He probably didn't need them; they were that close he could almost reach out and touch them.

The weather conditions continued to deteriorate, and Reg switched on his navigation lights to help keep the formation together. Bill Blessing, for one, was grateful, for he was steadily losing his way and the sight of Reg's lights enabled him to regain formation at the crucial point. Ted was still worried that they might literally fly into the ground and for the briefest of moments thought that the attack may have to be abandoned. Twenty miles short of the target, they dropped down into the valley of the River Saale and were able to pick out various landmarks which told them that somehow, miraculously, they were dead on track. Perhaps it was luck; perhaps it was skill, or a combination of both, for visibility was now down to around 1,000 yards and while they knew the target was just a few miles ahead, they still couldn't see it.

Reg was now at full throttle, the engines screaming, and his bomb doors were open. They came to the autobahn with just three miles to run. Guns mounted on flak towers 50-feet high began firing at them horizontally, for they were at the same height, bright streams of tracer dancing past them in the half light, unhealthily close. Balloons that had not been expected and not part of the briefing also now appeared as Ted shouted a warning to his captain. Reg spotted a gunner in a flak tower firing for all he was worth at one of the other aircraft, but he was now focused on the target ahead. The distinctive chimneys of the works made it easy to see, and Reg selected one of the tall buildings in front of him and pressed the bomb release at point-blank range. He pulled hard on the stick to climb over the building, missing the roofs by what seemed like inches, and then saw a violent explosion in front of his eyes and felt something tug at his hand and leg as smoke and fumes entered the cockpit.

Now the aircraft were in a veritable hail of tracer shells, dodging and jinking for all they were worth. More balloons appeared as if from nowhere as Ted shouted again, completely unaware that Reg's intercom lead had been severed just below his starboard ear and his pilot could not hear a thing:

> "Reggie had cut his hand and his leg, and a piece of shrapnel had come into the cockpit and ripped through the neck of his battledress. It had also cut the cable of the intercom, although we didn't know it at the time. I'm shouting at him to turn as we're heading straight for a balloon cable but somehow we missed it."

It was only as they left the target that Ted realised Reg had been wounded. The tug Reg had felt was the shrapnel from an exploding cannon shell, which had torn into his leg and sliced his hand, both of which were bleeding freely. Glancing out of the cockpit, Ted and Reg could see holes in the fairing in front of the radiator. Flak had pierced a hole just aft of the port radiator and close to one of the main tanks. A few inches closer and it would have been the end. What they couldn't see were two large holes in the fuselage close to the throttle box where some fittings had been blown away.

Reg was especially anxious about the port radiator and thought it was nothing short of a miracle that the aircraft was still flying. He'd been here before and paid close attention to the temperature gauge on the panel in front of him. Happily, it remained at a constant 97 degrees, and while the Mosquito was vibrating, it wasn't getting any worse. With luck and a fair wind, they should make it home. Both engines were running, and the immediate danger appeared to have passed.

Now clear of the target, Ted gave Reg a course to steer for home. Every aircraft was to proceed independently. Ted reached for the first aid kit and bandaged his skipper's hand to stop the bleeding. There was no need for any pain relief; Reg's hand and leg had both gone numb. It was a long flight home in a badly damaged aircraft, and there was still the damage they couldn't see that worried them. Reg continued to stare apprehensively at the engine instruments as well as the fuel. He had a moment to consider the attack. He was satisfied that his bombs had hit the target but wasn't sure how the others had got on. He would find that out later at debriefing.

They flew in cloud for a little way until it began to break. By now they were in near darkness, and Ted had some difficulty in picking out where they were. There was little ground detail by which to map read. They flew over one especially well-defended area and the flak opened up, Reg once again taking violent evasive action at full throttle and in fine pitch to avoid being hit, and praying that the airframe would hold together. Eventually they were back over the Netherlands, and towards the mouth of the Rhine they flew again over a large flooded plain, reaching the coast with just enough light to see the beach. He'd managed to find a spot that was undefended, and they crossed in relative peace. The petrol gauges suggested they had enough to make it to Marham, and so Ted went through into the nose to check the bomb gear to discover that a piece of the port airscrew had been forced through the side of the fuselage and smashed various parts of the equipment. It was another miracle that the explosion had happened just moments after the bombs had left the racks.

They were soon across the North Sea and in sight of home. The friendly lights of the flarepath were switched on and the Mosquito glided down for a successful landing. The station medical officer (MO) was summoned to look at Reg's wounds but was satisfied that neither was anything to worry about and Ted had done a good job in stemming the bleeding. A press photographer was on hand, snapping a photograph of Reg and Ted with their hands on the splintered propeller of a rather battered Mosquito, the strain clearly etched on their faces.

With his wounds now professionally attended to, and B-Beer in the loving hands of the ground crew, Reg and Ted went up to interrogation and a first chance to discuss the raid in detail after an eventful trip of only 20 minutes short of five hours. Other crews began to drift in to be debriefed by the senior intelligence officer and given a welcome cup of something strong in a white enamel mug from a mighty flagon.

Of the 14 aircraft that had set out, Ted knew that at least two from their section would not be coming back as he had seen them collide. Others had seen the collision too, and the fatal crash that followed, an enormous ball of flame rolling down the mountainside.[72] One Mosquito, flown by 'Smokey Joe' Stovel, successfully bombed the target and came home without incident. Another, with Vernon Pereira, a Trinidadian, at the controls, suffered the loss of the starboard engine (the nav, 'Taffy' Gilbert, put it down to a glycol leak) and was forced to leave the formation. He bombed a railway bridge near Kassel. He only narrowly missed the attention of half a dozen waspish Fw 190s to make it back to base. The sixth aircraft, flown by William Sutherland, successfully bombed the target and came home on one engine, but in coming in to land at Coltishall, just over the coast, he flew into a high-tension cable that he saw too late, if at all, and both he and his navigator were killed when their aircraft crashed near Wroxham railway station. Flight Lieutenant Sutherland was 29.

In the second formation of 105 Squadron aircraft which had bombed Zeiss, there were similarly mixed results. Despite Reg's best efforts in using his navigation lights to keep the formation together, at least three had lost contact with one another and bombed targets of opportunity. Only two, including Bill Blessing, could claim to have bombed the primary target. One other, flown by Flying Officer Alan Rea, was seen to fly over the target only to crash on its return to base, attempting to land on one engine. Another, flown by Ronald Massie, simply failed to return.

The raid on Jena has gone down in history as yet more proof of the rugged reliability of the Mosquito in carrying out operations that would have previously been impossible. But at what cost? Ten men were killed out of 28 taking part –

a loss rate of almost 36 per cent – and a figure that was clearly unsustainable. Two of the pilots lost – Harold Sutton and Alan Rea – had been decorated for gallantry, Rea for surviving a tour on Handley Page Hampdens – the famous flying suitcase – earlier in the war. In terms of damage to the target, only a handful of aircrew bombed the primary, making the loss rate similarly hard to justify. Ted was certainly doubtful:

"It was the kind of operation that was considered successful at the time. We hit the glassworks, which was obviously a key element. It made periscopes for submarines so was an attractive target, and the optical works similarly so, but we probably put them out of action for no more than a week or two. One wondered afterwards whether it was really all that important, and whether a nighttime raid by a larger force might have put it out of action for longer and been more useful. But that's the advantage of hindsight."

A day after the raid, Ted took a call from an intelligence officer at Bomber Command headquarters. The officer seemed somewhat doubtful about Ted's report of raised flak towers and a balloon barrage around the target. The inference was that if intelligence didn't know about them, then they couldn't have been there:

"He asked me: 'Are you sure they are there?' I replied: 'Look here, who was there? You or me?' He did at least have the decency to phone me up a week or so later once the photos of the raid had been processed to tell me I was right!"

The raid on Jena is described in the operations record book at the time as 'the most ambitious operation attempted by low-flying Mosquitoes to date'. It states: 'It was superbly navigated by Flight Lieutenant Sismore, in spite of the visibility which at times necessitated the use of navigation lights in order to maintain formation.'[73]

'Dim' Wooldridge was similarly keen to heap praise where it was due:

"The credit for the success of this raid must go almost entirely to Wing Commander Reynolds – he had only just taken over command of 139 Squadron – and his navigator Flight Lieutenant Sismore, who led the whole formation deep into Germany through the most filthy weather conditions to find their targets and then bomb them in the face of very stern opposition."[74]

Perhaps not surprisingly, several of the aircrew were recommended for immediate awards. These included a Bar to the DSO for Reg Reynolds, 'an outstanding operational commander', completing his 66th sortie. Ted's efforts were formally recognised with the award of his first DSO, the citation reading:

"On 27th May, 1943, this Officer was Navigator of the leading aircraft of a formation of 14 detailed to attack targets at Jena, Germany, in daylight. The total distance was 1,100 miles, over 500 of which were to be covered at very low level in daylight, through strong defences, both from the ground and the air, in occupied and enemy territory. Weather conditions were not as expected, being very clear over the first part of the route, but deteriorating badly towards the target. Visibility was reduced to less than a mile for the last 150, and was not more than half a mile for the last 40. In spite of these difficulties, Flying Officer [sic] Sismore navigated with extreme accuracy, and finally brought the formation up to the target along the pre-arranged run. The attack was made at low level in the face of very heavy anti-aircraft defences and balloons. Over the target itself, a light anti-aircraft shell burst in the cockpit, wounding the pilot. Flying Officer Sismore coolly rendered First Aid and helped the pilot to maintain control of the aircraft. He then continued his accurate navigation, and the aircraft returned safely to base."

The recommendation also referenced Ted's earlier 'spectacular':

"This Officer was Navigator of the leading aircraft of a formation which attacked Berlin in daylight, arriving precisely at the scheduled time. Since then, he has completed 11 successful sorties, all of which have called for the highest degree of navigational skill at low level. All crews of the formation which carried out the attack on Jena are unanimous in saying that it was a magnificent navigational feat in face of difficulties."[75]

It was indeed a magnificent feat, and more was to come. But in the immediate term, both Ted and Reg disappeared for some well-earned leave. Their return was marked by a change in operational profile, and a brief interlude with Pathfinder Force.

CHAPTER SIX
A CHANGE IN DIRECTION

TED KNEW SOMETHING WAS AFOOT. The comings and goings of various senior staff officers confirmed the rumours that both 139 and 105 Squadrons would be leaving 2 Group in a re-organisation ahead of the expected opening of a Second Front in 1944. They would instead become part of 8 Group, Pathfinder Force.

The Pathfinders had been established to spearhead the Main Force bombing attacks on the enemy in Western Europe. An analysis of bombing accuracy in the first two years of the war had identified serious shortcomings, and targets being missed not by the odd mile or two, but sometimes 50, 60 or even 70 miles from where their bombs were meant to be dropped. The reasons were many and varied: inexperience; poor training; poor aircraft. Some bomber crews had only a few hours nighttime flying under their belts before setting off to find and bomb a German city. The average standard of navigation was woeful, and navigational aids almost non-existent.

It was in this context that certain senior officers within Bomber Operations began agitating for change. Some, including Arthur Harris, wanted raid leaders to be appointed within each squadron. Others argued that a separate force was required, comprising the best crews in Bomber Command, to find and mark the target for the bulk of the bomber force to see and attack. It was an argument that went on for more than six months before a reluctant Harris was effectively ordered to form the new unit, asking each of the Bomber Groups to surrender one of their squadrons and their best crews to the new venture.

While originally referred to as a 'Target Finding Force' Harris decided on his own name, Pathfinder Force (PFF), and insisted the men should be given their own badge to mark them out as 'special' – a golden eagle worn on the breast pocket. Harris, a contradictory man in many ways, originally protested against the formation of an elite force because it would denude the Main Force squadrons of their best men which would in turn impact their operational effectiveness. He also believed it would be bad for morale. In being over-ruled, he then set about giving the aircrew of PFF the trappings of an elite body of men, with their own badge, and an advance in rank and pay to reflect the increased risk the men would be facing.

While PFF initially struggled, hampered by having to operate multiple aircraft types with very different performance envelopes, they soon got into their stride. In their leader they had arguably the world's best air navigator of their generation, Donald Bennett. Bennett, a somewhat humourless Australian, was the man for the moment. Unlike his contemporaries, he had flown bomber operations and led a bomber squadron earlier in the war, and so had current operational experience. He'd attacked the *Tirpitz* battleship, been shot down, and evaded capture. All of these experiences gave him a better understanding of his men, and the challenges they faced with the equipment they had and the environment in which they had to operate. While unpopular with many of his peers, not least because he was young, outspoken and prone to arrogance, he was popular with his men and respected on the front line. There was no doubting that results were improving, and bombing was becoming more accurate.

One of the reasons, beyond the better training and advanced navigation techniques now being deployed, was a new blind-bombing device called 'Oboe', which could identify a target even in thick cloud. Targets that were once missed by miles could now be found within yards. To carry the technology, and the crews to operate it, Bennett had access to 109 Squadron equipped with high-flying Mosquitoes.

Oboe was first successfully used operationally at the end of 1942, five months after PFF was founded and a few weeks before it was formally given group status (to become 8 Group). While early sets were prone to technical difficulties, the results justified the effort, and the investment in time and resource. The success of PFF allowed Bennett the luxury of being able to expand his force. Further squadrons and airfields were added to the group to support the 'main effort' on which Harris was now embarked. He had more aircraft at his disposal capable of carrying a much heavier weight of bombs a much greater distance. As the number of Main Force squadrons had grown, and the size, duration and frequency of bomber attacks increased, PFF was obliged to grow with it.

The expansion of 8 Group coincided with the unhappy demise of 2 Group, and its departure from Bomber Command's order of battle allowed 105 and 139 Squadrons to be transferred to PFF. For 105 that meant retraining to become the second Oboe-equipped squadron and share the workload with their colleagues in 109. For 139, it meant a different role altogether. They were to form the nucleus of what was to become the Light Night Striking Force (LNSF) which eventually grew to a strength of eight Mosquito squadrons and a mighty weapon in its own right. Their purpose was two-fold: to fly diversionary raids to fox the German defenders and lure the Luftwaffe night fighters away from the Main Force attack; and to fly the 'siren' raids referred to earlier, to keep the air raid sirens screaming at all hours of the night and rob the urban German population of their sleep.

The transfer to PFF meant a move from the familiar and comfortable surroundings of Marham to RAF Wyton, near Huntingdon, the spiritual 'home' of the Pathfinders and where Bennett himself had a house. The squadron flew its last operation from Marham on July 3, and while the Mosquitoes were in the air the ground crews and administrative staff began packing boxes and trucks for the 40-mile trip to their new home. Moving an entire squadron took significant time and effort and the rear party did not arrive until two days later when the move was finally complete.

The squadron was operational immediately, sending a small number on nuisance raids to Hamburg, Düsseldorf and Cologne. While Mosquito operations were generally considered less 'risky' than flying in Main Force, because of the speed and height at which the aircraft could fly, it was not especially 'safe' either. Searchlights and flak were still to be reckoned with, and on more than one occasion an aircraft would be 'coned' (i.e. caught in a searchlight beam) or return with some degree of battle damage. The squadron flew every night, all through the night, and were soon referred to in German broadcasts as 'Ghost Raiders', a soubriquet which was readily adopted by the aircrew and with the artwork on their aircraft. On July 14 the squadron suffered its first casualties since becoming part of 8 Group when 23-year-old Raymond Clarke and his 30-year-old navigator Eric Thorne disappeared without trace on their way back from Berlin. Thorne made a last desperate transmission to say they were baling out as the aircraft was on fire, and while the wreckage of the aircraft was reported on the sea, there was nothing to be found of the two men.

Reg and Ted flew their first LNSF sortie a couple of nights later with three 500lb and one 250lb bombs on board, returning exhausted after a trip of more than four and a half hours to Munich. The ORB diarist records the trip simply as 'long and successful'.[76]

On the night of July 24/25, 1943, Reg marked him and Ted down on the Battle Order for a further operation. It was an important one. Thirteen crews would be flying that night to attack multiple targets including Bremen, Kiel and Duisburg in the Ruhr. Ted's target was the pretty northern town of Lübeck, easily distinguished by its brick Gothic architecture which dated from its time as the medieval capital of the Hanseatic League. The crews knew the importance of the task they were to perform, for the intelligence officer had been very clear. That evening, Harris was opening Operation Gomorrah, an all-out attack on Hamburg, with the RAF bombing at night, and the Americans by day, to prove that a major city could be 'defeated' by air power alone. It was also an opportunity to try out his latest secret weapon – 'Window' – strips of foil which when dropped en masse rendered the German radar defences effectively blind.

It was a late start, the Mosquitoes flying ahead of Main Force to practise the deception. Pathfinder 'heavies' had evolved a technique where they would not only mark the target, but also mark the route, occasionally dropping yellow flares on a particular heading or at a turning point to keep the following bombers on track. It was a godsend to many a Main Force navigator, especially on nights where the wind direction or speeds may have been different from those given at briefing and relied upon to stop them from wandering unsuspectingly off course, and perhaps into a heavily defended area they had been routed to avoid. The flares dropped to help the heavy Lancasters and Halifaxes which now made up the bulk of Harris' principal squadrons were also of use to Ted, and he had little trouble in finding Lübeck and dropping his bombs to shake up the locals. Forty miles behind them, to the south-west, the first of the Pathfinders' markers were going down, and the start of a near hour-long onslaught on the German port city began.

The fires caused by thousands of tons of bombs cascading from above were both magnificent and terrifying, and later led to the now infamous firestorm which sucked the oxygen out of the air and the life out of thousands of Germans. Ted and Reg stayed briefly to marvel at the sight, before turning for home. Seen from altitude, the wild furnaces in the ruins shrank to patches of orange and gold in a black bed, 'like hot coals in a fireplace'.[77]

The fires that were burning below would still be ablaze two nights later and guide subsequent Mosquitoes to the city. But by then, Ted had made a decision. While not unhappy to belong to an elite group, the LNSF did not feel fully integrated within 8 Group Pathfinders. Having also spent almost his entire flying career at low level, he found high-level sorties a little dull. Had Reg been more enthusiastic, perhaps they may have stayed, but fearful that he may spend the rest of the war doing a job in which he had little interest, and perhaps didn't make the most of his skills, he requested to be transferred. His ops total now stood at 52.

His view was very much a personal one and not one that appears to have been widely shared. Eric Shipley, a fellow navigator who flew with Canadian Squadron Leader Donald Skene, one of 139's flight commanders, found the change in roles less of an issue. He does, however, agree with Ted that it was something of a culture shock: "It was a remarkable change for all of the ex-2 Group types used to low-level daylight operations to suddenly find ourselves so high up and at night, but we appeared to cope reasonably well."[78]

He also remembers being proud of their low-flying skills, evidenced in their move from Marham to Wyton: "The squadron flew in close formation, just to show these night flyers what real formation flying looked like and what 'low level' really meant – we didn't fly over the trees we flew around them!"

Ted put a call through to 2 Group Headquarters and spoke to the senior air staff officer (SASO), David Atcherley. Atcherley, very much a maverick who had once broken his neck in a crash and thought nothing of flying with a broken arm, was somewhat taken aback that Ted should be looking to leave a force that the rest of Bomber Command was so keen to join. Ted convinced him, however, that he was serious and so the wheels were put in motion and the paperwork sorted for him to rejoin his own spiritual home. He was posted out of 139 Squadron on September 12, attached on temporary duty to HQ 2 Group. Reg left a few days earlier, for a spell at 10 OTU as commanding officer of the training unit's satellite station. They would not be separated for long.

In parting company with Bennett, Ted was joining forces with another mercurial leader who had reputedly been offered command of PFF ahead of Bennett, but whose proposal was also reputedly rejected by Harris.

His name was Basil Embry.

Embry had joined the RAF as far back as 1921 and spent five years overseas in Iraq, serving under both Harris and Harris' deputy, Robert Saundby. A full and active pre-war career saw him awarded the Air Force Cross and the DSO, the latter for his command of 20 Squadron at Peshawar, taking part in the Waziristan campaigns of 1937 and 1938. When the world war finally came, Embry manoeuvred himself into the command of 107 Squadron. Always leading from the front, he undertook many hazardous operations, often at low level and in the face of fierce resistance, earning the second of an eventual four DSOs after the campaign in Norway. He fought the Germans in the Low Countries, his squadron suffering horrendous casualties, until Embry was himself shot down having been hit by heavy flak while attacking enemy troops advancing on Dunkirk. Captured by the Germans he was not held prisoner for long before making good his escape, killing two of his guards, evading recapture, and returning to England via Spain. He held senior posts in Fighter Command and in the Desert, before eventually being given command of 2 Group and immediately summoning his old friend David Atcherley to join him.

Embry arrived at 2 Group, shortly to be transferred from Bomber Command into Second Tactical Air Force (2TAF), to find it in a very sorry state. It was May 27, 1943; the same day as the attack on Jena. Morale was rock bottom, bombing results were low, casualties were high, and the group lacked ambition and purpose. He also shared some of the practical challenges that his counterpart in 8 Group had encountered in establishing PFF. When Bennett subsumed five different squadrons into Pathfinder Force, he inherited four different aircraft types: the Lancaster, Halifax, and Stirling – which were all four-engine aircraft – and the Wellington, with two engines. All were capable of different speeds, rates of climb, maximum ceiling, bomb loads and endurance. All had to be accommodated with service, maintenance and spares. It was inefficient and unsustainable, until Bennett was eventually able to rationalise his aircraft choice to just two: the Lancaster and the Mosquito, which hadn't been available when PFF came into existence.

Embry encountered a similar problem albeit all four aircraft types had two engines: 2 Group operated North American Mitchells, Douglas Bostons, Lockheed

Venturas, and de Havilland Mosquitoes. The first three were all American. The first was promising and had only just entered service with the RAF. Its two 1,350hp Wright Double Row Cyclone GR2600 A-5B engines gave it a top speed of more than 290mph at 15,000ft, and it could carry up to 6,000lbs of bombs. It was also well defended, with six 0.5 calibre machine guns. The Boston had been in service a little longer, introduced as a replacement to the battle-weary Blenheims. Boston IIIs had 1,600hp Double Cyclone engines which meant they were more than 10mph faster than the Mitchell but could carry only a third of the weight of bombs. The Ventura was the turkey of the three (Embry thought the Ventura 'thoroughly bad'[79]), and although its two 2,000hp Pratt & Whitney Double Wasp GR2800 S1A4-G engines gave it comparatively high speed (300mph), it could similarly only carry a modest payload (2,500lbs) and was generally considered vulnerable by the men who had to fly them.

The three American and one British aircraft not only had different levels of performance but also different numbers of crew, ranging from five in a Mitchell to two in a Mosquito. This meant there was no interchangeability in types, and therefore no efficiencies in training and replacements to be made. Embry, like Bennett, flew them all to make his own assessment, and noted the value of the Mosquito at once. He also recognised the importance of bringing pride back into the group and gave orders that station commanders and staff officers were to take part in active operations. As a result, quite a number of unlikely people found themselves in combat – doctors, engineers, intelligence officers, ops room officers, even a Church of England chaplain. Embry himself opted to fly at every opportunity and went by the name of 'Wing Commander Smith', two ranks below his actual rank of air vice-marshal, with dog tags to that effect. The Germans had put a price on his head after his escape earlier in the war, and he was well known to the enemy. He faced the very real likelihood of being executed if he was shot down again and captured, making his decision to fly even more remarkable.

David Atcherley and Basil Embry 'breathed the same kind of air'[80], and Embry sought to surround himself with like-minded people who shared his passion and zeal for prosecuting the war. He recruited Peter Clapham, his former navigator from his time in charge at Wittering, as well as Percy Pickard, a highly experienced 'bomber boy'. 'Pick', as he was universally known, was an impressive character in every sense of the word. Physically well-built, at 6ft 4in he towered over many of his peers, especially the diminutive Embry. Pick had been the star of an early propaganda film, *Target for Tonight*, and was something of a celebrity. He was station commander at RAF Sculthorpe, where Ted reported on September 12, 1943 for a spell at the Mosquito Conversion Flight. Ted felt immediately at home, and Ted and Pick shared a mutual respect.

Sculthorpe, in north Norfolk, was a satellite airfield to West Raynham, a few miles further south. It was a wartime field with wartime amenities, and some of the Bovis construction workers were still on site when Ted arrived, putting the finishing touches to the mess facilities and accommodation. It was, in the words of one contemporary, 'a bleak, windswept collection of Nissen huts. The mess was so cold that I had great difficulty holding a knife and fork.'[81] The Free French had been the first to use the station with their Bostons, followed by the New Zealanders (487 Squadron RNZAF) and Australians (464 Squadron RAAF) for conversion from Venturas to the Mosquito. On September 20, 21 Squadron arrived to join the other two squadrons and form what was to become known as 140 Wing. This reflected the reorganisation of the RAF's assets ahead of the planned opening of the Second Front which would ultimately lead to the Normandy invasion.

The concept of a 'Tactical Air Force' had been formulated in the desert, the military leaders recognising the benefit of their air force providing direct support to ground operations and supported by highly mobile supporting echelons:[82] Ted explains:

"The difference between the basic air force organisation in the UK and the Tactical Air Force was that the wings were mobile. So whereas traditionally you would have a station with a station commander with two or three squadrons reporting through station headquarters to group, in the TAF the group captain commanded the wing rather than the airfield itself. He could command the airfield, but if the wing moved then the group captain moved with it. That was the big difference. In the Tactical Air Force, we had a wing commander flying, and a wing commander operations. The wing commander flying ran the airfield, air traffic, and was responsible for the organisation; the wing commander operations ran the operations room and controlled the operational information and intelligence because there was more to do than you would normally have to do on a UK base. It was all very sensible."

While eminently sensible it was not without its teething problems. Ground crews, for example, who had previously been attached to squadrons were now attached to an airfield and responsible for servicing whichever squadron that happened to be there at the time. It did not initially go down well. While it took some time to settle, settle it did, and soon the practical advantages of the new organisation were being realised. On November 13, 1943, the Allied Expeditionary Air Force came into being under the command of Sir Trafford Leigh-Mallory, the force eventually comprising three components: the US 9th Air Force (similar in composition and purpose to the tactical force within the RAF's Fighter Command) was one; the two other units came about from the dissolution of Fighter Command. The tactical elements became the Second Tactical Air Force (2TAF), while the remaining squadrons became part of another new organisation, Air Defence of Great Britain (ADGB).

The Second Tactical Air Force was placed under the command of 'Mary' Coningham, who had led the Desert Air Force to victory during 1942. It was to comprise three groups: 83 Group, with primarily Spitfires and Typhoons led by Harry Broadhurst; 84 Group under the command of a South African, Leslie Brown, with primarily Spitfires and Mustangs; and the re-invigorated and repurposed 2 Group under Embry's command, and whose force now included the Mosquito FB.VI, a fighter bomber. As well as being able to carry two 500lb bombs internally and two on the wings, it also had four Browning .303 machine guns in the nose and four Hispano 20mm cannon in the belly. It was to become the most numerous and widely used of all Mosquito types.

In preparation, Embry moved his group to new headquarters at Bylaugh Hall, a rather splendid 19th century stately home near Dereham. Completed in 1852, the hall was not a happy home and eventually the house and its grounds were sold off to speculators in 1917, a portion being acquired by an American family who used the hall to entertain. Requisitioned by the RAF, the family moved out into Butler's Cottage while the military moved in.[83]

While still at Sculthorpe, and with the Americans as their near neighbours, Ted flew a number of practice formations with P-47 Thunderbolts and even went along for a ride in a B-17 Flying Fortress, which although considerably larger than the Mosquito, was only capable of carrying the same weight of bombs. The practice flying was in preparation for using Thunderbolts in a fighter/bomber role, but with a difference:

"The Americans found their Thunderbolts could take on the Bf109s and probably even the Fw 190s at heights above 20,000ft but they couldn't take them on at heights below about 10,000ft. So, they wanted to drop bombs. We went to a meeting with one of the American wings at an airfield in Suffolk and they'd had bomb racks made in the local village. They had problems aiming the bombs and so wanted a Mosquito to lead the formation and they would all drop their bombs when the Mosquito did. The targets would be airfields so the Germans would come up and fight."

The theory made sense, but in practice the idea was never tested for real; the squadron involved soon after re-equipped with Mustangs.

Among Ted's contemporaries at Sculthorpe was Charles Patterson, whose operational record very much mirrored his own. Both men had served on Blenheims in 1940/1941 and Patterson had been awarded the DFC after 40 operations including a deep-penetration raid on a power-generation station at Knapsack in the summer of 1941 which was at the time the most daring and hazardous daylight operation of the war. He began flying Mosquitoes in August 1942 and had been one of the crews on the attack on Jena before finding a niche flying a Mosquito with a cine camera in the nose. His duty was to arrive over a target five minutes after the main bomber force to film the results of a raid before dropping his own bombs. It was extremely high risk as the German defences were by then on high alert, but he was nonetheless proud of his role as the RAF Film Unit's unofficial pilot.

Ted flew a practice trip with Patterson at Sculthorpe and nearly came to grief. Their aircraft developed a technical fault obliging an attempted landing at Marham. Despite Patterson's best efforts, the aircraft crashed as the starboard undercarriage collapsed and it skidded to a halt on its belly. The Mosquito was declared category 'B' – beyond repair on site.

After six weeks at Sculthorpe enjoying the freedom of flying with pilots who loved to fly, and recovered from the crash landing, Ted joined Embry and his 2 Group staff at Bylaugh Hall on October 23, 1943. He was immediately taken in by the energy of his new commanding officer, and delighted when a few weeks later Embry asked him to fly as his navigator. They flew a number of practice bombing and navigational exercises, from the Norfolk coast to the Welsh borders and back again, getting to know one another's habits and idiosyncrasies. With

Reg, Ted had grown accustomed to focusing on his navigation, while Reg took it upon himself to manage anything to do with physically flying or operating the aircraft. With Embry, it was different and almost the complete reverse. The air vice-marshal focused on flying, but everything else – the opening/closing of the bomb doors for example – was left to Ted.

There was a buzz at HQ where it was obvious that a big operation was being planned for Embry's Mosquitoes. Two months earlier, in August, the RAF had mounted a huge raid on an experimental site in the Baltic known as Peenemünde where the Germans were developing a series of 'Revenge Weapons' (*Vergeltungswaffe*). These weapons included rockets and pilotless flying bombs, although at the time it was not known precisely what level of threat such weapons posed, or how they would be deployed. While the raid was deemed a success, and significant amounts of damage were achieved, actually production was probably only delayed by two or three months, and in the early winter of that year, intelligence was being gathered concerning a large number of 'construction works' being started across Northern France. Some of these works were comparatively small; concrete ramps and associated buildings and infrastructure from which large numbers of V-1 Flying Bombs – the so-called 'doodlebugs' – would be launched. Other sites were much larger and more substantial; permanent sites for storing and launching V-2 rockets, capable of supersonic flight that landed and exploded on their target before anyone heard them coming. The full dangers were not yet understood, but sources on the ground in France and across Occupied Europe suggested the enemy was close to unleashing a new and terrible bombing campaign against Britain, and if its flying bombs and rockets could be targeted at the gathering invasion forces, it could set back the opening of a Second Front for many months.

Embry had deployed his Mitchells and Bostons to attack the targets as they became known; he had more than 100 to choose from. The question was how best to deploy his Mosquitoes. Now he had a clear objective, a new site at Sainte-Agathe-d'Aliermont (formally listed in German records as *Feuerstellung Nr 680*) and was planning a major, low-level attack involving some 40 aircraft from Sculthorpe's 140 Wing.

Ten days passed, their desire to go frustrated by the weather. On more than one occasion the crews were roused and briefed before it was light, only then to have the operation cancelled moments before take-off. Tensions were high; nerves strained.

Duff weather and stand-downs were the order of the day. Ted was scheduled to fly with Embry. On December 21, they were once again briefed, Embry making the importance of the operation clear. The codename used to describe the target was 'Noball', and while he couldn't go into precise details, he could tell them that the destruction of their objective was of vital importance to the war effort. But then they'd heard that many times before and would hear it again several times in the coming months. Arthur Eyton-Jones, a navigator with 21 Squadron remembers:

"He told us that [the site] had to be destroyed 'at all costs'. When he said the 'at all costs' bit he looked at us with his piercing steel-blue eyes in a manner that I shall never forget. Those eyes bored right through us so that, although feeling like a condemned man, one would not for a moment consider the possibility of so much as a mild protest!"[84]

Ted's friend Charles Patterson received an additional briefing. On this occasion, rather than following the bombers he was to fly ahead and advise on the weather at the French coast. Patterson took off shortly after 0835 hrs. The weather was appalling with low cloud and drizzle, but he hoped it might be better across the Channel. He hoped in vain. As he hopped over into Northern France, the dense cloud persisted and there was no hope of finding the target. He radioed an abort, and the main strike force behind reluctantly turned about and headed for home. Ted recorded the disappointment blandly in his logbook: 'Recalled by Patterson at French Coast.'

The next day they tried again and had better luck. As the author of the 487 Squadron ORB records: 'Today was a good day.' The briefing that morning was a little later, and the hour rather less ungodly.[85] The ground crews had been busying themselves all morning, hoping that this time their efforts wouldn't be in vain. While the crews had been briefed before, they needed to be briefed again. Nothing was left to chance. The importance of the raid was reflected by the seniority of those taking part. Pickard would lead, with 'Wing Commander Smith' and Ted following, along with the COs of 21 Squadron (Wing Commander Richard North), 464 Squadron RAAF (Wing Commander Henry Meakin) and 487 Squadron RNZAF (Wing Commander 'Willie' Wilson).

Pickard led the force over the Channel and across into France, Embry and Ted keeping station as they crossed the coast just to the north-west of Dieppe and used the rivers, roads and railways to pick their way to the target. Maintaining a steady speed, Pickard began to climb gently to 1,500ft from the deck, so that he could attack the launching site in a shallow dive. Satisfied that he had the target in his sights, he dropped his bombs, turning sharply away with the engines now at full power. Embry and Ted followed moments later, dropping their four 500lb medium capacity bombs from 1,000ft and similarly powering away. Flak was present but limited in its effectiveness. The enemy had once again been caught napping.

Behind them not all was as well as it should have been. Of the 15 crews from 464 Squadron, only eight managed to find and successfully bomb the target. Four crews from 21 Squadron similarly turned back having made what the squadron diarist records as 'a bad landfall'. Eyton-Jones, in his memoir blames the navigator of his formation for the mistake which left him and his pilot circling off the coast for 20 minutes while the leader tried to work out where they were.[86] The New Zealanders had the most success, reporting several hits in the target area and all returning safely to base. Such was the importance of destroying the target that two hours later a smaller group of Mosquitoes returned to finish what they'd started. Embry was happy and the crews were in high spirits, but results were mixed. Charles Patterson flew over the target the following day and it seemed 'fairly well damaged'. Attacking Noball sites at low level in a Mosquito, however, did not seem to be a profitable business.

In the third week of the new year of 1944, Ted left Bylaugh Hall for the mock-Jacobian house of Mongewell Park, the new 2 Group HQ in Oxfordshire. Embry valued Ted's expertise and experience, despite his relative youth, and wanted him close as a planning officer to support all future 2 Group operations. The timing of Ted's appointment could not have been better. The outcome of a meeting between Embry and his AOC, the ever popular 'Mary' Coningham, in early February would test Ted's navigational and planning skills to the limit.

CHAPTER SEVEN
PRISON BREAK

From the moment the first German jackboot goose-stepped its way down the Champs-Élysées, pockets of French citizens began to resist. While initially passive, by being obtuse or deliberately misunderstanding a question when asked or an order when given, resistance steadily became more organised, hostile and effective. Although often depicted in adventure stories and films from the war as heroes from the start, the actual rise to power of the multiple resistance networks and their ultimate collection into a coherent fighting force, armed, supplied and occasionally led by the British, took many years. Men like Jean Moulin became legends and died for the cause; his nemesis Klaus Barbie became infamous for his barbarity which earned him the nickname 'the Butcher of Lyon'. But the resistance was so much more besides.

Perhaps more important than their fighting ability, however, and their military resistance, was their intelligence-gathering capabilities. Being 'on the ground', they were able to convey a regular flow of vital information back to the British, which was especially important in planning the Second Front. The building of The Atlantic Wall, for example, a huge complex of fortifications on the French coast to guard against an Allied invasion was not only consuming thousands of hours of French labour, but also exercising the minds of dozens of important leaders keen to keep the British informed of its progress. Those same leaders were also keeping the British planners apprised of new construction sites for the V-1s and V-2s that were then underway, and generally making a nuisance of themselves. But the tolerance of the German High Command towards their occupied peoples, if such tolerance ever existed, had long since disappeared, and hostages were being regularly taken out and shot in reprisal for resistance activities. A reign of terror not seen by the French for 200 years had now descended, and huge numbers of leaders and their networks were being rounded up and imprisoned to await trial and, most likely, their subsequent execution, for arrests rarely ended well for the prisoners taken away in the dead of night.

By the end of 1943 and the start of the new year, the situation in parts of Northern France had become critical. The German secret police, aided by a collaborationist faction of French, mounted an all-out offensive against the Resistance, intending to address the opposition question once and for all. Many dozens were arrested and imprisoned in the gaol at Amiens; resistance in the area was at the point of collapse, just when they were needed most; the Germans were on the point of victory, as one French fighter recalls: 'The Gestapo and Wehrmacht counter-intelligence were having a field day mauling the Resistance and filling prisons.'

The same eyewitness counted at least 70 resistance fighters that he knew of in the prison at Amiens, some caught by the French gendarmes, some by the German police, some by counter-espionage. Most had been betrayed, 'If invasion didn't come in the next few months, resistance action and intelligence networks in France would be virtually made ineffective. Already, comparatively few were left.'[87]

Embry was summoned to see Coningham at his headquarters in Uxbridge and was handed the exact same intelligence summary 'Mary' had himself received just a few hours earlier from his chief, Leigh-Mallory. It stated simply and starkly that hundreds of French prisoners were at that moment awaiting trial and almost certain execution in Amiens prison. The next batch of executions could take place any time. Incredible though it sounds, the brief was to get them out.

A ground attack was out of the question. The prison could be too easily defended, and the Germans garrisoned there could quickly summon help from the surrounding area, as well as air cover. It would have been suicidal. Which left an attack from the air. The RAF had been given the challenge, and the senior commanders gave it to 2 Group. Coningham thought that if they could bomb the walls of the prison, then some of the prisoners might be able to escape. It was an idea that had already been mooted and rejected, but now he was discussing the possibility with Embry. Might it be possible with a formation of low-flying Mosquitoes?

Embry went away to consider the idea carefully with his own people, Ted included. He recognised that the basic problem in planning the raid was how to bomb a prison without killing all the people in it:

> "The French had provided us with plenty of information about the construction of the gaol, so we knew what we were going to attack, but what we didn't have were any documents or facts about what a bomb did to a brick wall [when it exploded]. So Basil chaired a meeting to get our opinions about the types of bombs we should use and our tactics [for dropping them]."

Embry had an exact model made of the gaol from a set of original architectural drawings the Resistance had managed to smuggle out. It gave them the precise dimensions and thickness of the walls, as well as their construction. In the event, a mix of bomb types was preferred for the tactics deployed. Eighteen Mosquitoes from 140 Wing would take part, six each from 464, 487 and 21 Squadrons, who had recently moved to RAF Hunsdon in Hertfordshire from Norfolk to take them closer to the action. A further Mosquito would film events and assess the results as they unfolded.

Each Mosquito was to be loaded with two 500lb bombs fused with an 11-second delay. The New Zealanders were to breach the outer wall of the prison with their semi-armour piercing (SAP) bombs in two places, while the Australians were to hit the main prison buildings by destroying the German guards' annex at the base of the main structure. Only three minutes were allowed between each of these events. The six Mosquitoes of 21 Squadron were to be held in reserve, ready to complete any unfinished part of the job.

The plan was incredibly risky and there was absolutely no certainty of success. SAP bombs had been known to go through a wall and out the other side, and if they came into contact with anything too hard, they were known to bounce even higher than the aircraft that had dropped them. Ted had seen it happen when attacking railway lines and didn't fancy witnessing it again. For the inside buildings, medium capacity bombs were chosen, though again it could only be a best guess as regards how much explosive would be needed to achieve the desired result.

Ted was given the task of planning the route. He began as he always did, closely examining detailed maps and photographs of the target area and the approach:

"Route planning for low-level operations started with what was the lead-in to the target. Is there something like a railway or a road that we can see, or an obvious landmark like a church steeple that we could lock onto?"

To that end, Ted was lucky. The prison was out of town, and adjoined by a long, straight road running from Albert to Amiens. All the formation leaders had to do was find the road and fly along it for a few miles until the target came into sight. It was just a question of waiting for the target to come up; the navigation problem was solved.

What wasn't resolved, however, was the best way of avoiding the German fighters. One of the most famous German fighter squadrons, *Jagdgeschwader* (JG) 26, was based at Abbeville, just 25 miles from Amiens. The 'Abbeville Boys', as they were known, were some of the best fighter pilots the Luftwaffe possessed. Even with intelligent routing and a small diversionary raid, the Mosquitoes would be close enough to be seen, and there was every chance they would be intercepted. While a confrontation could not be avoided, the Mosquitoes would have surprise on their side, and the Germans would have to be quick to react. Each formation was also promised a squadron of powerful, heavily-armed Hawker Typhoon fighters as close-escort protection. The Germans may indeed come but were likely to have a fight on their hands.

For the 18 attacking Mosquitoes, the squadron commanders were told to select their best crews. Wing Commander Ian 'Blackie' Smith, who'd taken over as CO of 487, had the plum role, leading the first Mosquitoes to breach the walls; Wing Commander 'Bob' Iredale, the CO of 464 Squadron who'd been in tenure for a little over a month, would lead the attack on the prison buildings themselves; relegated to the reserve, the CO of 21 Squadron, Wing Commander Ivor 'Daddy' Dale, would sweep up the afters and only attack if either of the aforementioned squadrons failed. (Dale, also called 'The Grand Old Man of Hunsdon', was 39 and a pre-war regular.) In overall command of the operation, Embry decided he would lead, taking Ted as his navigator. Percy Pickard, who Embry feared had too little experience of low-level daylights to lead outright, would be their deputy, along with his navigator, Alan 'Bill' Broadly.

By February 8 the stage had been set and they had only to wait for more favourable weather to go. But they couldn't wait forever. Despite the wintry conditions and seemingly endless falls of snow, at some point they would have to take a calculated risk; otherwise, the prisoners would die. The French were becoming desperate, made more desperate still by the arrest of Raymond Vivant on February 14, the last big chief of what was known as the *Organisation Civile et Militaire* (OCM) and the *sous-préfet* of Abbeville. He had been the brains behind the establishment of the intelligence network in his area, and of all those who had information about the forthcoming invasion he knew the most. Time was running out.

By February 18, and with intelligence that suggested the first prisoners were to be shot the next day, they could wait no longer. Despite the crews waking up to low cloud and near blizzard conditions, the decision had been taken to go. By 0800 hrs they were in the briefing room, being given details of what had first been called Operation Renovate but had since been renamed Operation Jericho, hoping only that the walls would come tumbling down not to the blasting of horns from the Bible but to the sound of explosions from a swarm of Mosquitoes. Embry, however, would not be leading the attack after all. A meeting with Leigh-Mallory at 137 Wing at Hartford Bridge a few days before led to a chain of events that resulted in a direct order from his chief that Embry was not to fly. Embry protested vigorously to his immediate boss, Coningham, but Mary was adamant: "I am sorry," he said, "but those are Leigh-Mallory's orders, and he was most emphatic about it, so I am afraid you will have to accept it."[88] The decision had implications for Ted:

> "It was just before the raid that Basil was told by the commander-in-chief that he wasn't allowed to fly because he knew too much and if he got shot down, he might reveal his secrets. I rather foolishly said that I'd go down to the wing and fly with one of the boys to which he replied 'Oh no you won't. You know as much as I do so if I can't fly then you can't fly either.' So that was that!"

In the light of other events, Embry's decision to include Ted in Leigh-Mallory's orders and refuse him permission to fly appears a little churlish. No-one had stopped Ted joining a crew from 180 Squadron for an attack on a V-1 construction site at Bailly-en-Campagne on February 15, in the middle of planning for the Amiens raid. Flying a daylight raid as a supernumerary in a Mitchell must surely have presented the same and most likely an even greater risk than Ted's usual ops in a Mosquito.

The briefing, when it finally arrived, was shrouded in total secrecy. Only at the very end did Embry break the seals and lift the lid on the box in the room to reveal the beautifully made model of the gaol. For two hours the crews studied it from every angle, calculating heights, obstacles, gun posts, and exit routes. In his part of the briefing, Ted carefully and thoroughly explained the chosen route in and out, and the threat posed by the proximity of the German fighter base. He made it very clear that they could not afford to hang around after dropping their bombs.

At 1100 hrs, the roar of 38 Rolls-Royce Merlins could be heard across the airfield; if all went well, they would start their attack while the Germans were having lunch. On the ground, resistance fighters outside of the gaol were ready to help their compatriots make good their escape. Inside the prison, word had also got through to the resistance leaders that an attack was imminent.

Conditions on the flight out were appalling. At 100ft, the weather was such that pilots and navigators could see little more than a grey, soupy mist of snow and rain beating against the Perspex canopy.[89] The rendezvous with the Typhoons didn't go exactly to plan and four Mosquitoes lost contact with their formation and returned to base. A fifth returned with an engine fire, leaving only nine aircraft to carry out the attack with four in reserve. It was enough. Over France the weather cleared and by 1201 hrs the pilot of the first of the Mosquitoes was lining up his attack, using the tree-lined Albert–Amiens road to guide him to the target, just as Ted had planned. Some of the Typhoons had also made it through, one navigator almost jumping out of his skin as a 'Tiffie' shot across his nose at full bore.

Some of what Ted feared might happen did happen. At only 10ft off the ground, 'Blackie' Smith flew so low that his bomb skipped over the first wall, across the courtyard, and exploded on the wall on the other side. The smoke and debris from the opening attack also caused problems for the Australians following closely behind. But despite the challenges, as the photo Mosquito zipped over the target, the pilot could see that the operation had been a success. Both ends of the prison had been demolished and the surrounding wall broken down in several places. Large numbers of prisoners were seen scrambling over piles of rubble, rushing out onto the roads and running into the fields to freedom. As Raymond Vivant recounted afterwards:

"I had just taken off my jacket to go and wash my hands when there was suddenly the deafening roar of planes flying very low overhead followed by a tremendous explosion. At first I thought a German plane must have crashed just outside and was rejoicing gleefully to myself. When the first explosion was followed by several others, instinctively I crouched for protection in the corner of my cell while the window shattered to pieces. The left wall of the cell suddenly gaped open, and the air was filled with dust. I didn't move and by now I was thinking that there must be an aerial battle going on overhead and that planes were crashing to the ground with their bomb loads. But as soon as the dust cleared a little I saw that my cell door had been torn from its hinges. The corridor outside was a pile of stones and smoking rubble. To the right the prison building seemed to still be intact but to the left I could see my way open to the country, the snow-covered fields stretching as far as the eye could see. A wide gap had been torn in the high surrounding wall."[90]

Of the 700 or so prisoners held captive, 102 were killed and 74 wounded, but 258 escaped, including many of the most important members of the resistance movement. Of those who escaped, 182 were recaptured.

The Mosquitoes also suffered casualties. The aircraft of Squadron Leader Ian McRitchie, leading the second vic of Australians, was riddled by flak as he attempted to re-form after the attack. His navigator was killed outright and McRitchie was forced into a high-speed crash-landing which he was lucky to survive. It may have been this that distracted Pickard, for as he circled the wreckage looking for signs of life, his aircraft was suddenly pounced upon by a German Fw 190 flown by Wilhelm Mayer who had found his way through the fighter screen. Hit in the tail, Pickard didn't stand a chance; his Mosquito flipped onto its back and slammed into the ground, killing both pilot and navigator instantaneously. Pick had told his men at briefing that it was a 'death or glory' job, and in the event, he achieved both.

In the operations room at 2 Group Headquarters, Ted could only follow the drama of the raid as it played out on the plotting table. Their own intelligence and information regarding their aircraft's whereabouts was supplemented by 'Y' plots from the Germans' own reporting system, picked up by dedicated 'Y' listening stations along the south coast and then relayed to headquarters. Ted was alarmed when the plot suddenly revealed the presence of fighters, unaware that the RAF's own Typhoon fighting force had been seriously depleted. He watched as the German pilots started to close in on the Mosquitoes, powerless to do anything about it:

"It was really rather tense. It's the only time I had seen it happen and didn't like it very much. According to the reports we received, the German fighters were opening fire almost as soon as they raised their undercarriage, they were that close."

Embry had been right to be concerned about Pickard's suitability to lead the raid and says as much in his autobiography:

"I shall always regret that decision because, although he was an exceptionally experienced operational pilot at night, he had carried out only a few missions by day, and I believe this may have been the reason why he was shot down by enemy fighters. He stood out as one of the great airmen of the war and a shining example of British manhood."[91]

While not explicitly criticising Pickard, Ted shared similar reservations about Pick's actions that afternoon:

"The important thing with any low-level attack in daylight was to get away quickly before the fighters had a chance to find out where you are. The risks of being intercepted were quite significant. As I understood it, it was actually the pilot of the photographic Mosquito, flying right at the back, behind everyone else, who would decide whether the reserve formation was needed or not but in practice Pickard flew an orbit which he was not briefed to do. Doing that in sight of a German fighter airfield was not to be encouraged."

In assessing the tactics of the raid afterwards, and the lessons to be learned, it was perhaps always questionable whether so many Mosquitoes could conduct a quick 'in and out' given the presence of German fighters without coming to some harm. The issue was, however, that the RAF would only get one chance on this particular target and if they missed, there would be no going back a second time. The prisoners would either be moved or shot:

"Amiens was a one-off chance; if we'd failed, we wouldn't have been able to go back again which is why we always tended – unwittingly perhaps – to use too many aircraft and too many bombs. The bombing, however, was pretty accurate. They did remarkably well in atrocious weather and poor visibility, and I am still surprised at how many Frenchmen got out."

Ted says that the French underground movement's planning was also first class: "You couldn't have had two or three hundred prisoners all running around wildly; they needed somewhere to go and somewhere to hide."

Any sense of elation as to the success of the raid was tempered by a deep sense of shock at Pickard's loss, and 140 Wing were perhaps fortunate not to lose more of their number. In the 80 years that have passed since the raid, new theories have also emerged as to its true purpose, whether or not, for example, the French prisoners were actually about to be shot or whether there was some other political motive behind the attack. Perhaps in this case the truth isn't relevant: Operation Jericho has gone down in history as an 'epic' and will forever be so.

CHAPTER EIGHT
PREPARING FOR D-DAY

A NY DISAPPOINTMENT OR FRUSTRATION THAT Ted may have felt in not being allowed to fly on the Amiens raid was short lived. A few weeks before Operation Jericho, Reg Reynolds had been posted to 140 as wing commander flying, and nominally Ted was posted to 21 Squadron as navigation leader to join him. After Reg's wilderness years, he was delighted to be re-acquainted with his young friend, and they celebrated with an afternoon operation against some V-1 construction works on February 28, 1944. It was, for a little while at least, an ideal scenario. Ted knew that Reggie was coming back to 140 Wing at some time and was determined to rejoin him: "Through the generosity of the AOC, I still kept my planning job for major operations. If we had something special on, I would be recalled to headquarters; you couldn't really do any better than that."

No sooner had the old team been reunited, however, then Ted was taken off operational flying and planning and posted away to 1508 BAT Flight, to become an instructor for a Gee-H bombing course at Swanton Morley. It was far from his dream job.

Swanton Morley was four miles north of East Dereham, back in the bosom of Norfolk. Built to pre-war standards, it had excellent facilities and three, well-drained grass runways. It was at Swanton Morley that 105 Squadron had taken delivery of its first Mosquitoes and from where British and American airmen had set out back in the summer of 1942 to take part in the first combined bombing raid of World War Two, waved off by Churchill and General Eisenhower, later to become the supreme allied commander. In August 1943, a new unit had been established to teach pupil pilots blind approach and landing techniques, and which also served to explain to navigators the mysteries of a new blind-bombing device known as Gee-H.

Gee-H was a development of the basic Gee radio navigation system used widely by Bomber Command. Rather than the ground station transmitting to the aircraft, the addition of a new transmitter in the bomber enabled it to send signals to the ground which were then reflected to determine a fix. It was similar in concept to Oboe but unlike Oboe, which could only guide one aircraft at a time, Gee-H could support multiple aircraft at once. The set could also be used in two modes: for general navigation, the transmitter could be switched off, and switched back on again for the actual attack.

Operating Gee-H required training, skill and a not inconsiderable amount of patience, because as with all new technologies developed during the war it was prone to technical difficulties. When it worked, however, it was incredibly accurate. Gee-H was first used on the night of November 3/4, 1943. Düsseldorf was the objective. Thirty-eight Lancasters of 3 Group set out to bomb the Mannesmann Steel Works. Fifteen attacked according to plan, and of the remainder, 16 suffered equipment failures, five returned early and two went missing. Photographs after the raid, however, suggested that more than half of the bombs dropped by the 15 serviceable Gee-H aircraft had fallen within half a mile of the aiming point and caused considerable destruction. Faith in the equipment's development had been well placed.[92] The device was first used by 2 Group three months later and was to prove invaluable against larger targets when covered in 10/10th cloud.

Ted spent two months as an instructor, counting the days before he could return to operations. While he increased his flying hours and experience on Mitchells it was not what he'd signed up for. He'd been frustrated when obliged to attend a bombing instructor's course earlier in the war, and incurred the anger of Digger Kyle, but this was worse, because an invasion could only be just around the corner, and he didn't want to miss it. His logbook shows that he flew with some of the group's leading lights. These included Wing Commander Lewis Lynn, the wing commander (flying) of 137 Wing from Hartford Bridge who had recently been awarded the DSO for his leadership of 320 (Dutch) Squadron; and Lieutenant Commander Thijs de Groot who was recognised with the DFC while serving with the same unit at RAF Dunsfold.

Happily, Ted's purgatory ended when a vacancy came up in the middle of May for a wing navigation officer and he jumped at the chance. It meant re-joining Reggie and the boys of 140 Wing at Gravesend in Kent, where the three squadrons were now residing prior to moving to a more permanent if somewhat over-crowded home at Thorney Island in West Sussex. Gravesend was a civil airfield with a grass strip, just big enough for Mosquitoes:

> "One thing that amuses me is that the ground floor of the control tower was a public bar which we kept going. It was quite a good airfield, but we were forced out of there because, when the flying bombs started coming across in large numbers, quite a few landed in that area of Kent. That meant they increased the number of gun batteries, but the gunners had a habit of shooting at anything, including our own aeroplanes. I once saw them open fire on a Liberator that flew across at about 1,000 feet and could not have been mistaken for a flying bomb!"

Ted said that the move to Thorney Island had happened quite suddenly; it was a Coastal Command station and the Mosquito boys initially slept under canvas:

> "We had a gale once which blew most of the tents over and so we moved into the mess which was one of the big officers' messes that the air force had. I think there were only five or six of them, and the locals were not too pleased, but we got on very well with the local Fleet Air Arm squadron and a Coastal Command development unit that was also stationed there. It suited us very well."

Ted flew with Reg from Gravesend on May 28, a short hop across the Channel to attack a Howitzer battery near Fécamp. It was one of many thousands of sorties being flown to soften the defences ahead of the invasion, and to keep the Germans guessing as to the intended landing grounds. Hitler still believed the Allies would cross the Channel at the shortest point between Dover and Calais. The Allies, of course, had different ideas, but to maintain the deception, for every 'genuine' target they attacked in Normandy, they mounted two in the Pas de Calais. It required huge effort and resource and led to an intense period of activity for the Mosquito crews of 140 Wing.

A change in tactics came at the start of June. From thenceforward, the Mosquitoes would be used at night. With Gee and a two-man crew they were better suited to the task than the single-seater Typhoon fighter-bombers. Ted took the news in his stride and set about devising a new operational standard, albeit with an element of Heath Robinson built in:

> "Operating at night you couldn't really see that much or anything at all for that matter, depending on the state of the moon. We therefore organised things beyond the front line [of the advancing troops] into 'blocks', and each Mosquito was allocated a block, a time in and a time out. Our role was then to patrol that area for our allotted time and use our bombs and guns to try and stop any movement we could see. Sometimes when it was particularly dark, if we thought we saw something then we would fire off a Very pistol (which was like a flare and mounted in the roof). Then we'd turn the Mosquito about and if we were lucky, we might see a locomotive or a truck and attack it. If our luck was out, we saw nothing."

Philippe Livry-Level, a French navigator in 140 Wing, remembers:

> "We flew over enemy territory in night sorties covering over 1,000 miles at more than 250 miles an hour. We swept down low over roads and railways and canals. We spat fire at the least glow of light, the slightest sign of movement, at transport and convoys. Even if it was cloudy and there was no moon we still flew, keeping 300 to 600 feet higher to avoid any unexpected obstacles or forgotten hills or in case of any error in the altimeter."[93]

Much to his frustration, Ted was not allowed to fly on D-Day; he was grounded until the troops had landed on the beaches. In the meantime, his frustration was not in any way assuaged when obliged to surrender his parachute to a rather high-profile passenger, the BBC journalist Richard Dimbleby, who had managed to wangle a flight in a 2 Group aircraft to report 'live' from the Normandy beachhead. Ted was not impressed, and neither was the parachute section officer who accused him of losing it and refusing him a new 'chute until he coughed up. It took some time for the matter to be resolved.

It was not until very late on the first day of the invasion, June 6, 1944, that Ted set out with Reg and a full load of 500lb bombs to attack targets of opportunity in their allocated block. The moon was on their side for they returned with their bomb racks empty and machine-gun and cannon ammunition trays all but exhausted having attacked a railway bridge and shot up a steam locomotive. It was the order of things over the next few days as the ground troops became bogged down and needed all the help the air force could provide in preventing the Germans from regrouping. Losses among the Mosquito crews remained tolerably light, and Ted did not perceive the operations as particularly hazardous. They would become more dangerous as the front line moved, the Germans rallied their defences, and the terrain became less hospitable to aircraft flying low in the dark.

On July 14, a special operation was laid on, requested directly from the headquarters of the Special Air Service (SAS), the elite of the British army. Ted was summoned to 2 Group HQ by Embry to support with the detailed planning as the need for the attack was immediate and urgent: "It was a case of get the boys together, get a briefing sorted and let's go. A quick telephone call from somewhere and immediate action."

A few weeks before, the SAS had been parachuted into France as part of Operation Bulbasket, tasked with teaming up with the local French Maquis to create havoc behind the German front lines. Their camp in woods near the small town of Verrières, however, was discovered, and a group of dreaded SS Panzer Grenadiers based at Bonneuil-Matours was assembled to attack. Taken completely by surprise, the SAS men and their Maquis friends were slaughtered. Many of those who tried to surrender were gunned down or bludgeoned to death. A number were taken prisoner, interrogated and then taken out, shot and buried in mass graves. Only a handful survived to tell the tale, among them the commanding officer of B Squadron Captain John Tonkin. It was Tonkin who managed to get word back to the Allies and request a retaliatory raid on the SS base. The precise location was the Château de Marieville, a rather splendid 18th century castle overlooking the Vienne river.

Embry with Ted and the other 2 Group planning staff decided on an attack using 14 Mosquitoes, once again taking a handful of Mossies from each of the 140 Wing squadrons. The newly appointed leader and veteran of 21 Squadron,

Wing Commander David Dennis, would lead one section, 'Blackie' Smith from 487 Squadron a second, and Wing Commander Gordon Panitz, recently promoted, the remaining section of four from his force of Australians. They would be joined by Reg and Ted and the raid leader, Group Captain Peter Wykeham-Barnes, the dashing new 28-year-old OC of 140 Wing and worthy successor to the gallant Pickard.

The crews knew the reason for the attack but were sworn to secrecy. It would not play well if the Germans were later to learn that the raid was purely one of revenge. It would especially not play well given that some of the Mosquitoes would be armed not with 'conventional' bombs but rather a new and rather more terrifying weapon: napalm. Developed in the US, gasoline and aluminium naphthenate mixed with aluminium palmitate (hence na-palm) were packed into a shell case containing phosphorous and TNT. When the weapon exploded, it shot out thick, gooey globules of fire that would stick to anything with which it came into contact with horrifying results. Officially designated AN-M76, it was the first time that such a weapon was to be used by the RAF in action, and in the minds of the planners and those taking part, there were few more deserving targets.

The attacking force left Thorney Island in the late evening, Panitz having returned from an investiture ceremony earlier in the day at Hartford Bridge where he had received the DFC from the hands of the King. Their time on target was designed to coincide with when the Germans should be having their evening meal and allow the aircraft to make good their escape in the dark. On the way in they would have a fighter escort of a dozen Mustangs, but on the way back they would be on their own.

From base the formation climbed to 5,000ft as they crossed the Channel, descending to 2,000ft as they approached the Channel Islands. Luftwaffe flak batteries on Alderney had been informed of the approach of enemy aircraft and trained their 88mm guns on the lead aircraft. Heavy flak was not as feared or effective as rapid-firing light flak or even small-arms fire on aircraft at very low level, and although the raid leader felt a sharp thud on the airframe, they were otherwise untouched and dodged to throw off the gunners' aim.

With the enemy coast in sight, the Mosquitoes eased down to 1,000ft and began positioning themselves for attack as their escort peeled away and headed for home without a word, strict radio silence being maintained. The main target was the barracks itself in an area no bigger that 170ft x 70ft. It would be difficult to spot, hidden in the north-east section of a forest, and even at very low level it would be a challenge to deliver an accurate attack. The plan was for the Mosquitoes to approach from the east to avoid the risk of civilian casualties and damage to the nearby village should any of the bombs be off target.

To Ted, the conditions were perfect. It was a cloudless night and the visibility excellent. It had been an uncomplicated piece of navigation and within moments they were upon the target without the Germans being aware. The first bombs were dropped before they had time to man their defences. There was a slight delay; 11 seconds. A lull before a devastating storm. Then they exploded, and the terrible destruction began, the soldiers falling over themselves to grab their weapons, rush outside and fire blindly into the air. A single 20mm flak gun also opened up from the roof of a nearby house but the attack was over almost as soon as it started, and the flak position put out of action.

Ted and Reg dropped their own bombs, including two of the special weapons, into the broken mess that had once been distinguishable as a noble building sheltering an ignoble army. Reg eased the Mosquito around and dived back towards the target to strafe anything that was still moving on the ground. The formations led by 487 and 464 Squadrons had wreaked most of the damage, and by the time it was 21 Squadron's turn, seven barrack blocks had been blasted and were now engulfed in flames, causing one of the pilots to observe that 'there wasn't much left to attack'. That didn't stop them, however, for they were in no mood for mercy. Nine tons of bombs and thousands of rounds of machine-gun bullets and cannon shells had taken their toll. Subsequent reports varied but anything between 80 to 200 of the 400 or so SS troops quartered at Bonneuil-Matours had been killed and there were no reports of any civilian casualties, despite at least one or two of the bombs being seen to overshoot towards the village or roll down the east bank of the river. The success had been complete. On the return leg, several of the Mosquitoes shot up whatever they could see with their remaining ammunition to complete the night's work.

Before the attack, Embry had apparently urged his men to 'let the bastards burn'. He had achieved his wish. The SS murderers had themselves met a terrifying end, many dying in an agony of flames. There were few to mourn them.

Of those Germans who had escaped the carnage, their respite didn't last long. A few weeks later, John Tonkin, who was then still at large in France, called for another airstrike against a barracks near Poitiers where some of the SS were now stationed. It was also used as a training school for turning French collaborators into the *Franc Garde* – an armed branch of the dreaded French Milice.

Ted remembers it because of the speed with which the operation was called and planned. He said it was one of those quick reaction operations on an objective that was easy to find, unlike some of the V-1 targets that were extremely difficult to see:

> "If you could get enough information about a target, and its defences, then the chances of success were pretty good. That's why I remember it so well. It was a success because we had the right intelligence to start with."

On July 31, Ted did some local flying with Peter Wykeham-Barnes at the controls. It was the first time the two had flown together, and since they would be leading the raid the next day, it made sense to get to know one another's foibles. Ted recalls that the OC 140 Wing was 'a very, very good pilot': "It always used to surprise me that he never looked as if he was paying that much attention (to anything) but if I looked at the [control] panel it was always absolutely spot on."

Wykeham-Barnes was certainly an experienced officer. And an eccentric one. He'd started out as an aircraft apprentice (as Roy Ralston had done) and became one of RAF Halton's most famous 'Brats'. As a highly decorated fighter pilot he notched up 15 'kills' in North Africa and commanded what became known as 'The Malta Pirates' – a 'buccaneering and exceptionally successful' Mosquito intruder squadron based on the George Cross island. His favourite ruse was to panic enemy airfields at night, retire to a respectful distance, and wait until the flak started to open up either at its own aircraft or simply nothing at all. Tearing a cartilage while exercising, he returned to the UK and a stint as a staff officer at Fighter Command, prior to being given operational command of 140 Wing. Well-built and debonair, Ted couldn't but help liking Wykeham-Barnes for his larger-than-life character: "He was a bit of a showman. He had a Bentley and used to drive around wearing a red neckerchief and a large Alsatian sat beside him, looking absolutely marvellous."

The attack was executed on August 1 and the barracks totally destroyed. The SAS and their French friends had been avenged. One Mosquito failed to return.

CHAPTER NINE
GESTAPO HUNTING

A S A SEAT OF LEARNING, Aarhus University could trace its history back to 1928, with an initial enrolment of 64 students under the tutelage of one professor of philosophy and four associates in Danish, English, French and German. A university in Copenhagen had blossomed, and businesses and institutes in Aarhus were determined that their city should have one of its own. Their donations, and the supply of a million bricks and tiles from the United Tileworks of Aarhus, helped the first buildings to be constructed and the official opening in September 1933. Within a year the university was authorised to hold examinations and a year later appointed its first rector.

As the university flourished, so it became clear that further auditoriums and lecture theatres were required, and a new expansion plan devised. The occupation of Denmark by German forces in 1940 delayed the construction of a new main building, which was further and deliberately delayed with the arrival of the Gestapo in 1943 to establish their new headquarters.

The Gestapo chose Aarhus as its HQ to project terror across the whole of Jutland, under the command of its chief Eugen Schwitzgebel, a 44-year-old Bavarian bully who was feared by friend and foe alike. He shared a building, no doubt reluctantly, with the *Geheime Feldpolizei* (GFP) – the German secret field police tasked with counter espionage and counter propaganda. A large part of the GFP's work was targeting its own troops, to put down insurrection or defeatism with a firm hand, but its officers were also used in connection with the arrest and interrogation of local resistance leaders. The building was also home to the *Sicherheitsdienst* (SD), an organisation superior to the Gestapo in many ways and whose informants presented a great source of danger to anyone fighting for freedom. The local officer in charge was SS Obersturmbannführer Lonechun.

On the same site but in a separate building was the military intelligence organisation known as the Abwehr under the local command of Oberstleutnant Lutz. The Abwehr, which was part of the Wehrmacht, enjoyed an uncomfortable relationship with both the Gestapo and the SD, as its leader Admiral Canaris was later to find when he was arrested following the assassination attempt on the Führer in July 1944 and ultimately hanged. Once the most powerful of the secret organisations, it involved itself with military espionage, counter espionage, and the training of saboteurs.

A much lesser-known organisation, the *Deutsche Wochenschau*, completed the German presence. The organisation was perhaps less familiar for a reason, for it was the cover name for the German informer system and taken from the newsreel series of the same name. Chief of the department, Oberleutnant Bluhme, was a well-known organiser of intelligence services in Denmark, and the cover name wasn't fooling anyone, least of all the local resistance.

The danger represented by these organisations to the resistance cannot be overestimated. The fear of capture and torture and the implications for whole families was ever present, and filing cabinets were by now overflowing with interrogation and surveillance reports, observations and tip-offs that might lead to imminent arrest and execution. The net was tightening.

The summer and autumn of 1944 was a challenging time for the resistance in Jutland. The capture and interrogation of Jakob Jensen, a British parachutist, led to the arrest of more than a hundred men and women involved in the resistance movement and supplies of arms and ammunition quickly dried up. The use of informants also had a catastrophic effect on what little resistance remained. A further 50 resistance members were rounded up, interrogated and their networks dismantled. Soon – very soon, and unless something drastic happened – their organisation would fail to exist.

The chief of resistance operations in Jutland, Vagn Bennike, saw the writing writ large on the wall and with the capture of one of his couriers at the beginning of October recognised that urgent action was required. He knew that a dramatic blow needed to be struck, and that the RAF were the ones to do it.

A signal sent to London by Bennike dated October 15, 1944 tells its own desperate story. It recognises that while some of his people were already beyond help, many hundreds more were at risk from the information the Germans had gathered. It said simply:

'Underground in Jutland just about to be torn up by Gestapo. IT IS MORE IMPORTANT TO DESTROY ARCHIVE AND SAVE OUR PEOPLE THAN TO SAVE ARCHIVES AND HAVE OUR PEOPLE DESTROYED.'

The intelligence chiefs in London understood the dangers at once and asked for details of the enemy's defences within a kilometre of two specific buildings (colleges four and five) that had been earmarked for attack and were the two most westerly of the university block. The information was fast in coming – there were no anti-aircraft guns within a radius of one kilometre from the colleges – but then came a period of agonising delays as the weather closed in over the target making a low-level attack impossible. Every day that passed increased the risk both to the resistance fighters, and to the RAF airmen, since secrets never lasted for long.

Using a now tried-and-tested process, Embry set his model makers to work, constructing a scale model of the university based on recent reconnaissance photographs. Peter Wykeham-Barnes gave Ted and Reg the task of leading the raid and the two men immediately set about detailing a series of cross-country training flights to hone their low-flying skills:

"It all started when we got a call for us to go and visit the headquarters of Special Operations Executive (SOE) in Baker Street.

"I went up with Peter who may have known [what it was about] but I certainly didn't. We were introduced to some Danes and the question came up: could we attack the Gestapo headquarters in Aarhus? They produced all the information they had available. We looked at it closely and decided 'yes we could'. We could see which specific buildings we needed to hit and given that the university was outside of the town we were happy to do it. From our point of view, it was not a difficult target."

While it may not have been difficult, there were some hospital buildings nearby, and getting there and back caused Ted a few sleepless nights. It was a long leg from the British coast to Jutland, all at low level, and all across sea. Without visual references, Ted would have to rely on dead reckoning, which was notoriously tricky over long distances where even a tiny miscalculation could result in an aircraft being many miles off course. Gee was useful up to a point, but at 50ft it didn't help for long.

Flying alone was one thing, but Ted also had the responsibility of guiding the whole formation to the coast and then on to the target area. And once over the coast, his problems weren't over. Then they had to avoid the flak and, if possible, the German radar. Denmark was protected by many guns, and finding a path through their anti-aircraft defences was critical: "If you found [a gap] you might be lucky, but if not, you could suffer."

The distance itself was also an issue. Being based on the south coast, 140 Wing was a long way from Denmark for the unit's Mk VI fighter-bombers, even with drop tanks to extend their range. They decided instead to launch the attack from Swanton Morley in Norfolk, reckoning that they would have adequate fuel (for a round trip of c.1,250 miles of which 700 would be over water) and sufficient bomb loads to cause the destruction required. In addition, they were to have an escort of Mustang fighters, courtesy of one of the Polish squadrons (315 Squadron), to deal with any Luftwaffe trouble should it materialize. Given that the squadron was led by one of Poland's 'ace' pilots, Wing Commander Kazimierz Rutkowski, the wing leader of 133 Wing, they were in safe hands.

Reg takes up the story in his own words:

"The plan was as follows: Ted and I would be leading and there would be a deputy leader in No. 2 position. No. 3, incidentally, was Air Vice-Marshal Embry (Wing Commander Smith). There would be four flights ('boxes') of six aircraft and the attack would be at the lowest level with each flight attacking successively. Three Mosquitoes would bomb No. 4 building and three No. 5 building from each flight. The first two would have 30-second delay bombs; the remaining four would have a 11-second delay. This was decided upon so that there would be no risk of the last aircraft in the flight being blown up by the bombs of the leader or deputy leader.

"To string out the second, third and fourth flights, a geographical point was chosen – a lake – about 30 miles to the south of the target, around which the second flight circled once, the third flight twice, and the fourth three times. The fighters were to remain with the last flight, as they would be the most likely to be intercepted."[94]

After a frustrating but familiar ten-day wait for the weather to improve, Ted and Reg finally received the green light on October 30 when the decision was taken to attack the following day. Ted briefed the crews that evening. He spoke not only of the flight out, but also the points to look out for in their run-in to the target, and in particular a brightly coloured gas storage tank that would confirm they were on the right track. The timing of the attack was once again planned to coincide with the enemy's eating habits!

The briefing room was packed with senior officers, their breast pockets a patchwork of medal ribbons denoting huge operational experience. Besides Reg and Ted were the AOC, the OC of 140 Wing, and the officers commanding 21 Squadron ('Daddy' Dale leading the second box), 464 Squadron (now Wing Commander Arthur 'Bill' Langton leading the third box) and 487 Squadron (Wing Commander Roger Porteous leading the fourth box). The attacking force would comprise seven Mosquitoes from 21, eight from 464, and nine from 487 as well as a single Mosquito from 107 Squadron which Embry had 'borrowed' for the occasion. A Mosquito from the 140 Wing Film Production Unit would follow on behind to survey the damage.

Shortly after 0700 hrs on the cold winter morning of Tuesday October 31, and with the sun not yet in the sky, the first of the Mosquitoes began taking off for the 40-minute flight from RAF Thorney Island to Swanton Morley to bomb up and refuel. The plan was to fly in squadron formation but the weather determined otherwise. Within two hours of arriving, they were on their way again, heading for the coast and then the long, 360-mile trek across the North Sea, the Mustangs guarding their rear. Reg had nothing but respect for the 'gallant Poles', especially at the height they were flying:

"I say 'gallant' because they were skimming the waves down with us. They were eager and should they have engine failure, there was only one way they could go – down. At least we had two engines and could fly with one out."

The weather conditions were in their favour. By now the day had dawned and sunny clear skies were making their task much easier. Visibility was only hampered by a steady build-up of oily sea salt on the windscreen of each aircraft which the wipers struggled to clear. Reg had to peer through the scratches in his windshield to see what was ahead, but all he could see was an ocean of grey. Inevitably, one of their number struck a bird and was forced to retire; another just narrowly avoided being struck by a 50-gallon drop tank as it bounced off the sea in front of him.

In an expert feat of navigation, Ted brought the formation over the Danish coast where the weather deteriorated. The journey seemed to have taken an age and Reg was perspiring heavily from the intense concentration. He looked to his right to see his number two tucked in close behind. To see such a powerful force of Mosquitoes now screaming across the Danish countryside lifted the soul. There were so many he wondered whether there were any left in England, the formation seemed to stretch for miles! Bright sunshine gave way to leaden skies of dull, low cloud. The AOC was later to remark that the conditions were ideal for a low attack; visibility was sufficient in the target area but a cloud base of 1,200ft made an interception by enemy fighters unlikely.[95]

What had been a loose formation now began to close up as they thundered towards their next turning point – the lake at Skanderborg. Now four of the Mustangs peeled away to make height and prevent the Luftwaffe from getting between them and the attacking force; four other Mustangs stayed with the formation. Everything was now accelerating to its climax. Reg recalls:

"I commenced my turn to the left (north) to pick up the road which was to lead me directly to my target, the western-most building. Ted was navigating at his best for I think that we were never more than 150 yards from our predetermined track. He pointed out to me the road which I was to follow. We scooted down to 50 feet at a speed of 280mph and very shortly [after] Ted said: 'there's the target ahead'."[96]

The buildings were clearly visible, even in the gloom. They passed a German transport aircraft flying a reciprocal course just a few hundred yards to one side, too late to do anything about it. While two miles and just a few moments flying time from the target, Reg opened the bomb doors and Ted armed the master switch. Lights were burning through the office windows and figures could be seen moving around inside. A cyclist looked up as their Mosquito approached, Reg hoping he wasn't a local as he pressed the release button, aiming his bombs directly at the fleeing man. The bombs skipped into the base of building number four as Reg pulled up and away and the rest of the first box came in to attack. Only then did the first air raid siren begin its mournful wail.

One by one the Mosquitoes dropped their bombs as the first box made way for the second, about four miles behind. In the lead formation, Squadron Leader Frank Denton, a Kiwi, got a little carried away. Spotting a lone gunner about to open fire from a top-floor balcony he dipped his nose and gave the German a quick burst of machine-gun fire. So close was he now to his intended target that he didn't have sufficient height to pull up and managed to clip the top of the building as he passed. The impact rocketed the aircraft up 200ft as Denton struggled to gain some semblance of control. He knew the aircraft had to be badly damaged, but wasn't aware that his port tailwheel and tailplane had been ripped off, both engine nacelles had been damaged, and a lump of masonry was embedded in the fuselage.

'Bill' Langton, at the head of the third box, was drawn to the dust and smoke of the damaged buildings and as such had no difficulty in identifying his target. He made his approach in a gentle curve and dropped his bombs a little higher than intended. On reflection it was a good thing, for as he zoomed over the target his aircraft was lifted by the explosion of the bombs that had been dropped by the Mosquitoes in front of him. He also saw fires beginning to set and the black, powdery fragments of burned paper rising into the skies.

Only Roger Porteous, leading the fourth box, experienced any difficulty. He had somehow missed the road leading from the lake to the target and had led his formation back to the coast to re-orientate themselves. It was a risk, for it meant that the German defences were now wide awake and the timing of their run was out of sync. Flying at 100ft, Wing Commander Lew Thomas, a supernumerary loosely attached to 487 Squadron, caught the blast of a bomb bursting in front of him and his aircraft, K-King, lurched into the air with smoke streaming from a damaged engine. As the aircraft veered away, Peter Wykeham-Barnes drew alongside and began gesticulating wildly. Thomas seemed not to understand that his engine was on fire and his aircraft badly damaged until the OC 140 Wing broke radio silence and told him! Thomas immediately feathered the starboard propeller and took stock. Orders were that if the flight home across water appeared too risky, they were to make for neutral Sweden. Better to be missing and later reported interned, than to go missing without trace, remembered only as a name carved on a lonely memorial.

While there was little or no flak over the target, several of the Mosquitoes came under fire from a German warship – the *Nürnberg* – anchored in the harbour close by. The main attack was over inside of ten minutes but that isn't quite the whole story. Several of the pilots from the Australian 464 Squadron shot up a number of trains with cannon fire while en route – just because they were there. The Mosquito of the film unit also lingered to ensure suitable footage of the raid was obtained for further analysis.

By 1420 hrs the last of the Mosquitoes had returned safely to Swanton Morley and the excited crews began discussing the raid in detail. Ted remembers how easily the buildings appeared to collapse, so much so that he doubted whether bombs were needed at all, and whether they would have gone down with a firm shove. He also remembers the conversation with Frank Denton on their return:

"While we were still over the sea Frank called up and asked could he break formation. He needed to get rid of his ammunition because he had no hydraulics and would have to crash land. Permission was given and when we landed, we asked him what had happened. He said: 'Well, I saw a German leaning out of a window with a gun so I dropped the nose to shoot back at him. I then pulled back hard [on the stick] and I clipped the roof.' We asked what he clipped the roof with, and he told us the starboard engine and the tailplane. When we looked at the aeroplane, of course he'd landed without wheels, the back nacelle on the starboard side was missing. Some weeks later we were in Aarhus because the war had ended, and we went to look [at the buildings we had bombed]. In the wreckage of the target was the nacelle from Frank's aeroplane."

Reg also remembered the incident well: "There was always a Mosquito in every formation which seemed to have trouble in retracting that part of the landing gear, but that was carrying things too far!"

In the debriefing that followed, all agreed that the attack had been a success. The buildings had been left in smoking ruins and the nearby hospital untouched. Quite how successful the raid had been was made clear almost immediately. A message sent from Jutland to London on the day of the attack simply read:

'BOMBING OF GESTAPO AARHUS…COMPLETELY DESTROYED. ONLY ONE BOMB FAILED. BARRACKS LANGELANDSGADE ARE BURNING. CONGRATULATIONS TO ALL CONCERNED.'

Less than two hours later, a further message was transmitted:

'COLLEGES FOUR AND FIVE TOTALLY DESTROYED. MAIN BUILDING AND COLLEGE THREE DAMAGED.'

Further messages of deserved congratulations were received by Reg and the wing in the weeks that followed, including one from the deputy supreme commander (Arthur Tedder) and the AOC-in-C 2TAF (Arthur Coningham). On November 12 Tedder wrote: 'I want everybody who had a part in it to know of its tonic effect on the Danish Resistance movement.'

Basil Embry in a letter to Wykeham-Barnes (November 20) ended: 'It is amazing how successful the show was. It was well executed but luck was on our side.'

In the subsequent analysis of the raid, the success of the attack was confirmed as was the news that Schwitzgebel and Lonechun had been killed in the bombing, along with dozens of their men. Twelve women were also dead. By luck, a meeting was being hosted that day by the Gestapo involving various Danish Nazis and they too perished in the flames. While both buildings 4 and 5 had been destroyed, so too had the Langelandsgade barracks as the signal had read. While not a target, it was a welcome bonus. Regrettably, a small number of Danish civilians were also casualties, but their loss did not detract from the overall sense of euphoria that came from the Danish Resistance. The thin line between success and failure had once again been navigated thanks to the skill of Ted and his colleagues. And a large slice of luck.

Who lived and who died was also down to luck. One Danish patriot, Pastor Sandboek, gave a graphic account of what it was like to be inside the building when the Mosquitoes struck. He was at the time being beaten with a dog whip and tortured by Schwitzgebel and his deputy:

"Suddenly we heard a whine of the first bombs while the planes thundered across the university. Werner's face was as pale as death from fright and he and his assistants ran out of the room. I saw them disappear down a passage to the right and instinctively I went to the left. This saved my life because shortly afterwards the whole building collapsed, and Werner and his assistants were killed."[97]

For his part in the raid, Ted received a Bar to the DFC he had been awarded after the attack on Berlin 18 months earlier. It was joint citation along with his pilot who also received an immediate Bar to his DFC.

'As pilot and navigator respectively, these officers have taken part in numerous sorties against a wide variety of targets. In October 1944, they took part in a most successful attack on a vital German target. In this well-executed operation, these officers displayed skill and resolution of the highest standard.'

Ted and Reg also received the undying thanks of the Danish underground and the gift of an engraved match case bearing the coat of arms of King Christian X, along with a set of cufflinks. It came with a note from their Danish liaison officer and friend Captain Svend Truelson which described the gift as 'a token of the close friendship and esteem existing between our two countries – a friendship which your gallant deeds have strengthened even more'.

By January 1945 it was obvious that the war couldn't last much longer. The Luftwaffe had taken one last gamble with Operation Bodenplatte, an all-out attack on Allied airfields, and succeeded only in losing what little talent and experience it still had in its ranks. The raid coincided with a similarly futile attempt by the army to break through in the Ardennes in what was to become known as the Battle of the Bulge and also served only to squander what was left of Germany's once feared Panzers. By the end of the month, the Russians had advanced from the east and liberated Auschwitz, thus revealing to the world the full horrors of the Nazis' Final Solution.

After the excitement of the Aarhus raid, which prompted similar press interest to the attack on Amiens, Ted settled back into more routine planning punctuated with the occasional operation to keep his hand in. For Reg, Aarhus was his 89th and what was to prove his final sortie of the war. On January 8 he was posted from his role as wing commander flying (operations) at 140 Wing to RAF Staff College where he saw out the war. There was a further changing of the guard at 140 Wing with the arrival of Bob Bateson as the officer commanding.

Bob Bateson, much like the man he replaced, was everything an RAF hero should look like. Square of jaw and with a blond, handlebar moustache, he was rarely to be seen without a pipe wedged firmly between his teeth. 'Pinpoint' Bateson had joined the RAF in 1936 and was regularly assessed as 'above average' in his flying abilities. By the outbreak of war, he was already an experienced officer with almost 700 hours of flying time in his logbook, mostly undertaken in Egypt and the Middle East. It was not until Italy entered the war in June 1940 that Bob became operational, flying six sorties in 11 days with 113 Squadron. By October he had already recorded 34 ops and by the end of the year that had nudged beyond 50.

After serving time as a staff officer, he returned to operational flying as OC of 211 Squadron, and later left the desert for Burma to fight the Japanese before escaping to Ceylon (now Sri Lanka) from Java. Here he was given command of 11 Squadron before finally returning to the UK in the summer of 1943. Having flown Blenheims almost from day one, he now converted to the Mosquito and was posted to 613 Squadron first as a flight commander and then as its CO. It was Bateson who had led the strike on the Gestapo HQ in The Hague for which he was awarded the DSO and later joined 2 Group HQ staff at Mongewell Park. Itching for a return to operations he was appointed wing commander flying at 136 Group before taking over the reins from Peter Wykeham-Barnes as OC 140 Wing.

The pleasure that greeted Bob's arrival was somewhat tempered by the loss a few days later of Daddy Dale, shot down and killed while on patrol over enemy territory between Arnhem and Osnabrück. Philippe Livry-Level, who was a similar age to Dale, remembers him as one of the most winning personalities in the RAF:

"Dale was passionately devoted to flying although he was over 40 and most of his limbs had been broken at one time or another through various accidents. He had worn down the opposition of his friends and superior officers until they let him go out on operations again. He was in peacetime the perfect gentleman farmer enamoured of fox hunting and had once spent some time proving to me that France had not yet reached so high a degree of civilization as England because we didn't hunt the fox with hounds.

"That night we heard him on the radio telling us that his plane had been hit, his right engine was out of action and his machine was badly damaged. He kept us informed every two minutes and we gathered that his plane was practically out of control but he had reached our lines and was being guided towards Brussels. Then came the last few words in Dale's voice: 'It's too late.' Then silence. Later they found his body near Aix-La-Chapelle along with his navigator among the burnt remains of their Mosquito."[98]

Ted did some local flying with Bob as well as an operation on February 10 to shoot up and bomb a railway target near Paderborn. He also shared his flying with Bob Iredale, the Australian former Jericho pilot, who was by then attached to 140 Wing HQ and similarly keen not to be 'out of it'. It was with Iredale that Ted also had his first trial with LORAN, a hyperbolic radio-navigation system developed in the US that was similar to the RAF's Gee system but operated at lower frequencies and so had a greater range. His thoughts on the new technology are not recorded.

One evening, Ted was invited to Baker Street to toast the success of the Aarhus raid. Senior officers of the SOE, Danish agents and some of the RAF pilots and other navigators who had taken part in the attack were present and the alcohol was said to be flowing freely. Ted was speaking to Peter Clapham, Embry's long-time and long-suffering regular navigator when the old man himself strode over and with a twinkle in his eye asked innocently: 'Could we get to Copenhagen and back?'[99]

The situation in Copenhagen mirrored that of Aarhus, as did the rationale for launching an attack. The Gestapo had set up home in the Shell House in the centre of the city. It's filing cabinets were similarly bursting with damning information and intelligence regarding the local resistance. Destroying the records in Aarhus was only one part of a three-piece jigsaw; the Danes were also desperate for similar and in some cases duplicate records to be destroyed at the Gestapo headquarters in Copenhagen and at Odense on the island of Funen. Ted relates that no patriot could be safe until those papers were burned:

"We had got to know the Danes very well by this point. Our liaison was Svend Truelson, a Dane in the British Army. It was he who asked us whether we could attack the Shell Building. They were after the paperwork and afraid that if it wasn't destroyed, the Gestapo would themselves be able to destroy the resistance movement."

Ole Lippman, who worked with Svend Truelson in the underground's military intelligence network and was greatly liked and respected by the Allies, was the man on the ground assessing what was possible. It was Lippman who believed the attack was needed and needed urgently. He was too experienced to suppose that the bombing of Shell House would destroy the Gestapo organisation in Copenhagen but he was confident that the destruction of their records would disrupt and hinder their work and gain necessary time for the resistance to regroup.[100] There was, however, one significant difference between the attack on Aarhus and the planned attack on Copenhagen. Within the attics of Shell House, the Germans had constructed a series of cells, each cell holding a member of the resistance. It was, in the eyes of many, an impossible task to bomb the building and destroy the records without also killing everyone inside. Ted was horrified. The purpose of the raid, unlike for example the raid on Amiens, was not to free the hostages but to destroy the headquarters and its records. There was no expectation that any of the prisoners would escape alive.

Embry himself was similarly appalled by the prospect. Ted thought the idea little short of 'crazy' and was convinced they would kill them all. Both men had to overcome their scruples and focus on the job in hand. For Ted, what first looked impossible slowly began to take shape. For some bizarre reason, the Germans had decided to try and camouflage the building by painting it with green and brown stripes. In attempting to hide the headquarters it had in fact only served to make it more visible, for it was the only building of its kind in the vicinity. Once again, planning for the raid followed the now familiar, tried-and-tested pattern.

Truelson helped with the gathering of intelligence, providing Ted with a number of photographs and tourist guidebooks that Ted said proved surprisingly useful. It was clear from the start that there was only one way in and out if they were to see the target, but from the photographs provided, Ted wasn't sure if it was feasible. He asked Svend whether he could get another photo, taken from a particular bridge overlooking St Jørgen's Lake, as it might give him a better angle:

> "He just smiled and a fortnight later strolled into my office and laid some photographs on the desk in front of me and said: 'are these what you wanted?' He'd had the photos taken in Denmark and then smuggled out through Sweden and flown back to England. I thought 'well, I'm committed now, and I have no excuse for not finding the target!'"

Once again nothing was left to chance. The precise make-up of the building and its construction was analysed, and Embry's personal model-making team set to work. The positions of Luftwaffe fighter airfields and flak positions were all plotted, and intelligence gathered on their strength and number. It was Bob Bateson's responsibility to determine the route, the turning point and to decide upon flying speed, formation, and the number of aircraft required. This was itself a challenge, since the modern structure of the building made it difficult to calculate how many bombs – and therefore how many aircraft – would be needed to bring it down. It was then Ted's job to plot the detail, marking identification points and suggesting any alterations necessary that might simplify navigation.

Bateson decided that six Mosquitoes would be sufficient to do the job; Embry disagreed. They would only have one shot at this, and they couldn't take any chances. Even the loss of a single Mosquito out of six might jeopardise the attack and there was safety in numbers. In the event they agreed on 18, in three waves of six, with a mix of high explosives and incendiaries.

Ted proposed that to avoid detection, the Mosquitoes would fly at wavetop height across the North Sea and no higher than 200ft across south Jutland and Zealand. The three waves would fly in echelon formation and, continuing their left-handed turn over the target, return to base via north Zealand and the southernmost point of Samsø. Embry remembers:

> "Shortly before the operation took place, we learned that several units of the German fleet had anchored in Copenhagen harbour. This meant a very considerable increase in the anti-aircraft defences, but we worked out, by the help of our target model, that if we succeeded in gaining initial surprise in our approach to the Shell House and withdrew by following a main thoroughfare through the town, flying below the rooftops, the flak from the ships could not hit us. And this was to be our plan."[101]

'Special' raids had to be accommodated within 140 Wing's existing commitments, and 18 Mosquitoes could not be spared for more than 48 hours from their critical role in supporting the Allied armies in Europe. As such, it was determined that the crews would only assemble for briefing 24 hours before take-off, and to avoid the additional risk of such a long flight Fersfield in Norfolk was chosen as the base for

Above left: Ted with the family dog Bob in more peaceful times.

Above right: Ted's ops in a Whitley were enough to convince him that heavy bombers were not for him!

Below: While popular to fly, the Blenheim was vulnerable to the new generation of German fighter.

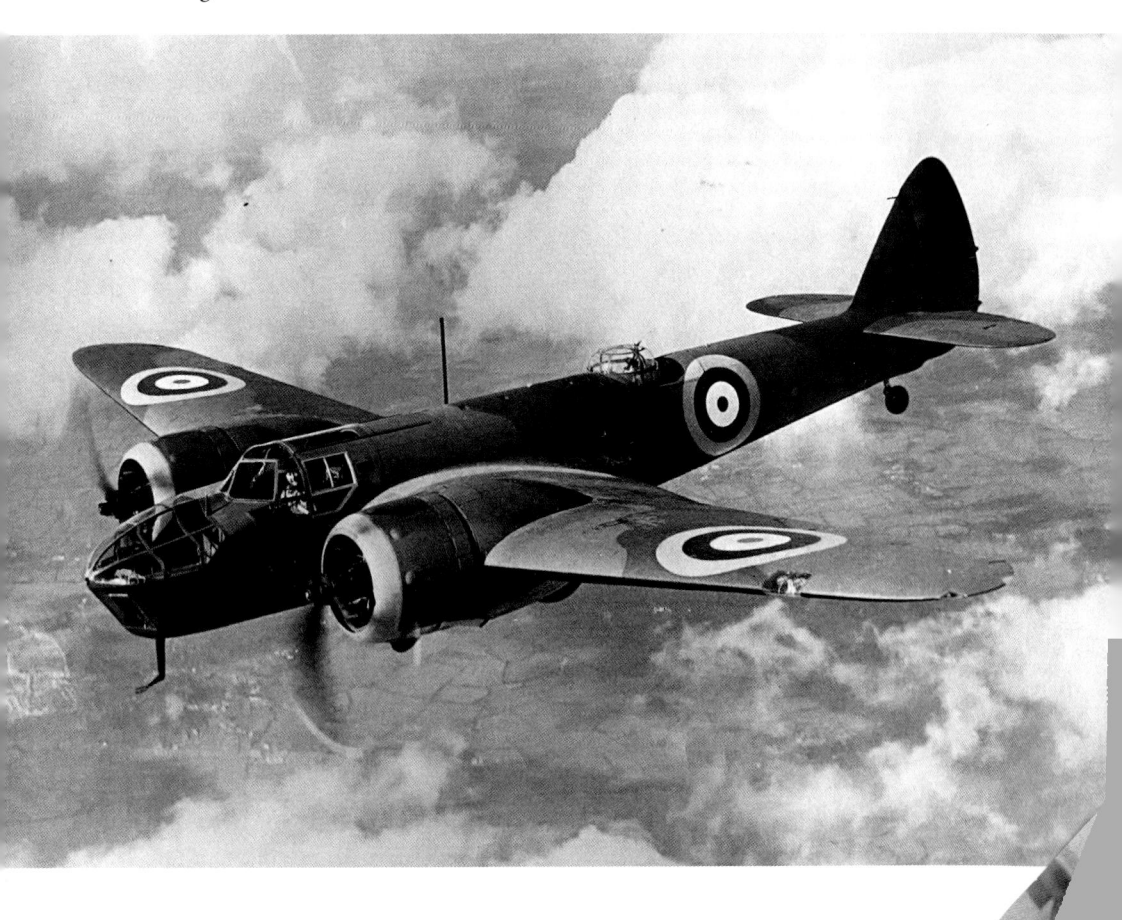

Left: The beautiful clean lines of the Mosquito are obvious in this classic shot of a 105 Squadron aircraft in flight.

Below: Ted with Reg Reynolds (right). When Reg arrived at Marham he was starting his third tour.

Right: Fighter-bomber variant of the Mosquito with one engine out.

Above: The surviving ten aircrew from the daylight attack on Berlin were officially congratulated by the CAS.

Right: Reg and Ted were praised for their calm courage, resolution and endurance during the Berlin raids.

Left: Ted as a young flying officer having recently been awarded his first DFC for the raid on Berlin.

Below: Planning for the deep penetration attack on Thionville in 1943.

Left: A last word of advice from the station commander prior to take off for Jena.

Above left: Ted lights up a Player's – untipped, one of his few vices.

Above right: Ted with the ribbons of the DSO and DFC, Marham, shortly after the raid on Jena.

Below: The smoking ruins of the college buildings at Aarhus.

Above: The accuracy of the Aarhus attack is evident as neighbouring buildings are left intact.

Left: Bob Iredale - former Jericho pilot and commanding officer of 464 Squadron.

Left: Low-flying Mosquitoes on their run into the target.

Above: A Mosquito (left of the picture) twists away at rooftop height.

Basil Embry (right foreground) appears to share a joke with his hosts in the ruins of Shell House.

A shot of Ted (far right) in the rubble of Shell House.

Bob Bateson (right) was everything an RAF hero should look like.

Above left: Odense where Ted broke almost every rule he had ever set!
Above right: Harold 'Mick' Martin, Dambuster and low-level supremo.
Below: A broadcast of thanks and condolences to the people of Copenhagen.

Above left: Long-range tanks are clearly visible in Ted's snap of the Mosquito en route to Cape Town.

Above right: Martin inspects the Mosquito's engines prior to the record-breaking flight to Cape Town.

Left: En route to Cape Town, the crew enjoyed a brief refuelling stop at Kisumu.

Below: The Mosquito taxies to a halt at Brooklyn airport.

Top: Ted and Mick Martin's arrival in Cape Town was greeted with great excitement.

Left: The award of the Britannia Trophy by the Royal Aero Club was a great honour.

Below: Prior to taking command of 29 Squadron, Ted (seated, second left) had to learn the ropes as a flight commander.

Top: Close up of a Meteor NF11 shows off the extended cockpit to accommodate the two-man crew.

Left: Meteor NF11s of 29 Squadron in tight formation for the Coronation Review.

Below: No. 29 Squadron Meteors in close formation. The aircraft nearest the camera (WD603) was later lost in the Channel.

Above left: Ted (second left) and fellow aircrew after a successful night-interception exercise.
Above right: Ted with his wife Rita (left) who had also been a serving air force officer in the war.

Above: Pilots of 29 Squadron. Flight Lieutenant Cottam (third from right seated) disappeared in the Channel.
Below: Pilots and navigators of 29 Squadron with their CO (seated centre).

Above: Ted used this Meteor 7, WL348, as a 'hack' during his time in Addis Ababa. It was later struck off charge at Khormaksar in December 1961.

Left: Formal duties with the commander-in-chief.

Below: Staff College where Ted (seated sixth from left) learnt the secrets of professional administration.

Above: Canberras of 139 Squadron. The Canberra proved the most elusive of the new generation of bombers to intercept at night.

Right: Wing Commander John 'Tommy' Thompson.

Below: An example of a Victor SR2 with cameras in the bomb bay.

Left: Ted as a Group Captain while serving as SASO at the Central Reconnaissance Establishment.

Below: Meeting Her Majesty the Queen at Bentley Priory. Ted was later mortified that he forgot to remove his sunglasses.

Far left: Air Commodore Ted Sismore as the 13th commandant of the Royal Observer Corps.

Left: A formal portrait with the ribbons of the DSO, DFC and two bars, and the AFC beneath his pilot's wings.

the operation. Bateson would be the raid leader, with Ted as the lead navigator. Embry and Peter Clapham would fly second, and the rest of the crews would be drawn from the most experienced pilots and navigators available at the time.

A message arrived from Denmark on March 15. Its contents were stark:

'Military leaders arrested and plans in German hands. Situation never before so desperate. Remaining leaders known by Hun. We are regrouping but need help. If any importance attached at all to Danish Resistance you must help us irrespective of cost. We will never forget RAF and you, if you come.'[102]

The one element of the raid that Ted couldn't control was the weather. They needed to know with absolute certainty that when they approached the target, they would not have to abort at the eleventh hour for there would be no going back. Embry was clear: "In spite of the urgency, I refused to attempt the raid until I was satisfied that the weather would be favourable, otherwise failure was certain and the patriots would be worse off than before."[103]

It was not until the 19th that Embry got the news they had all been waiting for, and the next day the attacking force comprising the usual suspects began to assemble, the Mosquitoes flying back to the UK from their airfield in Belgium. Frank Denton, recovered from his 'near miss' over Aarhus, was again taking part, and would lead the third section with his New Zealanders. Bob Iredale would lead the Australian contingent in the second wave. And joining Bob Bateson and Ted in the first wave was Peter Kleboe, who had only recently taken command of 21 Squadron.[104] This was to be his first 'spectacular'. Fighter cover was to be provided by Mustangs from 64 and 126 Squadrons, the pilots of which seemed particularly excited to be involved in such a 'hush hush' operation.

The long and thorough briefing was completed in its usual detail; what was unusual was that Bateson invited Svend Truelson to address the crews and stress the fact that the prisoners in the attic were all expected to be executed. They would prefer to die at the hands of the RAF, he told them, than continue to be tortured and then finally shot by the Nazis.

In the early hours of March 21, The Central Meteorological Forecasting Establishment confirmed its predictions of fine weather over the target. By 0830 hrs the crews were in their aircraft, going through their pre-flight checks. Twenty-five minutes later, the formation of 46 Mosquitoes and Mustangs were all in the air, and Bateson led them into a steep dive and levelled off at around 50ft for the long leg across the North Sea.

The journey out was especially challenging, Embry describing it as 'rough and boisterous', and at one point having to reach out of a side window to clear a small portion of the windscreen or else he couldn't see. Ted was being bucketed about so much by the wind that he actually thought the back of the aircraft was broken! Keeping station at 250mph under such conditions called for great concentration and physical endurance.[105] After a tense flight of an hour and 40 minutes, Ted saw ahead of him the first faint outline of the coast of Jutland. Immediately he began to search for landmarks; he and Bateson had brought the formation across 350 miles of sea to a perfect landfall. Another 40 minutes of flying would bring them to the target. Ted recalls:

> "We had by now become really quite good at reading the sea state. The wind lanes would give us the wind direction and the white horse would enable us to calculate the wind speed with a fair degree of accuracy and adjust course if necessary. What was essential was that the pilot was very precise in his steering and maintaining the correct compass course."

Ted had another essential weapon in his navigational armoury, the *North Sea Pilot:*

> "It was a sailor's book which had pictures of all the things that stuck out on a coastline like churches, windmills, and even tall trees – anything that is visible from a boat was featured. I carried a pair of binoculars with me, scanning the horizon to see what I could see. Sometimes it paid off in a big way."

It certainly paid off that day. The 18 Mosquitoes now rushed towards the centre of the city, sweeping over the green countryside of Jutland. Bateson deliberately exaggerated his manoeuvres to avoid high-tension cables and give those behind him suitable warning of any impending danger. 'I have rarely flown behind a better leader', Embry was to remark afterwards. Ted pointed to the lake and the bridge from which he had wanted a photograph, and there ahead of them was the target. He was justifiably pleased with himself: "My guesswork about what we would see actually worked!"

German ground defences opened up just as Bateson released his bombs and pulled clear of the roof, Ted clearly seeing their explosives strike between the first and second storeys. It was 1114 hrs. Embry followed, and similarly pulled up just in time before dipping back down again, almost to street level, to make good his escape, narrowly missing another Mosquito as it flashed over him, forcing him lower. Peter Kleboe should have been next but was no longer behind. His Mosquito had struck a light standard over the goods yard at Dybbølsbro station. The aircraft was seen to stagger in the air momentarily as if the pilot was fighting to regain control before crashing into the ground and catching fire.

Kleboe's crash was to have tragic consequences, for his burning aircraft smashed into the ground next to a catholic school. At least two aircraft in the second wave mistook the flames for the target and dropped their bombs accordingly. Amid all the confusion and harassed by the flak primarily from the German warships in the harbour, four Mosquitoes from the third wave did the same. As many as 89 children and 16 teachers and nuns died as a result.

After the raid, the usual messages of congratulations began flooding in. Operation Carthage, as it had been named, appeared to have succeeded. The Freedom Council in Denmark stated that the city was 'wild with excitement'. Lippman was more cautious. The building had been destroyed and was also on fire, the incendiaries having done their work well. But casualties among the Germans had been smaller than anticipated and as many as 123 innocent Danish men, women and children had been killed. Miraculously, however, and despite Ted's fears, many dozens of resistance fighters *had* managed to escape, many leaping from the wreckage of the fiercely burning building.

The cost to the attacking force had also been relatively high. Peter Kleboe and his navigator were dead, and two Mosquitoes from 464 Squadron flown by 'Shorty' Dawson and 'Spike' Palmer also failed to return, both the victims of flak. The loss of these 'well-tried veterans' was described as not only a shock, but also a severe blow to the squadron.

A further Mosquito from 487 Squadron also crashed trying to make for neutral Sweden. The pilot managed successfully to ditch his aircraft on water and clamber onto the wing but both he and his navigator died before help could arrive. Two of the fighter escort were also shot down. The Mustangs had done sterling work in supressing the German defences but paid the price. Bob Hamilton of 64 Squadron executed a successful crash landing and was quickly taken prisoner by soldiers of a nearby observation post; the Mustang of Dave Drew, one of the flight commanders with 64 Squadron, was hit by flak and crashed not far from the target area. He was killed. Many other aircraft were damaged. Frank Denton used up another of his nine lives, returning home to make a successful belly landing with the starboard flap in tatters and his hydraulics u/s. Flight Lieutenant Dempsey flew the last 400 miles on one engine. Four Mosquitoes and two Mustangs had been lost at the cost of nine men's lives.

The evidence available from the images taken during the raid were inconclusive; the subsequent report and photographs from a reconnaissance aircraft from 34 Wing confirmed the objective of the operation had been achieved.

In his role as the Gestapo's nemesis, Ted still had one last act to perform. Now permanently based on the continent, the wing was regularly on the move, often using primitive advanced landing grounds (ALGs) following a tactic that had been adopted so effectively in the desert some years earlier. B.87 (the 'B' denoting an airfield built for RAF use) was at Rosières-en-Santerre which had actually been built by the British in 1939 and later occupied by the Luftwaffe ahead of the Battle of Britain. Now it was safely back in Allied hands, and a springboard for operations deep into enemy territory. Ted was happy with his new home:

"Rosières-en-Santerre was a properly built field with runways and facilities for the aircraft. When we first arrived, we had to be very careful because the Germans had left boobytraps everywhere and that made life a little difficult. There was no living accommodation, so we commandeered some local housing and set up wing headquarters in a nearby chateau which was quite delightful. It was a little rundown but still very pleasant. We employed some local staff to work for us but most of the civilians were agricultural workers and neither healthy nor wealthy. They were very different from the Danes we would meet later who by comparison were well fed and organised, because the Germans had used Denmark as an example of what an occupation could look like. The French didn't seem to care."

Ted flew with Bob Iredale on April 5 to attack targets of opportunity and a week later was again asked to plan and lead a further raid on a Gestapo headquarters on the island of Funen, near the Danish city of Odense. The attack was at the direct request of the local resistance chief who felt the threat to his network was still very real. The war may only have a few weeks left to run, but many dozens of his fighters were still at risk should the Germans choose to have one last terrible hurrah.

The headquarters were situated in a large and once attractive country house known officially as the *Husmandsskolen* and more locally as 'the torture castle' – such was its grim reputation. In happier times it had been an agricultural college. On the one hand, the target should have been easy to find. However due to the panic instilled in the Gestapo by the success of Aarhus and Shell House, the Germans had gone to great lengths to make the building virtually invisible from the air. The house was in a thickly populated area and surrounded by trees. Clever use of camouflage netting managed to conceal much of the building's shape and structure. The Germans expected an attack; and they were not disappointed.

Other than its location, the headquarters presented little difficulty in planning. Bombs would be delayed action for the usual reasons. It was, to Ted and the expert crews within 140 Wing, a fairly routine affair. That said, Ted wasn't happy with the approach being proposed. Unusually he had been presented with a plan by the HQ staff, rather than creating the plan himself. In the staff plan, the Mosquitoes were to cross the coast at 20,000ft to avoid a build-up of flak defences over the Danish coast. Ted wasn't impressed. His strategy had always been to come in low, because at height a formation of Mosquitoes would be quickly and easily identified, and the likelihood of interception was very high. Embry allowed him the chance to present a new plan, which he did. Working closely with the 'Flak Major' Johnny Pullen, a Royal Artillery officer attached to Staff HQ who knew everything there was to know about enemy flak, Ted identified a gap in the German defences that was big enough to pass at low level. His new plan was accepted.

Six Mosquitoes were allocated: Bob Bateson and Ted would again take the lead, with 'Wing Commander Smith' slotting in as number two. The other four aircraft were taken in penny packets from each of the squadrons, including one flown by 'Willie' Wilson, formerly of 487 and now CO of 21 Squadron. (He had only recently taken charge following Peter Kleboe's death.) An escort of eight Mustangs would be provided from 129 Squadron who were also tasked with dealing with the flak.

The day chosen for the attack coincided with the wing's move to its new base at Melsbroek in Belgium which added an element of complexity. All six aircraft managed to get away in the early afternoon and at 1605 hrs the air raid sirens in Odense began to wail. Ted guided the small formation onto the target to make their first pass only there was a problem: they couldn't see it. Ted then broke every rule in the book: he decided to go around again:

> "The basic rule of low-level operations was that you NEVER went round again. At this stage of the war, and with no real opposition besides the odd machine gun, we thought we could risk it. I said to Bob 'let's go round again' and he agreed. He turned the aircraft around 180 degrees, flew back [to the starting point of the bombing run], and we tried again."

But still Ted couldn't see it.

The danger in loitering in the target area for too long was not just that the ground defences had time to get organised. It also gave the Luftwaffe vital minutes to scramble and make life difficult. Determined that the attack should be a success, and estimating the enemy defences to be minimal, Ted decided that further drastic action was needed and broke the second rule: "I pressed the R/T [radio transmission] button and asked if anyone else could see it. Silence."

Bateson led the formation around again, making the AOC somewhat anxious. 'We must have been in the target area at least half an hour searching and of course just inviting trouble from German fighters. Happily, they never appeared'.[106] At last, on the third pass, Ted spotted something. Then, he was sure. Once it was seen it suddenly became obvious what he was looking at:

> "The house was near some very tall trees, and they'd put a net across the top and over the top of the house which is why I had failed to recognise it. There was no main road or railway line for the run-in to help us."

Now sure of their objective, Bateson led the formation round for the fourth time and into the attack, dropping the first bombs right on target. The others quickly followed. One of the six, flown by Bill McClelland of 464 Squadron, was perhaps a little too eager and his Mosquito caught the blast of a bomb exploding beneath him just as he passed. Immediately one of his engines was knocked out and started streaming black smoke. Taking stock of the damage he headed for Eindhoven where he made a successful forced landing.

The remaining aircraft returned to base without loss or further incident. They were fortunate, perhaps, not to have been intercepted by German fighters, although Ted suspects their ability to react was now seriously diminished. "I rather suspect they had run out of fuel," he says.

Ted remembers the operation for another reason; while approaching from the sea, and having made such a fuss about it being safer to come in at low level, he realised he was about three miles off track. Using the *North Sea Pilot* and identifying a church steeple, he knew that if he carried on, they would run slap bang into the defences he was trying to avoid:

"We were over the sea with the formation of Mosquitoes and fighters and I realised that we were too far south and headed for a well-defended area. I told Bob that we needed to make an 'S' turn but that's not easy when the whole formation is at 50ft. Anyway, he executed a 90-degree turn to the port and held it just long enough for the formation to get settled, and then turned 90 degrees starboard so that we would come in at the right place. One of the fighter pilots said to me afterwards: 'I couldn't understand it as I couldn't see the land or anything. I just thought we were going home, and then suddenly we turned back again!' That made me laugh."

The attack on Odense was a complete success insofar as the Gestapo were forced out of their headquarters and many of their records destroyed. Two thirds of the main buildings had been completely demolished.[107] But again the raid did not come without civilian deaths. Later intelligence reports suggested that the explosive force from as many as 12 of the 28 bombs dropped were responsible for 20 homes being destroyed and another 150 being damaged. Nine Danes were killed and a further 20 injured. Some of the bombs had skipped off the rubble into the suburbs beyond, a phenomenon that was not uncommon.

Odense was Ted's 81st operation. Although he didn't know it then, it was also his last.

The war in Europe ended three weeks later. Since the crossing of the Rhine by the Americans at Remagen, Ted had always felt that victory was inevitable, and his thoughts began turning to peace.

On VE Day he was at Melsbroek when he received a call to go to wing HQ. He rang the MT section for some transport but all they could offer him was a 15cwt truck! He took it, driving though the centre of Brussels to the HQ which was then housed in an old calvary barracks:

"Every time I stopped the vehicle, at a crossroads or some traffic lights, people started jumping in the back until the whole truck was filled with Belgians, all cheering and bouncing up and down and waving handkerchiefs, having a quite lovely time. When I finally arrived at HQ they all jumped out again, said thank you very much and disappeared! By the time I got to the mess there was quite a party going on."

Some days later Ted and his former AOC went to Denmark and the scene of the attack to attend a memorial for those children and their teachers who had been killed in the raid on Shell House. He was slightly disconcerted by the appearance of so many Germans, many still in uniform, walking the city streets. The British Army had not yet arrived in any force, and while the Germans were disarmed, it was still an incongruous sight. Ted recalls:

"It was a very funny feeling at that stage in my life. We were guests of the Danish government and took time out to visit the nearest German airfield to have a look around and ensure that the Luftwaffe who were still there were complying with the terms of the surrender. The Germans had been typically German. Everything they were supposed to have done they had done. The aeroplanes were lined up with their rudders removed and propellers taken off. The airfield was guarded by a couple of Danish civilians wearing armbands."

A little after the war, in July, Ted and Embry met the parents of some of the children killed in the school:

"It was a most harrowing moment. They were marvellous and kept saying to us that they understood [why it had happened]. To me it took the edge of that particular operation. Yes, it was successful, but the penalty was that so many children had to die."

CHAPTER TEN
BREAKING RECORDS

IT WAS ONE OF THE early pioneers of British aviation and a founding member of the Royal Aero Club, Captain Horatio Barber, whose idea it was to present a trophy for aviators accomplishing the most meritorious performance in flight.

The first recipient of the Britannia Trophy, as it was styled, was Captain Charles Longcroft of the Royal Flying Corps, for his non-stop 445-mile flight between Montrose and Farnborough. That was in 1913, and from that moment on the names engraved on the trophy's base read like a who's who in aviation history: John Alcock – awarded the prize posthumously for his attempt to cross the Atlantic in a Vickers Vimy; Jim Mollinson for a flight of 4,600 miles from Lympne to Brazil. Alan Cobham's name appears three times; Jean Batten's twice.

Arthur Clouston endured a flight of some 45 hours between London and Cape Town, and more than 57 hours for the trip home. The legendary Alex Henshaw, in his famous and beautifully crafted Percival Mew Gull, set a new record the following year, completing the 6,377-mile outbound flight in 40 hours and making the return leg in almost exactly the same time. He completed the whole 12,754-mile round trip in four days, ten hours and 16 minutes, and by the end he was so tired he had to be lifted out of the cockpit.

The London to Cape Town record stood for eight years. In the spring of 1947, the record was smashed by a Mosquito flown by Mick Martin, of 617 Squadron Dambusters' fame. Accompanying him on the flight as navigator was Ted.

In the winter of 1945 and having applied for and been granted a permanent commission, Ted attended a staff navigator course (128 Course) at Empire Air Navigation School, qualifying with a 1st Class Navigation Warrant and rated as 'a very good instructor with an easy, confident manner'. He was subsequently posted first (briefly) to HQ 12 Group at Watnall and shortly after, in June 1946, to the staff of 47 Group at Milton Ernest in Bedfordshire, part of Transport Command. At the time it was mostly flying Avro Yorks and Consolidated Liberators, both four-engined and both capable of long duration flights. The Liberator, like the B-17 Flying Fortress, had been the mainstay heavy bomber of the USAF during the war, as well as being used by the RAF in Coastal Command for long-endurance submarine hunting patrols:

> "Mick and I were both on the staff of 47 Group and got on very well. His main task was a daily flight to Singapore. A request came through to take a Mosquito down to South Africa to take part in an air display. Somebody suggested that if we were going to send a Mosquito to Cape Town, then why didn't we try and break the record while we were at it?"

While there were no models to be built, or flak positions to be considered, the trip required careful planning. Ted knew that the quickest way would be to go via Kano in Nigeria but was nervous about trying to find the city when they would be low on fuel and every minute counted. He decided instead to go by way of El Adem in Libya and Kisumu in Kenya, before dropping down to the Cape. In advance of their flight, they flew out in a Dakota to test the ground for themselves and look at a number of airfields they might use on the way. These included Khartoum, Juba and Muglad. Ted stuck with Kisumu, however, keeping the others in mind in case of emergency.

The Mosquito in which they would make their world record attempt was a PR.34 (coded RG238), a high-altitude reconnaissance aircraft chosen for its very long range. Fuel was not going to be a problem: the PR.34 had bulged bomb-bay doors originally designed to accommodate a 4,000lb bomb but in this case housed an 869-gallon auxiliary fuel tank. It could also carry a 200-gallon 'slipper' tank under each wing. The total fuel capacity of Ted's aircraft, therefore, was 1,267 imperial gallons, which would provide it with a range of anything up to 3,340 miles, all things being equal.

Powering the aircraft were two Rolls-Royce 113/114 V12 engines which produced 1,430 horsepower at 27,250ft with 18 inches of boost. They gave the aircraft a maximum speed of 422mph at 30,000ft. The Merlin 114 was slightly heavier than the 113 and drove a second supercharger to keep the cabin pressurised. Both engines had been recently serviced, as had the whole aircraft, and while Ted was a little concerned that the aircraft had been left standing in a field, it appeared in good shape.

On April 17, the two men took the Mosquito up for an air test and flew to Manston. A few days later they took a rather longer flight to Fayid in Egypt, to test optimum speeds and fuel consumption. From Fayid they flew to El Adem and then home to Bassingbourn in Cambridgeshire. Ted recounts that preparations for the flight were not restricted to ensuring the health or performance of the aircraft; the medical staff were also concerned about the welfare and performance of the crew:

> "We still had food rationing in the UK at this time and the medical team decided that we should be put on a diet of special rations ahead of our flight. We were given meat, butter, eggs and milk (all of which were still in limited supply) and anything else you could think of to take home to build up our strength. We were also given food to take onto the aeroplane including two thermos flasks, one containing tomato soup and a second with cold milk in it. We were encouraged to drink milk because it created less water."

With their provisions stowed, the two men took off from Heathrow in the late evening of April 30, 1947. Take-off time was officially logged at 2006 hrs. With the additional fuel, Ted noted that the aircraft felt very heavy on take-off, his pilot requiring more of the runway than usual in getting the Mosquito into the air.

The flight out was something of a pleasure cruise for the pair and they reached El Adem ahead of schedule at 0130 hrs. The aircraft was checked over and refuelled by German prisoners of war, yet to be repatriated almost a full two years since they had surrendered. More food was also provided, even though neither pilot nor navigator felt they needed it. They were on the ground for no more than 20 minutes before taking off again at 0150 hrs.

The onward, seven-hour flight to Kisumu similarly passed without incident. Kisumu had nothing much to commend it to passing travellers. It was little more than a large, open space with few buildings save for a distinctive control tower that might easily have been mistaken for a Baptist church. Situated on the shores of Lake Victoria, it had once been a major airport for land planes and Imperial Airways flying boats but was now well past its heyday.

Again their stopover was brief. With their aircraft turned around by a local team, and with the early morning sun on the horizon, the two men clambered back into their aircraft for the second leg. It had been refuelled and a new radio set installed. It was now 0915 hrs. Ted recalls the subsequent take-off was a little 'dodgy' on account of the change in temperature and some nearby dwellings:

"In the UK, with the cool weather, the take-off wasn't so bad. Neither was it too bad taking off from El Adem because we left during the night. But at Kisumu, in the heat of the morning, it was a little different. There were a group of huts at the end of the runway with straw-covered roofs and how we missed them I will never know!"

Flying south over the lake and deeper into southern Africa, Ted spotted, some way off, a gathering storm, the biggest he had ever seen. He estimated it to be something in the region of 120 miles in length, but just far enough away to be avoided.

The flying conditions were almost perfect as they flew over the northern borders of Tanzania and across Zambia into Botswana, marvelling at the sight of the magnificent Okavango Floods which were then just beginning to creep their way into the Okavango Delta and breathe new life into the scorched earth. Mick varied his height between 20,000 and 27,000ft, according to the winds, and with no automatic pilot, was obliged to keep his hands on the controls all the time. The weather was kind and as they started the final leg from the Okavango Floods, Ted gave Mick a course to steer: "I told him that when he runs out of land, that'll be Cape Town!"

Thirty miles out from their final destination, Brooklyn airport, Ted called the control tower to let them know they were due north and about five minutes flying time away. Shortly after, their aircraft could be heard in the distance and then seen as it flashed by in what was described in contemporary reports as a 'victory dive' after skirting the northern range of mountains in the sunset for a final brief lap.

Blue smoke was pouring from the engines, partly the result of one of them having a smashed exhaust manifold. Fortunately, it had not impacted their time.

Their arrival in Cape Town in the early hours of May 1, 1947 was greeted with great excitement by the South Africans, who turned up in large numbers to applaud their achievement. As the aircraft taxied to where the crowd had gathered, Air Commodore Bill 'Crack'Em' Staton, the ebullient commander of 46 Group, who had flown ahead to organise the flight, stepped forward and saluted. He and a number of other service chiefs had waited several hours to welcome the record breakers and clapped enthusiastically. There was more applause and cheering as the legs of the pilot appeared from the aircraft, and Staton helped Mick to the ground with the words: "Come on you old slowcoach, you're 31 minutes late!" Mick joked that they might have got there sooner, 'but thought it advisable to conserve petrol by not flying faster'.[108]

Both Ted and Mick were somewhat bleary eyed and unsure on their feet after so long in the cockpit but delighted to be on terra firma and rid of their oxygen masks which had begun to chafe. They were quickly surrounded by local press and well-wishers, keen to hear of their adventure as light bulbs flashed and the film cameras started rolling. Mick produced a furry, koala bear mascot from his crumpled tunic – a mascot that had been given to him by his mother and which had shared all his adventures. The press lapped it up when he told them: "He brought me safely through the wartime ops and so I carry the little chap with me everywhere I go. He's my best pal."[109]

Ted was asked about the trip and claimed that everything had been arranged to such a pitch of perfection that the trip was 'all too easy'. He explained that the leading exhaust manifold had burned off but had not given them any trouble and they had not been in danger at any time:

"Eager journalists could scarcely believe that only hours before, the two of us had been in England. They kept saying 'is it true that you had dinner in London last night?' It was true in the sense that we'd had a fairly early dinner so of course said 'yes'. They couldn't believe it. To them it was a ridiculously short time."

The two men had flown 6,717 miles (10,810km) in 21 hours, 31 minutes and 30 seconds, recording an average speed of 312.02mph. This was inclusive of the

20-minute refuelling stop at El Adem and 25 minutes spent on the ground at Kisumu. Had they failed, a second Mosquito was on hand to have a go.[110]

Hopes of breaking the record for the return leg, however, were quickly dashed. The authorities were uncomfortable at the thought of sending the two men off without the aircraft being properly looked over and claimed that they lacked the facilities to do so. Neither Ted nor Mick believed it to be true, but let it pass. In the event, they left Cape Town two days later and flew to Baragwanath in Gauteng near Johannesburg to take part in an air rally before returning to England in stages. This included stopovers at Zwartkop, South Africa's oldest air force base, south of Pretoria, and Belvedere north-west of Salisbury (now Harare). They then flew from Kisumu to Khartoum, Khartoum to El Adem, and El Adem to Istres in the south of France. From there they flew to Manston before a short hop to Bassingbourn. They arrived home on 12 May although this time without the crowds to greet them.

Their record was recognised not just by the press but more formally by the South African Air Force (SAAF). After their press interviews, Ted and Mick were handed a telegram of congratulations from Brigadier James Durrant, the SAAF director general who commended their 'most excellent performance'. They were also recognised by the Royal Aero Club with the award of the Britannia Trophy – recognition that Ted acknowledged as a great honour. The previous record holder for London to Cape Town was Alex Henshaw, one of the world's greatest aviators who Ted much admired. As stated earlier, Henshaw had set the record in a single-engined Percival Mew Gull, and Ted felt somewhat embarrassed to have taken his crown in a more powerful twin-engined aircraft:

> "We had the privilege to meet Alex Henshaw while we were in Cape Town and apologised to him for taking his record in a modern, twin-engined two-seater aeroplane compared to his magnificent solo flight in the Mew Gull. I consider his attempt down the west coast of Africa was one of the most outstanding flights of all time."

Bill Staton thought it unlikely their record would be broken until faster jet planes had been developed. He was right.

While with Training Command, Ted sought the opportunity of completing what he'd started almost ten years earlier and begin training as a pilot. His application for a course in Flying Training Command, however, was flatly refused. A letter in response to his request simply read: 'The Air Ministry has stated there is no possibility of Squadron Leader Sismore or other officers in a similar position, being given a course in Flying Training Command.' The letter was signed by Group Captain Ulic Shannon and the sorry duty of informing Ted fell to his friend, Mick Martin.[111]

The letter, though discouraging, did not prevent Ted from taking the first step in his ambition to become a pilot. On June 6, 1947 he took his first dual in a Tiger Moth with Wing Commander Frank Griffiths, a very well-known special duties pilot, as his instructor.[112] He flew the short distance from Milton Ernest to Little Staughton. Happily, Ted experienced none of the difficulties which had held him back previously, although he did fall foul of one of the senior officers at Milton Ernest, Eugene 'Tubby' Vielle, for leaving his Tiger Moth unattended and unaccounted for, and received quite a rocket when the group captain at last tracked down his man![113] Not to be put off, Ted continued to receive instruction from Griffiths for a further 11 hours before at last being ready to make his first solo. His logbook records a 20-minute circuit of Little Staughton and a safe landing. The date was July 16, 1947.

Although now part way to fulfilling his dream, it would in fact be another four years before Ted was formally accepted into the RAF's pilot training regime. Until then, he continued his duties in Transport Command, spending some time with the Transport Command Examining Unit (TCEU), visiting squadrons within the command to ensure the navigators responsible for training were themselves fully aware of the standards to be maintained and the methods to be used in checking these standards. As an article in a contemporary edition of the *RAF Transport Command Review* asserts:

'The unit does not exist for the purpose of ruining careers nor is it a terror weapon or a Gestapo. It exists for the sole purpose of ensuring that the high standard of efficiency is maintained among transport flying personnel.'[114]

From Transport Command, Ted was posted to the Air Ministry, reporting to Group Captain Johnson who in turn reported to the Director General of Manning. Despite what might appear to be a desk job, Ted flew regularly with Johnson and Wing Commander (later Group Captain) Hughes, including an interesting trip in a Vickers Valetta twin-engine transport aircraft on February 15, 1951 to check the Calvert high-intensity light installed at London Airport. Developed by Edward Calvert, an Irish engineer in the electrical engineering department of the Royal Aircraft Establishment, the Calvert system consisted of an illuminated centre line with horizontal bars of light running transversely across it at even intervals. This pattern consists of two basic elements – a line of lights leading to the runway threshold, and horizontal lights to define the attitude of the aircraft. Calvert was the first to realise that it was easy to confuse lateral displacement with angle of bank. To that end, the Calvert system does not indicate a defined glide path; the widths of the horizon bars are such that, if a pilot maintains a glide that will take him to the correct touchdown point, each bar will appear to be the same width as the previous one as it disappears under the nose of the aircraft. Such was its success, that the basic form of Calvert crossbar lighting system still forms the basis for high-intensity approach lighting systems today.[115]

In the spring of 1951, Ted was at last given the news that he had been so desperate to hear. His entreaties to learn how to fly had at last been listened to. He took the train from London to RAF Syerston, to the east of Nottingham, and home to 22 Flying Training School. Here he quickly graduated from the Tiger Moth to the Percival Prentice, a beautiful little single-engine monoplane with an enclosed cockpit that was a delight to fly. It was a radical departure from the training aircraft of the past, with a more powerful engine and such added complications for the pupil as a variable-pitch airscrew, flaps and a radio. Also innovative for the time was that the pupil and instructor could sit side by side.[116]

Ted had no problems mastering the Prentice, qualifying as a first pilot on July 27, 1951. He then progressed to flying the North American Harvard, a workhorse trainer that remained standard equipment at flying training schools for more than 16 years.[117] Again, Ted sailed through his examinations in the air and on the ground, qualifying as a first pilot on November 19, 1951 and being awarded his flying badge on February 12, 1952. Wing Commander Wilfred Burnett, the OC Flying Wing at 22 FTS and an accomplished wartime leader assessed Ted as being 'above average' in his instrument flying and as a pupil pilot. As a pilot/navigator he used one word: 'exceptional'.[118]

Then came the tricky task of converting from piston engine to a jet at 206 Advanced Flying School at Oakington. The school had not long been in existence, established at a time when the country was deeply engaged in bitter conflict on the Korean peninsula, and the government keen to accelerate the training of more fast-jet pilots. Under the command of Wing Commander Charles Tomalin, a former Olympic diver and night-intruder pilot, each pilot was given 18 weeks to make the grade.

Ted's first flight in the Gloster Meteor, Britain's first jet fighter, was an experience he would never forget:

> "My first ride was as a passenger in a Meteor T7 to be shown what the aircraft could do. It was exhilarating. Sometime later, after I'd qualified, I took an American friend who was a marine fighter pilot, up for a ride. When we got back, I heard him talking to one of his colleagues. He described the aircraft as having a straight wing and a long canopy, and all looking fairly ordinary. But when he got in and we took off, he said he had never got to 40,000ft so quickly in his entire life!"

The Meteor T7 was indeed an exciting aircraft to fly. It had been the first jet trainer to go into service (in 1948), its introduction coinciding with the virtual completion of Fighter Command's conversion to jet aircraft where the Meteor F4 and Vampire FB.5 were then standard equipment and the only piston-engined aircraft being used were the night-flying Mosquitoes and a few Spitfires with the auxiliaries.[119] The aircraft had originally been produced as a private venture and differed from the fighter version by having a longer front fuselage to accommodate a second cockpit. Full dual controls were fitted, and all armament taken out. The two Derwent 5 engines gave the aircraft a remarkable performance: it had a top speed of 585mph and an initial climb of 7,600ft per minute which was superior to the operational fighter. The first T7 for the RAF made its initial flight on October 26, 1948 and more than 500 were delivered before production ceased in July 1954. While Ted describes the T7 as 'fun', his first jet solo (on March 13, 1952) was in a Meteor F3 which was disappointing by comparison. Although Ted believed it to be very easy to fly with few vices, it lacked the power and performance of the trainer version. The engines were liable to surge leading to a loss of revs per minute (rpm) and thrust:

> "It had far less power and was a much less advanced aeroplane generally. If you tried to do aerobatics in the Meteor F3 it took both hands on the stick and plenty of strength, though it could be a lot of fun."

Ted successfully completed his flying training and was again rated 'above average'. Now came the transition to an operational squadron, successfully navigated at 228 Operational Conversion Unit (OCU) at RAF Leeming. Leeming, in North Yorkshire, had been an airfield since the 1930s but opened as an RAF station in the summer of 1940. In 1943 it had been assigned to 6 Group Royal Canadian Air Force. After the war it had become a night-fighter base, initially equipped with the Mosquito and then the Meteor. More recently it had become home to 228 OCU equipped with both the Meteor T7s and the Meteor NF11s, a fighter that was radar equipped and could operate in all weathers but was principally developed as an interim night fighter. The radar (the AI Mk 10), however, was limited by lack of range and was said to need a good navigator to get the most out of it. Ted had a good navigator in Pilot Officer A. M. Pollard, and the pair began flying together as a crew. It was no surprise when Ted graduated from the course with his 'above average' and 'exceptional' ratings still in place.

Ted's seniority (he was a squadron leader) would ordinarily mean command of a squadron, but at the time the leap was considered too great until he had more hands-on fighter experience. As such, on October 15, 1952, Ted and Pollard journeyed to West Malling in Kent, one of the RAF's foremost night-fighter stations, on attachment to 85 Squadron to learn the ropes.

The spirit within 85 Squadron was exceptional; it had been the squadron in the First World War that could count Billy Bishop and 'Mick' Mannock in its ranks, the two highest-scoring fighter aces of the time. Both men had been awarded the Victoria Cross. In the Second World War it also attracted some outstanding personalities, not least Peter Townsend, the Battle of Britain 'ace', and John Cunningham, an outstanding night fighter and test pilot. The squadron had only relatively recently converted from the Mosquito NF Mk 36 to the more powerful and capable Meteor NF11 and was now under the command of Squadron Leader John Hawkins AFC.

Life for Ted on a fighter squadron in the 1950s was one of continual training in preparation for war and the annual RAF Review. Ted arrived as the squadron was expanding to two flights, and was basking in the glow of Exercise Ardent, the annual autumn training exercise in which it had given a good account of itself and chalked up an impressive 89 'kills' – at least in theory. His arrival also coincided with an almost immediate move to RAF Coltishall, in Norfolk, while the runway at West Malling was resurfaced, and a trip to RAF Acklington on the

Northumberland coast near Morpeth for the annual Armament Practice School. Air-to-air gunnery was practised just a few miles away out over Druridge Bay in the North Sea which had radar-controlled ranges to allow gunnery at higher altitudes and above cloud. In December, Ted also found himself called upon to take part in a search for a Vampire NF10 which had gone missing after a low-level night interception exercise on the 18th. The search was in vain; the aircraft crashed into the Channel, killing the pilot (Flight Lieutenant Cecil Smith) and his navigator (Flying Officer James Adams).

With the new year came a formal posting to 85 Squadron (the date was January 19, 1953) and with the departure of Flight Lieutenant Vasse to Leconsfield, Ted assumed command of B Flight. While the weather left much to be desired, and severely restricted his flying, Ted was nonetheless gaining experience with every day that passed and learning from the squadron commander. In February, disaster struck the south coast of England.

In what was the worst natural disaster Britain experienced during the 20th century the low-lying housing on England's east coast was devastated by a huge tidal surge which left 307 people dead and 40,000 homeless.[120] The RAF provided help both in the air and on the ground, in time-honoured fashion in any emergency. This support included Operation Floodlight, a massive programme of aerial reconnaissance to allow the rapid survey of a large swathe of the country that was difficult or impossible to reach by land. It helped identify the location and size of hundreds of breaches to sea walls, enabling engineers to focus their efforts where they could be of most immediate use. The support also involved more prosaic work, airmen from West Malling airlifting thousands of sandbags to the Isle of Sheppey in the wake of the disaster to make temporary repairs to the sea wall.[121] Hawkins in his squadron commander's summary for the month remarks 'all personnel put in some sterling work in connection [with the floods] in a most cheerful and co-operative manner'.[122] At a practical level, the absence of many senior NCOs and ground crew meant the pilots and navigators were obliged to undertake the primary inspections of their aircraft themselves before they could get airborne.

On the night of April 25, the squadron took part in a Bullseye against aircraft from Bomber Command. It was their first opportunity of getting to grips with an aircraft with which Ted would later become very well acquainted, the English Electric Canberra, built as a successor to the Mosquito and the RAF's first jet-powered bomber. The exercise did not go well; while the Meteors claimed eight Lincolns (the successor to the Lancaster and the last piston-engine bomber to be operated by the RAF), the Canberras escaped them. As the ORB states: 'Only one was intercepted and killed which re-emphasised the need for an all-weather fighter with a vastly superior performance to that of the NF11.'[123]

After a few short but informative months in charge of B Flight, Ted was at last given his own squadron to command. He and Pollard said their goodbyes and departed for Tangmere on the south coast and a posting to 29 Squadron. Ted took over from Squadron Leader Peter Horsley who'd flown with 140 Wing in 1944 and survived a ditching in the Channel having been shot down near Cherbourg.[124] In terms of aircraft, the squadron also had Meteor NF11s, making the transition to their new home much easier.

Once more, Ted's days were filled with air-to-air and air-to-ground sorties and practice interceptions as well as an increasing amount of night-flying training for the squadron's night-fighter role. Detachments to other squadrons and airfields were common practice, as were visits from experts in ground-control interception and signals. The squadron also shared their experience of night-time interceptions with their counterparts in the Fleet Air Arm.

Pete Hills, one of Ted's squadron pilots, describes a typical night operation:

"We would be on the operational readiness platform at the end of the runway and plugged into the telly scramble (a special phone attached to each aircraft) on two minutes' readiness with, as far as possible, all cockpit checks completed. The first indication of likely activity would come with a click in the earphones as the sector controller opened his line to our station ops room. Sector ops would then issue instructions along the lines of 'Tangmere scramble two aircraft vector 180 angels 30 call X [the GCI call sign] on X [the frequency]'.

"Tangmere ops had the list of those on the ORP and the order they were in so they would pass on the instructions to the first two aircraft on the order list. We knew who was next so as soon as sector had called the scramble we would be pressing starter buttons without waiting for the order to be relayed by Tangmere ops. As soon as the second engine was winding up we would wave the ground crew to disconnect the battery cart and remove the chocks (they most likely would have already done that) then a quick look to make sure they were clear and up with the power to move on to the runway for a rolling take-off. Air traffic was monitoring station ops so knew what was happening and would only intervene if there was an urgent need to stop the take-off for safety reasons.

"After take-off you would change frequency to GCI and tell them you were airborne. GCI would then control the intercept and tell us details about the target's height, speed and position. We would tell GCI when the navigator had contact with the target and then when he could take over the intercept by calling 'Judy'. On a moonless night it was usually possible to visually identify the target by about 600 feet from the six o'clock position from where we could carry out a simulated attack. On moonlit nights visual identification was possible at much longer ranges particularly if one was looking 'up moon'. On completion of the intercept with a 'murder' call to GCI they would issue details of another target or instructions to recover base."[125]

After taking part in the Royal Review Flypast in July, for a week in August 1953, the squadron was engaged in an exercise called Momentum, operating from Tangmere and West Raynham. Ted was disappointed with the results, most of the 'kills' being achieved against targets at medium level and low speed. They did better the following month during an exercise known as Window Box in which they recorded a number of successful and satisfactory night-time 'victories'.

Interestingly, the squadron also provided observers and marker aircraft for test pilot Neville Duke's attempt at breaking the world air speed record on September 7 in a Hawker Hunter Mk 3 (WB188). The attempt was successful, Duke achieving a recorded speed of 727.6mph. As the beautifully red-painted aircraft raced across the three-kilometre course and over Worthing pier, Ted was also in the air flying 'chase' in a Meteor at a pre-determined altitude with a barometer strapped uncomfortably to his ankle to measure the outside pressure.[126]

In the spring of 1954, Ted returned to RAF Acklington. In the three weeks they were there, the squadron diarist recorded only 'mediocre results' which Ted blamed partly on the poor weather. He had happier news on returning to Tangmere with the arrival of seven new aircraft. Since taking over command, his squadron had been constantly under-strength and under-resourced. The arrival of the new aircraft meant he now had a full complement of 22 fighters, but not the engine and airframe mechanics to keep them in the air. 'The prospect for the next month cannot be happy', he noted.

Despite such issues and a dip in squadron morale, the annual Air Defence Exercise (Dividend) in July 1954 proved to be something of a turning point in giving confidence to crews who had previously been struggling. The concept of the exercise was a simulated attack on the UK by a 'hostile' force comprising aircraft from the RAF and NATO allies. More than 6,000 sorties were flown by the 'enemy' over three days, operating at heights of up to 40,000ft.

The exercise saw Ted and his crews pitted against some of the best British and American aircraft then in service. They included Lincolns and Canberras; the North American B-45 Tornado, the first operational jet to enter service with the United States Air Force and used for both conventional bombing and aerial reconnaissance; and the Boeing B-47 Stratojet, a massive, long-range, six-engined turbojet strategic bomber capable of flying at high subsonic speeds and at very high altitudes to avoid fighter interception. Of them all, Ted reckoned on the English Electric Canberra as being the most difficult to intercept. Nothing had changed since his time at West Malling.

The 29 Squadron ORB for the period records its pilots being obliged to operate both at night and during the day, and recording 'kills' not only for B-47 bombers but also the escorting F-86 Sabre fighters – an impressive and much-loved swept-wing aircraft out of the same stable as the Mitchell and Mustang.[127] Three out of every four sorties resulted in claims of an aircraft destroyed 'giving a boost in morale to all ranks', and the aircrew gained confidence in themselves and their aircraft after operating continuously against high-speed targets and at high levels. As Ted says: "Air defence exercises were great fun involving the RAF in the UK and Germany, and our allies the Americans, the French and the Belgians. We'd be operating 24 hours a day for sometimes five or six days."

Ted remembers one particular exercise involving an attack on a US Convair B-36, a mighty six-engined strategic bomber ironically christened 'The Peacemaker'. It was the largest mass-produced piston-engined aircraft ever built, with the longest wingspan (70m):

"The B-36 had a wingspan that was far too big for the controlled gunsight that we had which was a hand control, so we had to use the tailplane as the measurement of range within the gunsight. The trouble was that if you did an attack on a B-36 tracking the gunsight on the tailplane (as we had been taught), the wings were so large that you were convinced you were going to hit the aircraft even though you were still several hundred yards away!"

Fighter tactics had evolved little in the ten years since the war had ended. Despite having more sophisticated weaponry, it was still necessary to 'see' an aircraft in order to attack it, other than at night with radar:

"In those days we had to see it, assess what kind of attack might be possible, and then organise and carry it out. Tactics were much the same as they had been in World War Two. The only real change was the speed and height at which the aircraft could fly, the speed especially. On one exercise I had my whole squadron flying in battle formation and we were told to keep climbing because the incoming raid was delayed. As we levelled off the squadron was at 48,000ft, which for a Meteor was doing well."

In October 1954, Ted was posted to West Raynham to attend the Day Fighter Leader School (DFLS), Flight Lieutenant Leon Scholfield assuming temporary command. For a man who wanted to fly all day, every day, the course was nirvana:

"The objective was to train people to fight as a unit (and not just individually). So you flew in whatever position you were allocated which meant one day you might be flying number two, the next day number four and so on. You might be leading a Finger Four or a section of eight or even 16, and your performance analysed on your return including your camera gun results. We were tested thoroughly by staff instructors who were very good and highly experienced, so it was of tremendous value. I enjoyed it because it was all action. We flew Meteor 8s, two flights a day, which for peacetime flying was the absolute peak."

Ted left the squadron again in February 1955 for a short, guided-missile course at Manby and returned to confront the same issues with serviceability of his aircraft that he had experienced from the beginning. The last major exercise he took part in was 'Beware' in the autumn of 1955 in which the squadron acquitted itself well, claiming 124 'kills' from 205 sorties.

Ted very much enjoyed his experience as squadron CO. Their 'neighbours' at Tangmere at that time included 1 Squadron and (later) 34 Squadron to form the Tangmere Wing, and the rivalry was both friendly and intense. As the author of the history of 1 Squadron Mike Shaw writes: 'Splendid chaps though they were, 29 flew Meteor night fighters and carried navigators. As such they were quite beyond the pale as far as No. 1 was concerned!'[128]

Ted knew the 1 Squadron CO, Freddie Lister, very well. Fred was not only a highly experienced pilot, having won both the DSO and DFC during the war, but also had a reputation as a tremendous party man and considerably enlivened the squadron social life. He was also happy to share aircraft: "Some of his pilots would come and fly my aeroplanes and I flew his," Ted recalls.

Not all of Ted's duties were pleasant ones. Peacetime flying was not without its dangers. Early on in his role, on October 20, 1953, Flying Officer Sneddon was obliged to ditch his Meteor five miles off Ford. Luckily, he was wearing a new type of rubber immersion suit and was only in the freezing water for a few minutes before he and his navigator were rescued by helicopter. Flight Lieutenant John Cottam and Flying Officer David Lovell were not so fortunate. They died in the Channel towards the end of Ted's time with 29 Squadron, on May 20, 1955, when their aircraft (Meteor WD605) fell out of the sky and crashed into the sea during an air-to-air firing exercise. Only the body of the 22-year-old navigator was ever found. The tall, dashing figure of his pilot has no known grave. The cause of the accident has never been discovered.

On being posted from 29 Squadron and handing over command to John Aiken, a former Spitfire pilot, Ted attended RAF Staff College in Bracknell, a rite of passage for those destined for higher rank.[129] He lived in family accommodation, for he was now married with two children. He'd met his wife, Rita, when she had been serving as an RAF officer during the war. She had run the plotting table at Tangmere (and later at Chichester) for a time and knew many of the most famous wartime fighter pilots well, including the one-legged ace Douglas Bader and one of his loyal pilots, 'Cocky' Dundas. An unusually (for the time) tall woman, Ted had spotted her in the canteen and made a point of being introduced. Originally from Yorkshire but brought up in Bournemouth, Rita was at first somewhat cool to their relationship, but soon warmed to Ted's soft voice and manner. They were married on April 6, 1946, Ted's friend from school, Don Sinclair, standing in as best man. Their first born, Martin, was named after Mick Martin who became his godfather. He was born in 1948. A daughter, Fiona, followed in 1953, while the family was sharing a house in Audley End (Cambridgeshire) prior to their move to Tangmere.

Fiona was born in Ely Hospital, which at the time was an RAF establishment. A near neighbour offered to take Ted and his young son to visit, and the three dutifully piled into the friend's black vintage Bentley. The car had coach-built 'suicide' doors, hinged at the rear edge, and no seat belts, and as they were driving through Ely High Street, one of the doors sprung open and Martin fell out, rolling underneath a Morris post office van. Although knocked unconscious, he otherwise escaped serious injury. Like father like son, it was an early scrape that happily didn't prevent further progress.

Ted's time in charge at 29 Squadron was one of the happiest periods in his career in the RAF, and he was delighted that his role in developing modern night-fighting techniques was recognised with the award of the Air Force Cross in the New Year's Honours list of 1956. He was even more delighted with his next posting back to RAF Leeming. On his first stay he had been the pupil; now he was the master, tasked with running the Advanced Training Wing, and with specific responsibility of streamlining the introduction of the RAF's new all-weather fighter, the mighty Javelin. The station commander was Group Captain John Innes-Crump, who was at the time overseeing a six-month renovation and refurbishment programme that included resurfacing the main runway.

The Javelin was the Gloster Aircraft Company's latest baby, and its birth had been a long and painful one. Its genesis was in the Air Ministry Specification F.4/48 for a two-seat twin-engined night-time and all-weather fighter to replace the night-fighter version of the ageing Vampire. Two aircraft were in the running: the de Havilland DH110, a less than revolutionary twin-boom tailed aircraft powered by two Rolls-Royce Avons; and the GA5 delta-wing twin-jet fighter from Gloster, officially christened the Javelin (though to some forever 'the flying flatiron').[130] Following competitive trials, the Javelin won out, thus becoming the first aircraft of its kind in the world to enter service and giving the RAF a weapon with very high performance, long endurance, and the ability to intercept bombers at great altitudes and high subsonic speeds. Electronic and radar devices enabled it to operate in all weathers, night and day.

The first Gloster GA5 prototype (WD804) flew on November 26, 1951. The test pilot at Gloster, Bill Waterton, was far from comfortable with the flying characteristics of the new aircraft and was not backward in coming forward to voice his opinions:

> "The Javelin was easy to fly, had an excellent performance, and showed great promise. But she had some dangerous tendencies too, such as reversing her longitudinal control [the stick had to be pushed instead of pulled] near the stall, tightening into the turn and pitching strongly nose-up when the flaps were extended. In these and a host of other control stability and engineering problems which I reported only lukewarm interest was shown."[131]

Frustrated at not being listened to, Waterton tendered his resignation in April 1952, but was persuaded to stay. Eight weeks later, on Sunday June 29, Waterton was taking the aircraft up for its 99th flight when the elevators experienced a severe flutter and broke away, making the aircraft extremely difficult to control. With superlative skill, the pilot managed to get the aircraft back onto the ground, performing a high-speed landing that caused the undercarriage to collapse and for the aircraft to burst into flames. Waterton made it out by the skin of his teeth, and the subsequent award of the George Medal for his cool action did little to mollify his mood.

Testing experimental aircraft has always been a hazardous occupation and in the decade after the Second World War it appears to have been especially dangerous. Bill Waterton was lucky; John Derry, a test pilot at de Havilland was not. While demonstrating the Javelin's rival at the much-anticipated Society of British Aerospace Companies' trade show at Farnborough only ten weeks after Waterton's crash, Derry was killed along with his observer when their DH110 broke up in mid-air and exploded on the ground, killing a further 31 spectators and injuring many dozens more.[132]

Waterton describes the controls of the second Javelin prototype (WD808) with a redesigned wing as being, if anything, worse than those of its predecessor. He was particularly unhappy about how the aircraft performed at low speed. On June 11, 1953, his number one experimental pilot, Peter Lawrence, was killed when WD808 stalled and ultimately crashed near Bristol. Eyewitnesses say the pilot could have ejected but stayed with the aircraft to avoid crashing into some school cricket pitches.

Accidents and further teething problems with the controls, the canopy and the electronics delayed the introduction of the new aircraft, and it was not until February 1956, almost three years after Lawrence was killed, that the Javelin finally entered service – 46 Squadron at Odiham being the first to receive their new charge.

Ted had already 'met' the Javelin prior to his posting to Leeming. In May 1955, he and his navigator had flown to Moreton Valence in Gloucestershire, the home of Glosters, to see the Javelin in production, but more than a year on and now planning for its wide introduction, he had still not flown one for himself:

"We started to write the training syllabus but of course no-one in my unit had flown [the Javelin]. I had been told I could fly it at the Central Fighter Establishment at West Raynham, but they kept putting me off, for good reason, as they were still busy with the trials. Eventually I got the call to say I could go down and fly her, so I read the pilot's notes, asked a couple of questions, and was ready to go."

It was not, as it happens, quite as easy as that. If the CFE was to surrender one of its aircraft for the afternoon, then Ted was going to have to sing for his supper. Rather than simply flying the aircraft, he would take part in a practice interception, and kill two birds with one stone. If he had enough fuel once the exercise was finished, he was told, then he could fly a few circuits:

"They gave me as a navigator, Tony Aldridge, who'd been a flight commander of mine at 29, so we were old friends. I took off and went straight into a trial interception. When we came back, I flew a couple of circuits and thought she was a pleasant aeroplane to fly with a nice comfortable cockpit. It could go higher and fly faster than a Meteor, and would go supersonic in a dive, so it was a significant step forward in technology."

Ted formally took up his post in January 1957, at which point 228 OCU reorganised on a two-wing basis: a 'Flying/Basic' Wing, commanded by Wing Commander John Gard'ner, and the 'Advanced' Wing, the latter ultimately expanding to comprise four squadrons.[133] Ted's first issue on taking command was the lack of any available aircraft. For the first six months, his Javelin conversion programme suffered from having no Javelins on which to convert!

A short stopgap – the Javelin Mobile Training Unit (JMTU – also referred to as the Javelin Mobile Conversion Unit – both titles are used in the operations record book from the period) – was already in play, having been set up prior to Ted's arrival and with Squadron Leader Patrick Street as its officer commanding.[134] A Javelin cockpit trainer was also installed in the Airmanship Hall.

The JMTU comprised two pilot instructors, two navigator instructors, 16 ground crew and two Vickers Valetta pilots. The Valetta was increasingly being pressed into service as a navigational trainer. Of the two attached to the JMTU, one was used in its original guise as a transport and the second as a flying classroom with an AI Mk 17 radar (which the navigators had to master) in the nose.

The unit led something of a nomadic existence, travelling from one airfield to the next, helping to convert various squadrons of Meteors and Venoms without the need to detach aircrew to Leeming.[135] While it allowed for some progress to be made, Group Captain John Thompson, who took over as station commander in March, noted that 'the tempo [of training] was not likely to increase until the arrival of the first Javelins'.[136]

'Tommy' Thompson and Ted became firm friends, helped by having families of a similar age and daughters who attended the same school. Thompson's wartime career had been spent on fighters. He'd been the CO of 111 Squadron (the famous 'treble one') in France and narrowly escaped with his life after his Hurricane was damaged by a Bf 110 leaving his engine overheating and 'everything off the clock'.[137] He remained in charge of the squadron throughout the Battle of Britain before leading 131 Squadron which at the time had a Belgian Flight. So popular was he with his Belgian comrades, that when they departed to form the nucleus of 350 Squadron, the first Belgian fighter unit in the RAF, they requested that he take charge. They also awarded him the Belgian Military Cross. He later went to Malta at the direct request of Sir Keith Park, the former AOC 11 Group with whom he'd served as a staff officer, ultimately taking command of all three of Malta's fighter wings (Takali, Hal Far and Luqa). He survived being shot down a second time, on this occasion by one of his own pilots. By the end of the war he was a wing commander with the DSO and two DFCs, having shot down at least ten enemy aircraft and maybe many more. Like Ted, Tommy was a keen golfer, and the pair would escape whenever they could for a quick nine or a longer 18, and a drink in the bar afterwards. Tommy was not only a friend, but also a tremendous mentor, and advised Ted to be patient.

Ted's patience was finally rewarded in June, with the triumphant arrival of the first of two Javelin FAW5s and the formal commencement of the OCU re-equipment programme. In quick succession and on virtually consecutive days, Ted managed to try out the differences between the Javelin 2, 4 and 5, usually with Tony Aldridge as his back-seater.

Within a month, the Advanced Wing had nine of the new FAW5 aircraft on which to train, and apart from interruptions brought about by various NATO training exercises, Battle of Britain flypasts, and the SBAC annual show, Ted was able to make significant progress in converting his crews. Not everybody made it, however. Despite the experience of the crews passing through Ted's hands, some were washed out for failing to achieve the necessary standard of airmanship, especially the navigators, and a good few were forced to abandon the course through airsickness.

On one occasion, Ted was leaned on to ensure one particularly senior officer passed the course. He point-blank refused, arguing – quite rightly – that if any accident should subsequently befall said officer, then fingers would start pointing in his direction, and the integrity of the training course would be called into question. The officer would have to take his chances with the rest of them. He did. And passed.

It was not until January 10, 1958 – a full year after Ted had taken charge – that the first Javelin course (No. 192) passed out, but by the April, Javelin flying time topped 300 hours and by June this figure had reached 500. Geoff Moores, one of Ted's instructors, remembers the FAW5 had additional fuel capacity: "The extra airborne time this gave crews undergoing conversion on type allowed more to be crammed into each sortie, and a safety margin given the claggy weather we could experience around the Vale of York."[138]

Events on the world stage, and particularly in the Middle East with British troops being deployed in Jordan and US troops in the Lebanon, were lending a new urgency to Ted's work, and the Advanced Wing provided instructor aircrew to take part in the three-day Exercise Sunbeam, claiming a very high level of interceptions of assumed enemy aircraft. His time at Leeming also coincided with further advancements in flight-simulator development and training and he spent two days in May with his senior navigator, Squadron Leader Reginald Hawtin, at the Ministry of Defence and at Redifon, exploring the latest modifications to the manufacturer's technology.

As well as the Javelin FAW5s, several Javelin FAW7s also began to arrive, with Ted arranging the necessary training, but it was in fact the introduction of the first T3 dual-control variant of the aircraft in February 1959 that proved to be a game changer.[139]

The main differences between the T3 and the fighter variants were a redesigned canopy with improved visibility for the instructor who sat in what was the navigator's position, with the radar display being replaced by a set of controls for the instructor. In addition to this, a periscope was added for the instructor in order to monitor gunnery practice and provide extra vision during taxiing, take-off and landing. The more sophisticated AI radar was removed from the nose section and replaced by a simple ranging radar for the guns similar to that used in the Hawker Hunter. To counteract a new centre of gravity the fuselage was lengthened which also allowed for extra fuel tanks. The Javelin T3 also accommodated the all-moving tailplane of the FAW4 in order to ease stick movements at high speed.

Ted was excited to lay his hands on a T3 to accelerate the training programme. The alternative was to have a Hunter T10 for instrument ratings, but in Ted's assessment the two aircraft were so dissimilar that he decided to press ahead with requesting the T3.

One morning he received a phone call from Fighter Command telling him to get down to Boscombe Down, home of the Aeroplane and Armament Experimental Establishment (A&AEE), as quickly as he could. The good people at A&AEE, the principal research facility for British military aviation, were to have a meeting about the future of the T3 and Ted was invited. The T3 programme appeared to be a hair's breadth away from being cancelled. Delayed by thick fog, it was not until later that day that Ted arrived, by which time the meeting was in full swing. The nub of their concern was the ability of the instructor to see enough to be able to fly the aircraft, especially in an emergency, and their only solution was to double the width of the runways. Ted thought their concerns somewhat hysterical; although not a flying instructor himself, he'd flown plenty of aircraft with poor forward visibility, not least the Harvard, and the Javelin had a periscope system fed to the central display on the instrument panel that enabled the pilot to see ahead:

"By now I'd had quite a bit of experience flying Javelins and so asked if I could fly the aeroplane myself. Unfortunately, the aircraft developed a hydraulic leak and since all of the flying controls were hydraulic, this was a serious issue, so I returned to Leeming, still with doubts in my mind."

A day or two later and the phone rang again. It was Dickie Martin, who was now chief test pilot at Glosters.[140] Martin had taken up where Waterton had left off and done sterling work in further developing the Javelin and building it into a successful programme. Ted's frequent visits to Glosters meant that the two men knew each other well: "I've got a T3 sitting outside my office and understand you want to fly one," he said. "How soon can you get here?"

Within an hour, Ted was sitting in the back cockpit of a Javelin T3 as Peter Varley, one of the company's most accomplished test pilots, put the aircraft through its paces and simulated approaches for Ted to be satisfied that the aircraft did not represent a risk to his instructors nor their pupils:

"If there was a slight crosswind, then you could see perfectly well out of the side of the canopy and the periscope allowed you to see straight ahead. I wrote a very short report to Fighter Command, making it clear that my findings were only based on a single flight and a few days later had the commander-in-chief on the phone asking me if I wanted the aeroplane. I said, 'Yes I do' and about two weeks later the first of the T3s was delivered."[141]

Pilots passing through Ted's care spent the first three weeks in intensive ground school before starting the flying phase. After typically three dual sorties in one of Ted's precious T3s, pilots were sent on their first solo. Flying the Javelin solo was thereafter a rare event.

Mel Evans, a young pilot officer at that time, remembers that a happy feature of the Javelin was the large cushion of air it created beneath it just before touchdown:

"This made hard landings almost impossible. Not so popular particularly with the old hands converting to the Javelin were the toe brakes and Maxaret anti-locking units. During the course at Leeming, we witnessed a number of accidents that were attributed to the brake units. Another unique feature of the Javelin was the power of its air brakes. At 430 knots, the maximum speed at which the air brakes extended fully, the retardation was 1g – the equivalent of 100 per cent braking in a car. For this reason, it was essential to warn the navigator before using them unless you wanted to have all his pencils."

After a brief period becoming familiar with the handling characteristics and performance of the aircraft pilots were given a concentrated period of instrument flying to achieve the necessary standard to operate in the 'night all-weather' role. As Mel Evans recalls:

> "Fundamental to a successful air interception was the need for the pilot to follow accurately the commands from the back-seater as he interpreted the indications from the radar. There was a standard set of commands that instructed the pilot to manoeuvre the aircraft precisely in turn rate, height adjustment, and speed control. If the pilot's response did not match the navigator's expectations the radar picture could then be misinterpreted giving rise to incorrect subsequent action. Even in perfect visibility it was vital that the pilot responded accurately and quickly to the navigator's commands. This technique was strongly emphasised from the very beginning, and I determined that I would follow it religiously and only look out when the navigator handed control of the intercept to me by declaring that the target was 'dead ahead at 200 yards'."[142]

Accidents at Leeming during Ted's tenure were mercifully few. The brakes to which Mel Evans refers could be a problem, and led to one Javelin being damaged during taxiing while another suffered damage to its pitot head (which helped measure an aircraft's speed) due to fatigue. It was shortly after Ted had been posted away that a more serious incident occurred that might have proved fatal. Pilot Chris Cowper was on his second trip of the day when the starboard engine caught fire at 30,000ft after turbine failure and the second engine was shut down after a fire warning. Chris and a 'spare' navigator, an American, ejected and while descending with their parachutes were so close that they could shout to each other.

Peter Masterman, Cowper's regular navigator, was not flying that day on account of a sore throat. Later that evening Cowper marched into Peter's bedroom demanding they go to the pub. At the Guardroom, the RAF police told them they had to wait for a bus that would take them up onto the Moors to help put out a fire caused by a Javelin crash: "Fuck that," said Cowper, "I was the pilot". Peter recalls:

> "The Javelin had a very bad reputation and killed a lot of people, and I was very lucky to be ill when my pilot bailed out. Ejecting from a Javelin could

cause a serious back injury and I don't think many people bailed out without incurring one. I remember those accidents but when you're young you don't worry."[143]

Ted and his family lived the peripatetic life familiar to all service personnel. At Flying Training School, they'd lived briefly in a small wooden bungalow in Syerston and at the time of the Great Flood of 1953, were in slightly larger accommodation in West Malling. Ted was never happier than in places and with jobs that enabled him to fly, but for the time being he was posted back to a desk, or rather for further staff training. His command at Leeming gave way to a posting in March 1959 to the Joint Services Staff College at Latimer House, a small stately home in the beautiful Chess Valley on the Buckinghamshire/Hertfordshire border.[144] Here he learned how to think more clearly and write more concisely. The course had little to do with aviation or flying an aircraft but was more about organisation, administration, strategy and tactics.[145] It meant moving his family again to the pretty village of Chalfont St Giles, where his near neighbour was his good friend Mick Martin. He was not at the college for long before he was once again uprooting his family for a posting overseas, as part of the Joint Planning Staff with the headquarters of British Forces in the Arabian Peninsula.

British presence in the region dated back to 1839 and the capture of the town of Aden (now part of Yemen) on the Arabian Peninsula. The occupation of Aden was strategic, rather than commercial, guarding as it did the lines of communication with India. Along with British Somaliland on the Horn of Africa, Aden gave the British control of anyone entering the Red Sea. Following the opening of the Suez Canal in 1869, Britain established protectorates in the hinterland of South Arabia to act as a buffer against the Ottomans who occupied Yemen. In 1937 Aden was separated from British India to become a crown colony.[146]

Following her humiliation in the Suez Crisis of 1956, a campaign described as a military success but a political disaster, Britain granted independence in February 1959 to the Federation of South Arabia.[147] This had been formed from the Aden colony and the surrounding protectorates in order to stabilise the region which had been dogged by years of unrest fuelled by Arab nationalism and anti-colonialism.

Having replaced Cyprus as the base of Middle East Land Forces, Aden was of even greater strategic importance to Britain in maintaining (with Far East Land

Forces in Singapore) its global presence. The new command was what was known as a 'unified' command which comprised a commander-in-chief (typically of three-star rank) with a small secretariat, an intelligence staff and a joint planning staff to which Ted was posted.[148]

Ted moved with his family to RAF Steamer Point, an oasis in an otherwise desolate space that was considered by the rank and file as 'one of the least desirable RAF aircrew postings'.[149] Off duty, there was little to do in the desert, but at least at Steamer Point there was a well-equipped NAAFI, sea swimming behind a shark net and walks along the beach. They played tennis and cricket in the summer months, and then football in the autumn, and had plenty of time to socialise with the opposite sex.

When he arrived, the senior RAF officer was Sir Hubert Patch who was instrumental in setting up the tri-service command in Aden.[150] Ted's principal duty was one of planning counter-insurgency exercises and actual operations, assuring the appropriate number of aircraft were available and suitably armed.[151] It was the beginning of a long and sustained interest in Middle East affairs, influencing future policies and thinking.

His stay in Aden, however, was short-lived, and in 1961 he was appointed air attaché to Addis Ababa, the capital and largest city in Ethiopia. Addis Ababa had been occupied by the Italians before the Second World War and liberated by British forces under Major Orde Wingate (later of Chindit fame) in May 1941, paving the way for the return of the Ethiopian emperor, Haile Selassie. An air attaché's life was considered by some to be the kiss of death in a general duties (GD) career.[152] Ted seemed to thrive, however, in a role that was essentially representational with other foreign delegates in the capital, but his tenure did coincide with a conflict between Ethiopia and neighbouring Eritrea, a former British protectorate that had originally been federated to Ethiopia and subsequently annexed, triggering an armed struggle that was to last 30 years.

Haile Selassie was a tremendous eccentric and a huge admirer and supporter of the British Royal Family. Ted was expected to drop everything to accede to the emperor's requests, and because of the latter's personal friendship with Prince Philip, the then Duke of Edinburgh, could not understand why Ted appeared to put so many barriers in the way of his desire to fly in and out of Heathrow at a moment's notice. The emperor was also amused one evening to witness Ted's discomfort at a state banquet when Africa's self-styled 'Lion King' allowed a number of the beasts to mingle with the dining party. Despite the lions being restrained by thick metal chains, they were still allowed to roam disturbingly close to the extent that Ted could feel their hot breath on his neck.

Ted spent a busy 18 months in the role and was given use of his own aircraft (a Meteor T7 WL348) with which to keep in touch with his bosses in Aden and in which to ferry his commander-in-chief back and forth to important meetings. He was, however, clamouring for a return to the UK and another operational command. He did not have long to wait.

CHAPTER ELEVEN
BACK TO BOMBERS

During his posting overseas Ted spent very little time airborne, his logbook showing a paucity of entries. He did, however, manage to squeeze in a trip in a Lightning T.4 with Wing Commander Bernard Howard DFC, wing commander flying at RAF Wattisham, giving him the chance to go supersonic, but otherwise his flying hours had dwindled significantly. One of his first actions, therefore, on his return was to seek out a Meteor refresher training course at RAF Strubby in Lincolnshire, to oil out any rustiness he may have felt. Then he began to contemplate his next move.

While at Staff College and before Leeming, Ted had discussed the possibility of commanding one of the RAF's front-line 'V' bomber squadrons. The increasing conversion to an all-jet air force had been exemplified in the previous year when at the Queen's Coronation Review, in which Ted had played an active role, 640 aircraft had performed a meticulous and highly impressive flypast and review parade for the sovereign. Two thirds of the aircraft present were jet engine. In January 1955 the RAF entered a fresh era; the first V bomber – the sleek Vickers Valiant – came into service with Bomber Command. The Valiant was the first of three major V designs. The second was the Avro Vulcan and the third the Handley Page Victor. The three aircraft were intended to transform Bomber

Command into an awesome deterrent force capable of instant retaliation, in depth, against any would be aggressor. Intended and designed to lift a nuclear or conventional war load, the Valiant remained the only V bomber in service for two years before it was joined by the Vulcan and Victor in squadron service after the summer of 1957.[153]

In turning down the opportunity, and wishing instead to stay with Fighter Command, Ted felt he may have blown his chances of achieving higher office. But having now been promoted group captain, he was given the opportunity of not just commanding a squadron, but rather an entire RAF station, and a plum posting to RAF Brüggen in Germany. Ted assumed command from Group Captain Ivor Broom, one of the war's most exceptional low-level pilots who had later gone on to command a Mosquito Pathfinder squadron. Ted and Ivor shared many similarities, not least that they both held the DSO, three DFCs and an AFC.

Brüggen, on the Dutch/German border, formed part of the RAF's contribution to NATO's 2nd Tactical Air Force. Along with Geilenkirchen, Laarbruch, and Wildenrath, it was at the centre of gravity for the RAF throughout the Cold War and home to two Canberra squadrons.[154] Ted recalls:

> "One was photo reconnaissance, that really had a tactical role, and the other was a bomber/interdictor. They had a wartime role with a bomb load and a semi-wartime role with a gun pack. They spent most of their time doing air-to-ground exercises or dive bombing, whereas the PR squadron flew mostly at low level doing tactical photography and weren't far off being fighter-type aircraft."

The two squadrons to which Ted refers were 80 Squadron and 213 Squadron. The former flew Canberra PR.7s and was supported by a mobile unit capable of developing and producing prints within a few minutes of one of their aircraft landing. It was a party trick that Ted's predecessor often used to impress visiting dignitaries. The latter was equipped with a dozen Canberra B(I)6s, six of which were capable of carrying either conventional or 'atomic' weapons.

The English Electric Canberra, which Ted had tried so hard to shoot down in his days as OC 29 Squadron, became one of his favourite aircraft to fly. He converted to the type at 231 OCU, Bassingbourn, taking the controls for the first time as pilot on October 15, 1964 and flying both the T.4 and the B.2.

In some ways, the first Canberra shared similarities with the Mosquito, in that it was unarmed and relied upon its high speed to escape fighters. The low aspect ratio wing was chosen to give maximum fuel economy at the highest possible cruising altitude and bestowed the aircraft with remarkable manoeuvrability.

Designed to Spec B.3/45, the Canberra prototype first flew on May 13, 1949, in the very safe hands of test pilot and former fighter ace Roland Beamont. The importance of its introduction at that time cannot be overestimated:

"If the B.3/45 failed there was no immediate alternative replacement for the ageing piston-engined bomber force of the RAF. If it failed, the new design department of the English Electric Company must go with it as it was not only their first but their only project in existence; and finally, from the outsider's point of view, and perhaps for some of those inside as well, the prototype of Britain's first jet bomber was the initial effort of an entirely new design team which had never worked together before."[155]

Happily, it didn't fail. Quite the opposite.

The first of the B(I)6s started to come on-line in the summer of 1954, and had 7,500lb static thrust Avon 109s, increased tankage and even greater range than the earlier marks. As a type they became the first jet bomber in the RAF to drop bombs on an enemy, during anti-terrorist strikes in Malaya. In terms of weapons, the B(I)6 had a Boulton and Paul gun pack containing four 20mm Hispano Suiza cannons in the rear of the bomb bay. Each gun was provided with 525 rounds, enough for 50 seconds' firing. In addition, three 1,000lb bombs could be carried in the bomb bay and two more on underwing pylons.

The photo-reconnaissance variant was a natural evolution, and the PR.7s became the first to be located in the Middle East. It was also a PR.7 that as Aries V completed a special return flight from the UK to Tokyo following the great circle route through Alaska. The PR.7, like the B.6s, had two of the Avon 109s giving it a top speed of 580mph at 40,000ft and a range of 4,340 miles. The official service ceiling stood at 48,000ft. The aircraft carried no armament, of course, but rather six 35in F52 cameras plus one vertical 6in F49 or four 20in F52s and one 6in F49.

Wing Commander Colin Adams describes the Canberra PR.7 as the backbone of the photo-reconnaissance force:

"The plane was originally designed for high-level reconnaissance with a set of six cameras for vertical work but it could also do oblique and low-level work. Normally in the Canberra the navigator takes the pictures lying in the nose where there is a sight for him. He has to be very accurate particularly for mapping work where you have to get the photos overlapping to complete the picture. Some of the early versions had an extra navigator taking pictures out of the back of the plane as the pilot cannot see behind him."[156]

Air Commodore Graham Pitchfork agrees: "The arrival of the Canberra with its suite of high- and low-level cameras, its two-man crew and its long range at low level brought a new capability to RAF Germany's tactical-reconnaissance force."[157] Ted took command shortly after the Cuban Missile Crisis, one of the chilliest moments of what was then an already freezing Cold War, and unrest in the US following the assassination of President Kennedy. He did not underestimate the role his men would play in helping to avoid a nuclear holocaust or contributing to it if ordered to do so. As such, the station maintained a very high state of readiness, such that it could respond to any major threat within minutes. Two Canberras from 213 Squadron (known as Quick Reaction Alert aircraft) were ready for immediate action with nuclear weapons loaded in their bomb bays. Aircrew and ground crew slept by their aircraft in a special hangar, such that the aircraft could be in the air and on their way to attack a target within 15 minutes of an order being received. The nuclear weapons themselves were of US construction, and closely guarded by a US major and an attachment of men permanently based on the station. They also protected the aircrew. An aircraft with a nuclear bomb on board could only take off if both the RAF and USAF commander at the highest levels had authorised it.[158]

In taking over command, Ted continued where his predecessor had left off, with training and practice regimes to keep his men at the top of their game. Dummy nuclear bombs (known as 'shapes') were used that were identical in size and weight to the real thing; aircrew only knew once they'd reached their aircraft whether an alert was for real or an exercise.

Brüggen was something akin to a small town, with a 'population' of around 3,000. As well as a school and a nursery, it also had three churches to cope with different denominations and some 36 different clubs and societies run by the residents and their wives. It occupied, Ted recalls, a considerable tract of land with a huge barbed-wire perimeter that was constantly patrolled. To Ted's delight it also had its own 18-hole golf course on which he could often be found when time allowed, with his son Martin carrying his bag. While on the fairway, Ted would listen out for approaching aircraft, and based on the noise they were making and the howling of the engines as they came into land, could invariably identify the individual pilot!

Given the size of the site and its amenities, Brüggen also required a sizeable civilian workforce for routine repair and maintenance and the upkeep of station infrastructure. Ted was not surprised to find that many of these men had only years before been fighting against him, and some had been highly decorated.

While 213 Squadron was at Brüggen primarily as part of NATO's nuclear deterrent, it also kept itself prepared to act for Britain in a conventional bombing role. The calls upon the RAF at this time were many, with small wars and insurgencies in many regions where Britain or its Commonwealth partners still had an interest. Exchange visits to RAF bases in Cyprus and North Africa were commonplace, as were exercises on bombing ranges not just in the UK and Europe but also as far afield as North Africa. Ted would often go with them, having now also gained experience in both the B(I)6 and the PR.7:

> "We used to practise in Libya, on a range there, with the Canberra flat out at 50ft and an indicated airspeed of 420 knots. It was quite exhilarating. The aircraft had a low-altitude bombing system (LABS) where you flew directly towards the target and then at a given range you pulled up and the bombs released automatically. We'd then go over the top of a loop, roll out, and then head back the other way which was all good fun."

While Ted loved flying the Canberra and everything about it, he never underestimated the strength it was sometimes required to fly:

> "The Canberra control system was on portion bars and at fast speeds it took all your strength to bend the portion bar or you couldn't move the control surfaces very far. The shallow dive-bombing technique they used was like being back on Mosquitoes. I hit the target once in an attack and was rather pleased with myself."

Although the station commander, Ted also brought his wartime operational experience to bear at a squadron level:

"Within 80 Squadron, its wartime role would have been one primarily of damage assessment. I spent some time with both squadrons in helping to improve the tactics of their wartime task, improving the routing and approach, and applying new tactics where it was appropriate and right to do so."

As well as British aircraft, the base was also regularly visited by American aircraft, the most remarkable that Ted recalls being the Lockheed F-104 Starfighter. The single-engined, supersonic air superiority fighter was distinctive for its needle-like fuselage and short, stubby wings. USAF pilots would drop in to 'trade' with their RAF counterparts on unofficial 'gin runs', swapping various US liquors and cigars for tax-free gin from the British NAAFI.

Ted's time at Brüggen was overshadowed by two fatal incidents, the first of which he could do nothing about. Canberra B(1)6 WT324 of 213 Squadron flown by Flying Officer Thomas Clapp was on a training exercise over the Netherlands on July 14, 1965 when a bird was ingested into one of the engines causing a loss of power and control. Despite the valiant efforts of the pilot to keep the aircraft in the air, the Canberra was too low and crashed into an orchard. Eyewitnesses had heard strange noises coming from the aircraft's engines and saw two of the crew jump clear (the two navigators) but both were killed when their parachutes failed to deploy in time. The pilot stayed at the controls, possibly in a deliberate effort to avoid crashing into nearby housing, and was dragged clear of the burning wreckage by a brave Dutchman but later died at the scene. By the time the RAF rescue team arrived there was little left of the aircraft other than a smouldering wreck and a trail of debris, and the crowd that had gathered were kept back by the heat of the flames and the risk of exploding ammunition.

The second fatal incident occurred seven months later. The crew, who were new to 80 Squadron and comparatively new to the Canberra, were detailed for a hi-lo-hi training flight from Brüggen that would take them over Scotland.[159] The flight was deferred for a few days because of bad weather, and in their final briefing they were given a forecast for the route and instructions that appeared to contradict what they had previously been told. A report on the accident reads:

'The briefing they received contradicted some instructions given during earlier briefings probably due to this being the first briefing that officer had given. Also, the weather forecast was not as accurate as it could have been as the meteorological officer did not know the exact boundaries of the low-flying area and had to give a more general forecast. This forecast gave conditions as marginal for the pilot's instrument rating but the authorising officer had not made sure that the crew was suitably experienced for the flight before signing it off. Having done a high-level transit from Germany to the north-east coast of Scotland the crew descended to low level but was still in cloud when the aircraft struck rising ground at the base of Sron Gharbh to the west of Berriedale, gouging a large scar and breaking up over approximately 250 metres, the wreckage only coming to rest as the slope becomes much steeper.'[160]

Local villagers spotted flashes coming from the hillside shortly after midday and a mountain rescue team was called in to investigate by Inverness Police. It was not until first light the following day that the wreckage was spotted by a helicopter from Leuchars, and the rescue party arrived to a scene of total devastation. The bodies of the 22-year-old pilot, David Girling, and navigator, Rowland Smith, who was also 22, were found soon after and evacuated by RN helicopter to RAF Kinloss. Further parties arrived over the next two days to make safe the armaments and other explosive devices associated with the engine starters and ejector seats.[161]

Wing Commander Colin Cummings writes:

'The aircraft was on a hi-lo-hi sortie from RAF Brüggen and had passed Lossiemouth at 1025 hrs and was due to return for refuelling about two hours later before returning to base. Having been overhead Lossiemouth at 10,000ft, the pilot was cleared to descend to 2,000ft where the reported he was IMC2[162]. A further clearance to descend to 1,000 was given and shortly afterwards, the pilot was given a position. Nothing further was heard from the aircraft but its wreckage was found the following day on high ground five miles north of Berriedale on the slopes of Scarben. The approach controller at Lossiemouth had misunderstood the let down and approach request from the aircraft's captain and then failed to safely control the aircraft, which he knew to be IMC and approaching the coastal hills.'[163]

Ted declined to discuss the latter incident in any interviews, but it led to an unpleasant exchange and harsh words with Sir Denis Spotswood, the C-in-C RAF Germany, and a disappointing end to an otherwise productive and enjoyable command. As the station commander Ted was well aware that he had to take ultimate responsibility. Some several years later, the two men found themselves on the same table at a charity event. Their conversation is not recorded.

The family returned to the UK in the spring of 1966, Ted's place being taken by Charles Browne.[164] For a brief time they were accommodated at RAF Honington in Suffolk while Ted actively sought his next posting, visiting old friends and colleagues and keeping his name visible. He did not have long to wait. Within a few months of returning to the UK, in the autumn of 1966, Ted took up his post as SASO at the Central Reconnaissance Establishment (CRE) at RAF Brampton under the command of Air Commodore Brian Young. He'd been in charge of the CRE since April 1964.

The CRE had been formed at Brampton seven years before in January 1957. It was the central body responsible for all of the RAF's strategic photographic and electronic reconnaissance and radio-intelligence gathering, and gloried under the motto *Ex Caelis Scientia*, generously translated as 'knowledge from the skies'. Given Ted's recent experience in Germany with a reconnaissance squadron, it was rewarding work.

The establishment shared Brampton with HQ Training Command and the Joint Air Reconnaissance Intelligence Centre (JARIC), the latter being one of three units under the command of the CRE AOC. The other two were RAF Wyton which operated a number of reconnaissance squadrons, and the Joint School of Photographic Interpretation (JSPI) at RAF Bassingbourn.

The three units were not only training for war; they were also actively engaged in various productive peacetime activities. Wyton, which was only a few miles up the road, had three squadrons on its strength: 543 (Victors), 58 (Canberras) and 51 which still had Comets; all three squadrons had peacetime operational roles. These included high-level photography for survey, at home and abroad, and for intelligence purposes; high-level radar surveillance, for instance for tracking naval fleets (the Russian navy was particularly active); low-level photography for a variety of users, military and civil (and including various government departments); recording of radio and radar frequencies; tracking and analysis of nuclear tests in the atmosphere; 'listening' on all frequencies near eastern borders; and the testing and evaluation of new reconnaissance equipment, be they cameras, radio, radar, as well as their installation and ongoing support.

The second unit under CRE – JARIC – was co-located with CRE and was well-known in the intelligence community, nationally and with NATO and the USA. Their principal task was that of photographic interpretation (PI), much of it on material coming from satellite photography. The staff were tri-service and were all experts in matters photographic and, most importantly, stereoscopy. Since this was still very much in the Cold War era, the work at JARIC was of vital significance.

JARIC was heavily dependent on the products of the third unit in CRE – JSPI at Bassingbourn – a small outfit whose sole purpose was to train photographic interpreters to the highest possible standard for all three services. CRE thus carried out specific peacetime tasks of reconnaissance and intelligence operations. It also enjoyed direct links with much of the intelligence community in both the UK and the US.[165]

Ted threw himself into his new role with his customary vigour. Although he had direct experience of the Canberra, he wanted to understand more about the operational aspects and capabilities of the Victor which equipped 543 Squadron. Not long after joining CRE, he spent a few weeks at Wittering on attachment to the Victor Training Flight, qualifying as a first pilot on October 14, 1966.

Ted worked very well with his commanding officer. He respected his war record, having been badly wounded in the Battle of France, and that he'd won the Sword of Honour at Cranwell.[166] When not deputising for Young, Ted was accompanying his AOC on a series of briefings and presentations on the latest reconnaissance and photographic techniques or hosting senior officers from other branches of the services (and sometimes from other countries) at Brampton. He was on a tour of Malta and Cyprus at the end of January 1967 and as such missed a visit by his wartime nemesis, 'Digger' Kyle. Kyle was at the time AOC-in-C Bomber Command.

The establishment was blessed with a highly capable and experienced staff, including dedicated PI and engineering specialists. Visits to the RAF's Trials and Tactics Cell were organised to further their understanding of the use of the Hawker Siddeley Harrier and McDonnell Douglas Phantom in a reconnaissance role (both the Harrier and the Phantom entered service with the RAF in the summer of 1969). New technologies were explored, including low-light television equipment being developed by Marconi (with whom Ted would later become directly acquainted) and the trial of new monochrome and colour films, the latter being developed by Kodak. Trips to the manufacturers themselves, Hawker Siddeley in Hatfield and Handley Page in St Albans, were also arranged, the former to discuss the use of the lightweight infrared line scan camera equipment for future reconnaissance; the latter to discuss the technical aspects of the new Victor B/SRII.

For this he was accompanied not only by the AOC, but also the OC 543 Squadron (Wing Commander Robert Redfern) and the OC Engineering Wing at Wyton. The B/SRII had replaced the Valiant and had a range that was at least 40 per cent greater, and a significantly enhanced photographic capability. With its radar it could map an area of 750,000 square miles in six hours. It was equipped with the F96 camera which unlike its predecessor, the F52, had the advantage of including an image movement compensation capability, minimising the effect of airspeed and giving a superior performance to those carried in the Valiant and Canberra PR.7.[167]

The tasking channels for Ted's work were 'a trifle odd'. Orders could come in not only from HQ Bomber Command (and later Strike Command after it came into being on April 30, 1968) but also direct from the MoD or one of the sister groups in Signals (90 Group) or Coastal Command (18 Group). They might also come from GCHQ in Cheltenham, or 'from anybody else on an "old boy" basis if time and effort would allow'.[168]

Several examples illustrate the point. In late January 1967, the establishment was asked by the Admiralty's Surface Weapons Establishment in Cosham to help evaluate the operational capabilities of a new type of radar installed on the aircraft carrier, HMS *Hermes,* while the ship was at sea off Malta. A Victor from 543 Squadron joined Buccaneers and Sea Vixens from *Hermes* in the trial which was completed to the Admiralty's satisfaction.

A few weeks later, and the CRE's Victor squadron was requested to take part in an exercise sponsored by the Commander-in-Chief Eastern Atlantic area mounted in the sea areas from the Azores through the Bay of Biscay to the English Channel. Exercise Wicked Lady, as it was called, required the Victor to conduct three days of surveillance of the 'enemy' fleet and cooperate with low-level probe sorties made by maritime aircraft. On the third day of the exercise, information about the fleet position and movement was also passed to 'friendly' submarine forces.

In the middle of March, it was the Headquarters Coastal Command who called upon the services of the CRE to provide photographic reconnaissance of the area around the Seven Stones Reef, 15 miles west of Land's End, where the 61,000-ton super tanker SS *Torrey Canyon* had run aground and was spewing vast gallons of crude oil into the Channel. The ironically named Exercise Mop Up lasted for more than a week as Victors from 543 and Canberras from 58 Squadron tracked the path of the spillage which within days had reached the Channel Islands and eventually impacted hundreds of miles of coastline in the UK, France and Spain. CRE was not the only group involved; aircraft from other groups and the Fleet Air Arm were tasked with attempting to set the spillage alight to minimise the damage but met with limited success. Eventually the ship sank, but not before an estimated 36 million gallons of crude had seeped from her tanks.

Overseas trips were not uncommon. At the end of April, Ted flew to Washington and on to the Tactical Air Reconnaissance Center at Shaw Air Force Base (AFB) in South Carolina before moving on to the Avionics Division at the Wright-Patterson AFB in Dayton, Ohio – the location of some of the Wright Brothers' earliest experimental flights. He returned in time to oversee the CRE's part in Operation Kendal to deliver coordinated surveillance of the summer exercise being enacted by the Russian fleet. NATO's response involved the military from the UK, the US, Canada, Denmark, France, the Netherlands and Norway. He also oversaw CRE's participation in photographing the launch of a Blue Steel nuclear stand-off missile over Cardigan Bay, a task that had originally been requested seven months earlier.

In November 1967, Brian Young was promoted air vice-marshal and posted to become Commandant General of the RAF Regiment. His place was taken by Air Commodore Michael Giddings, with whom Ted shared a similarly productive relationship. Giddings was a decorated fighter pilot from the war, who like Ted had served in Malta. Unlike Ted, however, most of Giddings' flying had been in single-seat Spitfires and Mustangs, though he had been an instructor at the Empire Test Pilots School and had well over 2,500 hours to his name when awarded an AFC for experimental flying work.

With Giddings there was no let-up in pace. Ted was regularly engaged with the CRE's role in various 'Mick' and 'Mickey Finns', as well as organising their own Howler exercises and flying whenever given the chance. Given that NATO forces were constantly being goaded by their Russian neighbours, preparation for war was a constant feature of service life. With the future war looking set to be a nuclear conflict, speed of response (both pro-active and re-active) was everything. A Mick was designed to test the ability of the V-Force personnel to generate aircraft and weapons on the main bases and 'to practise air crew and operations staff in alert and readiness procedures'; a Mickey Finn – the first of which was held on December 5, 1961 – was the annual 'no notice' dispersal exercise the purpose of which was to test the readiness capability of the V-Force whose dispersal was supported by all the Home Commands.[169] As well as the command-wide exercises, CRE squadron aircraft also practised their own element of a Mick or a Mickey Finn called a Howler – 'exercising the UK Reconnaissance Force under simulated war conditions'. This included using various bases as safe havens in the event their own airfield had been destroyed.

Giddings was still AOC when Bomber Command was stood down and Strike Command came into being in 1968, effectively 'merging' Bomber Command with Fighter Command, and with the ubiquitous Kyle as its first AOC-in-C. Ted accompanied Giddings to rehearsals for the stand-down event on April 26 prior to the formal ceremony taking place three days later. He was also with Giddings for the 50th Birthday Review of the RAF by HM Queen Elizabeth II at Abingdon a few weeks later, and the pair had the pleasant task of returning to Marham at the end of June to present the prizes for the Strike Command Bombing and Navigation Competition.

After only eight months in the role, Giddings was posted in July 1968, leaving Ted to break in his third AOC in quick succession. Air Commodore Edward Crew had visited the establishment for an introductory conversation at the end of June and formally in the second week of July. Crew had flown both Blenheims, Bristol Beaufighters and Mosquitoes during the war. Indeed, he was one of the most highly decorated day- and night-fighter pilots of the RAF having shot down 15 German aircraft and more than 30 'doodle bugs' which was no mean feat. Like Ted he had flown the Javelin (at the Central Fighter Establishment) and been station commander at Brüggen, so the two men had much in common.

Crew's arrival coincided with one of the more extraordinary events in which the CRE was asked to take part – a series of nuclear tests by the French government determined to follow its British and American allies in becoming a stand-alone nuclear power. Controversial then, and even more so now, the tests were to be conducted in the French Polynesian Archipelago over a four-month period. Among the bombs they were testing was a thermonuclear device 150 times more powerful than those that had destroyed Hiroshima and Nagasaki.[170]

The CRE had been made aware some months before that the tests would be taking place and planning its response had to be undertaken in great secrecy on a 'need to know' basis. Its mission was to provide aircraft equipped with the very latest radiation-sensing equipment which would take radiation readings in the atmosphere and within clouds after the various devices had exploded. After considerable debate, Lima in Peru was chosen as the most suitable site for the CRE detachment which would include 543 Squadron personnel, support staff, meteorologists, and scientists from the Atomic Weapons Research Establishment. The choice of Lima was not without its difficulties; the Peruvian government took some persuading to accept the detachment (which included two Victors) on their soil and the first personnel to visit the country from the CRE had to do so as tourists! Only when the British were certain in their choice did they formally approach the Peruvian authorities (the MoD, the air force and the Peruvian airport authority). Finding little joy they sought more productive assistance from the local BOAC manager, without whose help, Ted would write later, 'it would have been almost impossible to base the detachment at Lima.'[171]

The haste with which arrangements had to be made led to a number of challenges, mainly in relation to engineering support and communications, neither of which was wholly satisfactorily resolved. Ted flew out to Lima from RAF Wyton on July 30, to liaise with a Dr Reid, a scientist from the MoD, to review the situation and take charge of any issues that needed to be addressed. With the first of what would actually be a series of tests imminent, Ted decided to stay on to provide both practical and moral support to the men in the air and on the ground, while Dr Reid returned home.

In his report, Ted concluded that the detachment had been highly successful in almost every respect, in spite of their previous lack of experience and the difficulties of coordinating scientists and RAF staff. He did, however, make a series of recommendations, mostly around the requirement for improved communications, on the ground and in the air, and the need for a single authority for future detachments such that any advice, instructions, or orders to a detachment commander should be channelled through the CRE as a single source of truth. He also noted that the decontamination procedures for aircraft exposed to radiation needed to be enhanced in line with the higher levels demanded by their counterparts in the US Air Force.

A world away from Peru and nuclear testing, a similarly unusual task befell the CRE in September when it was called upon by the Ministry of Housing and Local Government, along with various rover authorities, to help survey flood damage in the south-east of England and East Anglia following heavy storms. Fifteen sorties were flown over seven days, generating more than 500 photographs for the authorities to review and use in planning future defences.

Crew was in office for only five months before he too was replaced, and Jack Furner appointed as the new (and what was to be the last) AOC. Ted was visiting Headquarters Near East Air Force at the time, spending a week in Cyprus discussing future reconnaissance operations, planning and intelligence matters.

Jack Furner was a no-nonsense former bomber boy, who'd completed a tour as a navigator with 214 Squadron in 1943. He returned to 214 and flew B-17 Flying Fortresses equipped with early electronic countermeasures as part of the highly secret 100 Group whose mission was to confound and destroy. He later described the unsatisfactory nature of his new appointment:

"I was conscious of the fact that there had been rapid turnover in the post. I recall that three people had gone through CRE in the previous 18 months. It was symptomatic of the possibly ephemeral nature of the headquarters – it was continually being sniped at by the financiers."[172]

Ted's final months at the CRE also coincide with the decision to disband the establishment, its responsibilities being integrated within 1 Group.[173] Ted was posted to the Central Defence Staff and on promotion to air commodore became commandant of one of the most famous of all of RAF establishments, the Royal Observer Corps (ROC).

The ROC could trace its roots back to the First World War and the foundation of the Metropolitan Observation Service (MOS) led by Air Vice-Marshal Edward Ashmore. Ashmore, a career soldier who had taken part in the Relief of Kimberley in the Boer War, had later transferred to the RFC and trained as a pilot. Given responsibility for the defence of London, which was then being challenged by night-time blitz raids by Zeppelins and Gotha long-range bombers, he set about devising an improved system of detection, communication and control. The MOS which initially covered London was extended towards the coasts of Kent and Essex, and while it enjoyed limited success, many valuable lessons were learned in how the country could be warned and defended against aerial attack. On October 29, 1925, the Observer Corps came into being.

Originally a volunteer civilian service, it became the uniformed ROC in 1941 as part of the RAF, belonging first to Fighter Command and latterly Strike Command. Ted became its 13th commandant on January 4, 1971, taking the baton from Air Commodore Dennis Rixson, a man described as an 'outstanding personality' who had fought in the ill-fated campaign in Greece.

Ted once again threw himself into the role with his customary quiet energy and understated vigour. Now living in Harpenden, a small town near the historic Roman city of St Albans in Hertfordshire, he had a driver take him round the multitude of bunkers and observation posts dotted around the country, meeting the men and women under his command. He also embarked on various overseas visits to fellow NATO countries to better understand their approach to civil defence in the nuclear age. He went first to France, meeting with his counterparts at the French civil defence headquarters in Rennes, before heading to Germany and Scandinavia. He also forged a close working relationship with the Danish air reporting corps (*Luftmeldekorpset*) which endured until 1992 when the ROC was stood down. The partnerships included an annual exchange and regular sharing of ideas, the Danish frequently sending parties of 50 or more observers to spend a week at the annual ROC summer camps. A friendly rivalry was also established between the two organisations, which manifested itself in a hotly contested aircraft recognition competition with honours remaining roughly even throughout its duration.

Two years as commandant passed quickly. When time allowed, he also gave air-experience flights from RAF Little Rissington in the Cotswolds in a de Havilland Chipmunk (attached to 6 AEFS at Abingdon) to cadets of the Air Training Corps and Combined Cadet Force, thrilling those who wanted it with some gentle aerobatics and allowing them briefly to take control. With his time served, he handed over the reins of the ROC to Roy Orrock, a former Mosquito pilot.[174] Ted's final appointment was a director of the Air Defence Environment Team (ADET) with Strike Command which involved planning a significant upgrade and re-equipment programme for the UK's air defence organisation including new early-warning radars and control and reporting systems. It was to prove the perfect introduction into a new life.

CHAPTER TWELVE
COMMERCIAL ENTERPRISE

TED WAS STILL ONLY 56 when he retired from service life, and still some way short of the retirement age of the average worker in Britain at the time. Thoughts had already turned to how he might continue to find an outlet for his energy, experience and military and government contacts, and in the winter of 1976, he joined Marconi with the general title of 'special advisor'.

The name Marconi was (and still is) synonymous with the development of wireless telecommunications named after the inventor Guglielmo Marconi and could trace its roots back to the beginnings of the 20th century. Through multiple mergers and acquisitions, the Marconi Company was acquired by English Electric (the firm behind the Canberra) in 1946 and reorganised into four divisions: telecommunications; broadcasting; aeronautics; and radar. By 1965, this had expanded to include a further nine divisions and reorganised into three groups: telecommunications; components; and electronics.

A further significant event occurred towards the end of the 1960s, and an attempted takeover bid by Plessey. In the event, the business was sold to the General Electric Company (GEC), and the core Marconi Company businesses effectively continued to operate as the primary defence subsidiary of its new parent (eventually emerging as GEC Marconi).

One of the many acquisitions during this time involved the takeover of Associated Electrical Industries (AEI) which included, amongst many others, Metropolitan Vickers and British Thomson Houston. AEI had particular expertise in various aspects of radar and electronic controls, and in August 1969, Marconi Radar Systems Limited (MRSL) was born, and the company's facility in Writtle Road, Chelmsford chosen as its headquarters. John Sutherland was to be its managing director.

MRSL merged various disciplines from several disparate entities, such that it had locations and factories not only in Chelmsford but also Leicester and Gateshead. For a short time, it also had operations in Borehamwood although as many people as possible were persuaded to relocate to its headquarters in Essex. To give some idea of its size, at the time of its formation it employed almost 4,000 people.

Ted's arrival at Marconi Radar Systems coincided with the firm's involvement in developing the new United Kingdom Air Defence Ground Environment (UKADGE) – intended to make any attack on the UK's air defences survivable. Marconi employed many ex-servicemen at the time because of their natural 'fit' in procuring new military business, and Ted was already connected with some of the Marconi and Plessey teams from his time as director of ADET.

Ian Gillis who spent many a pleasant afternoon in a mutual watering hole ('The Cats' in Curling Tye Green) says that Ted was remembered with respect and affection both inside and outside of work:

> "Ted was a man apart. Most of the members of the Old Boys' Club had some nickname or other in the ranks of the scurrilous proletariat (the Admiral, the General etc.). Ted's was AC1 (Acey One) – not aircraftman but air commodore first class! The most I had to do with him work wise was in California when Marconi was preparing a joint bid with Hughes for UKADGE. Ted was gentlemanly and unassuming but with a vast fund of operational experience combined with a charming manner. The Americans loved him."[175]

The roving nature of Ted's remit meant he was constantly travelling and pressing the flesh when required. He spent a short time in the Hughes Aircraft Company facility in Fullerton representing MRSL in a senior management capacity, casting a particular eye on the development of the US combative proposal system in which

Hughes, MRSL and Plessey all had a hand. Tensions between the UK team and their US counterparts had been present from the beginning, and Ted's arrival acted as a soothing balm for the disgruntled Brits. A satirical piece from the time captures the mood:

'Now it came to pass that, according to dispatches, the Marconi expeditionary force were running amok and indulging in heinous crimes such as booking early morning tea to their expense accounts, and taking less than five people in a rented car. So Jonlor Rence (aka John Lawrence – the Marconi UKADGE program manager) summoned his trusty cohort Acey One and urged him with all dispatch to travel to the Yewess of Ay as team coordinator, to restore morale and bolster flagging spirits. Now Acey One was a Very Important Person, having flown in the days when the Yukay had more than one flying machine, and being a founder member of the Yukay Old Boy's Club. Seizing command with a firm hand, immediately he organised the chairs around the swimming pool, and took the men to expensive eating houses where they used knives and forks, and they became once more content with their lot.'[176]

Nearer to home Ted was a regular at both the Farnborough and Paris Air Shows, the shop windows for the world's aviation, military and defence manufacturers to show off their wares. Alan 'Matty' Matthews, a former apprentice in a junior sales position at the time, recounts one particular trip with his boss:

"We were going to the Paris Air Show from Southend in a 12-seater twin light aircraft with a group which included John Crispin (a senior sales executive and former RAF regular complete with red silk-lined cloak) and Ted Sismore, who I did not know very well, but was my boss several levels up. I was in sales at a fairly junior level.

"When we got into the plane Ted asked the young pilot if he would mind if he sat with him up front. 'Fine,' said the pilot, and off we went. But when we landed at an airfield near Paris, the pilot said to us: 'Who was the old guy who sat with me on the way here – he seemed to know every church, road, bridge and other feature in France, and knew quite a bit about flying.' So we told him he was an RAF air commodore and had the reputation of being the best navigator in the RAF during the war and was also a top pilot with multiple DFCs. The pilot was horrified that his efforts had been seen by such an eminent flyer and asked if we could make sure Ted travelled in the back on the way home – though I am sure any of Ted's comments, if any, would have been kind ones.

"On the way back, in France, John Crispin stopped the bus and bought many cases of wine to take home and these were packed into the big boot at the front of the aircraft. It must have exceeded our duty-free allowance many times over but John with his impressive scarlet-lined cloak managed to convince the customs men that the cargo was legitimate and we later shared the spoils."[177]

It was some years into his role at Marconi when Ted was asked to head up one of the new divisions. Colin Latham, a senior executive within the business, recalls the sequence of events, and being summoned by the managing director to take charge of a new Military & Airspace Division:

"This was one of several small divisions (staff less than 100) created in a new MRSL organisational scheme. I was responsible to Peter Way (director) who also had four similar-sized divisions for other product ranges (I was also the chief engineer across all five). Each of these divisions had sales, contracts, business and systems departments with appropriate managers for each, but not development engineering which was still a separate large division acting for all (under H. N. C. Ellis-Robinson – known affectionately as 'E-R').

"My division was not successful. For one thing I was ill-matched to the job and my division was fundamentally at loggerheads with another division, reporting to another director, with the similar title of Military & Airspace Division (Export). Tension arose from NATO radar procurement for use in UK. Which division was that business?"[178]

That organisational restructure was the first of several that followed.

"The next plan was the creation of a much larger Airspace Control Division (nearly 1,000 strong) under Air Commodore Sismore. At the same time a comparably large Naval Division was created. Each was to include engineering, so a significant outcome was that E-R's comprehensive and long-established Development Division had to be split between airspace and naval. Evidently it was thought that by so doing a more responsive project-like approach would be achieved."[179]

While the theory was tenable, in practice there were snags, not least the need for duplication of expensive facilities such as specialised laboratories and test gear:

> "Sismore's two seniors were E-R and myself: we had worked together well in the past and respected each other; thus the inevitable splitting up and sharing of our staffs and responsibilities, which might well have been contentious, was achieved amicably."[180]

Colin says Ted advised the company on the most fruitful connections among the senior staff of the government and the various military services in the interests of developing national defence: "He encouraged staff by clear direction, good mentoring of their efforts, support when needed, but never undermined their efforts by interfering within their departments. Neither was he ever heard referring to his wartime successes."[181]

Ken Perry, consultant HF Radar Marconi Radar Systems, 1982–1995 remembers that in the late 1970s and early 1980s, the UK still had concerns about hostile aircraft approaching its shores at flight levels perhaps 500ft above the sea surface:

> "Studies were undertaken of the use of radars operating in the short-wave radio band which would track ships and also aircraft flying very low over the sea. Ted would have been exceedingly aware that survival could necessitate flying below the cover provided by microwave radar.
>
> "UK shore defences subsequently demanded an ability to track low-flying intruders and to guide our own interceptors below the normal radar horizon. While airborne early warning aircraft can fulfil such duties, they cannot be everywhere all of the time. Air Commodore Sismore, as manager of the Airspace Control Division, zealously encouraged the study and building of prototype high frequency (HF) radar systems (both Surface Wave for shoreline protection and Skywave for very long-range ship and aircraft tracking). He was also instrumental in guiding Marconi Radar/Research expertise into UK Surface Wave trials and into the proposals for the Australian Skywave radar network subsequently built in the 1990s."[182]

Both Surface Wave and Skywave systems fell into the category of over the horizon (OTH) radar (or sometimes beyond the horizon [BTH] radar) with the ability to detect targets at very long ranges and, as the name suggests, beyond the radar horizon. Marconi's research, with Ted very much as its champion, led ultimately to the development of the Jindalee Operational Radar Network (JORN) operated by the RAAF to monitor air and sea movements across 37,000sq km. (The decision to build JORN was announced in October 1986 with Telstra and GEC Marconi as prime contractors.)

Ted's passion for Surface Wave and Skywave systems led to an interesting but little-known project in the South Atlantic, immediately following the ultimately doomed invasion of 'Las Malvinas' by Argentinian military forces in 1982. Ted had already achieved fame during the conflict for securing in a matter of a few weeks the availability of a mobile air-defence radar, something which would normally have taken several years to procure. His contacts within the MoD, the RAF and Marconi expedited the sourcing and despatch of an S259 (Type 95) air-surveillance radar which was deployed in Punta Arenas in Chile, adjacent to the Argentinian border and which provided coverage of the two air bases. It gave the British Task Force early warning of aircraft launching from Rio Grande and Rio Gallegos.[183] Now with the war won, but the threat of further action still a possibility, HM Government sought to better prepare the islands against future attack. Air Staff Requirement 901 (ASR 901) was issued to explore Surface Wave OTH radar, with the ability to detect sea-level targets up to 160km from the coast. The deputy director of Operational Requirements, Group Captain David Barnes wrote:

> "The Argentines' ability to mount surprise low-level air attacks is the major threat to the Falkland Islands. Gaps in the low-level coverage of the planned microwave radars could be filled by the installation of HF Surface Wave radars. This ASR will provide the basis for the development of a suitable HF Surface Wave radar system."[184]

Barnes' rationale was endorsed by his superior, Air Commodore Derek Hann, who described it as 'the cheapest and most effective way of providing continuous low-level warning for the Falkland Islands'. The programme was authorised three days later (on March 20, 1983) by the assistant chief of Air Staff Operational Requirements, Air Vice-Marshal David Harcourt-Smith.[185]

The deadline for the new system was tight; it was required to be in service by the end of the following year and the team – led by Squadron Leader R. H. Griffiths of the RAF Technical Branch and including a propagation specialist from Marconi – lost no time in heading south for an initial site survey. MRSL had in fact been studying the feasibility of an HF Surface Wave radar for the Falklands for some time and had developed a pilot system as part of Project Heartbreak. While no-one expected the Argentinians to be capable of launching a full-scale invasion for at least another five years, limited attacks were still viable. The fluid nature of the political regime meant nothing could be ruled out. The devastating attacks by A-4 Skyhawks and Exocet-carrying Dassault-Breguet Super Étendards on Royal Navy warships (including both HMS *Sheffield* which was sunk and HMS *Glamorgan* which was badly damaged) and British merchant vessels (most famously *Atlantic Conveyor*) during the Falklands' conflict was still a recent and painful memory. The threat analysis reads:

'Unrefuelled the Argentine air force Skyhawks, Mirages and Super Étendards are capable of approaching the Falkland Islands at low level only from the west or the north-west. The Argentinians are acutely aware that during Corporate we felt safe on the east side of the islands, and they have therefore given emphasis to the development of air-to-air refuelling techniques. They are now judged capable of attacking in limited numbers from any direction at low level. Furthermore, whilst they may not wish to risk their carrier flagship against our submarines, they have experimented with flying Super Étendards from their aircraft carrier and could therefore launch carrier-based raids of up to 18 aircraft, including Super Étendards, from any direction. There is therefore a requirement to provide all-round low-level early-warning radar cover to cater for both harassment raids, and to protect important garrison assets against a larger attack.'[186]

Until the instigation of ASR 901, the islands planned to use three conventional microwave radars on hilltop sites, with early warning provided by naval picket ships. The flaws in the plan were obvious: microwave was limited in its low-level capability by line of sight, and the system suffered poor performance when looking down on moving water. The use of picket ships was not only expensive, but also made those ships extremely vulnerable to attack. Airborne early warning (AEW) was also considered but rejected as impractical.

The concept of a 'trip wire' detector that would give fighter aircraft stationed on the islands suitable time to scramble and pick up any incoming raiders on their own radar systems was considered the solution. Skywave radar based on the Ascension islands or South Georgia was an option, but one that came at considerable cost. An HF Surface Wave radar based on the islands itself was deemed capable of detection to an acceptable degree of accuracy and an acceptable level of cost.

Six radars were to be manufactured, shipped and installed, developed from the original Heartbreak prototype. Even with perfect seas and a fair wind, it would not be until at least the middle of 1986 that all six systems would be operational.

The benefits and the frailties of the system were explored at length. Jamming was a threat, but with six sites operating on different frequencies that were poor for Skywave propagation, the threat was deemed minimal. There were practical considerations; each site required nine personnel to operate, and a garrison of 30 men to defend, since they would become prime targets.

Then there were the benefits of developing the new system beyond the Falklands:

'The sales opportunities for OTH radars could be very good. Their military applications include early warning and over the horizon targeting of weapon systems. In the civilian field they offer some potential for sea-lane control and sea-state sensing. The University of Birmingham has been active in the latter field for several years. For these reasons many countries including France, the United States, Australia, and India have an active interest in Surface Wave radar systems. The UK has carried out investigations into radars for UKADR (Project Digest) and Saudi Arabia is interested in a system for the Gulf.'[187]

It was perhaps a very good thing for Ted and Marconi that the work they were investigating for the Falklands would have commercial benefits elsewhere. While the theory of HF OTH for the Falklands was sound in principle, the practical considerations were insurmountable. What was considered a 'cheap' alternative was working out to be incredibly costly. Poor ground conditions, site access challenges, and lack of basic utilities added up to a programme that simply wasn't viable, and Ted was disappointed to learn that on October 3, 1984, ASR 901 was withdrawn.

Throughout Ted's time in the business, the GEC empire had been led by the mercurial but divisive Arnold Weinstock, a man seemingly praised and despised in equal measure. He had joined what was to become GEC in 1954 and took over as managing director in 1963. It was Weinstock who oversaw the acquisition of AEI and EE, which at the time was the biggest merger in Britain. Dubbed by Hugh Scanlon, the leader of the AUEW engineering union as 'Britain's largest unemployer', Weinstock's style was one of vigorous financial control which generally involved closures and wholesale redundancies. Culturally the business was challenged, as Colin Latham attests: "I cannot hope to remember, let alone describe, the very many organisational changes that occurred in the early and mid-eighties."

Such constant reorganisation led to uncertainty and lack of clarity in proposition and mission, which was to manifest itself soon after Weinstock handed over the reins to George Simpson. Ted eventually fell victim to one reorganization too many and was ousted 'at indecently short notice' to be replaced by a much younger man with no radar experience but apparently impressive business credentials – who, in turn, was soon discarded. "It was a time of much change and distress," Colin recalls.

Ted was more disappointed than upset, and particularly so for the people he had left behind, and with whom he had enjoyed working. Never a selfish man, he was nonetheless somewhat put out by the shabby way in which he had been dismissed and that his contribution to the business had not been recognised by Weinstock and his acolytes. Weinstock was said to have put a courtesy call through to Ted not long after leaving the business but rang off before Ted could answer and never tried again.

While Weinstock perhaps failed to realise Ted's talents, others were not so reticent. He had impressed the Americans during his time on the UKADGE project and was soon after headhunted by the Hughes Aircraft Company as a director of the Eutronic Consortium in Brussels. The consortium included Marconi, CFTH (France), Telefunken (West Germany), and Selenia (Italy), and had previously been the NATO Air Defence Ground Environment Corporation (NADGECO). It was a part-time role and suited him well, especially with John Burke as his able deputy and close friend. John, a radar expert who had been closely involved in the development of UKADGE while at the MoD, would later say how much he valued Ted's leadership and sound advice – a common theme expressed by many of Ted's friends and colleagues.[188]

Despite the unsatisfactory way in which he left the Marconi family, he kept in touch with his MRSL peers and continued to show great interest in their work.

Keith Chittenden, who 'inherited' Ted as a senior member of the management team when he took over as managing director of MRSL in 1982, similarly valued Ted's experience and friendship:

"I often felt how lucky I was to have him at my side in Brussels (where 'General' Sismore was much revered) and I recollect lengthy visits to UK sites (such as going to RAF Boulmer by helicopter) and how greatly and rightly he was feted by the Royal Danish Air Force when we went to Bornholm (an air force station with a Marconi S723 radar) together."[189]

David Emery remembers Ted accompanying Ken Perry on a visit to a radar test site at Bradwell, formerly known as Dengie, where they were working on a new multi-frequency HF Surface Wave radar system. It was 2006: "It demonstrated his continued interest in low-level radar detection right through to old age," David says.[190]

At home in Woodham Walter, a small village three miles to the west of Maldon in Essex where he had moved with Rita for its proximity to Marconi's offices in Chelmsford, Ted settled into retirement. A neighbour who worked for British Gas employed him as an official/unofficial consultant. At the time, the energy provider was looking to target service establishments, and Ted knew the right people to speak to and how. Joint visits to see old haunts and make new friends amused him enormously and provided more than just pin money for the odd pint at the local. He kept his mind active by keeping up to date with affairs in the Middle East and writing various papers for The Royal United Services Institute, the defence and security think tank, some of which were published.

He also took *The Times* newspaper every day, paying particular attention to the weather section, his fascination with meteorology a constant sense of entertainment. If the weather was fine, he was often to be found walking along the Blackwater Estuary looking at the barges and boats, diving into the local hostelry and striking up a conversation with whoever was at the bar at the time. Frequently he would discover they were ex-servicemen like himself and treated everyone as equal, regardless of rank.

With time on his hands, he travelled the UK playing golf, meeting up with many of his former service friends including Ivor Broom, who was then president of Moor Park Golf Club in Hertfordshire, a popular venue for many former RAF officers because of its close proximity to NATO's Northwood HQ. Closer to home, he joined The Warren Golf Club which formed part of the nearby Warren Estate, inviting Sir Ivor and John Burke to play and gathering together a group of like-minded players of similar handicaps (Ted played off 21) to form a group known collectively as 'The Dawn Patrol'. They included, among others, a retired bank manager, a Fleet Air Arm pilot, and former sales manager of Decca Radar. This was particularly ironic given that Decca had been one of Marconi's fiercest rivals chasing the biggest contracts. Ted became a familiar face in the clubhouse, often sought out by younger members who knew something of his wartime work. He had to smile and had an answer 'off pat' for every time he was asked what it was like to fly a Spitfire! (Not long before he died, Ted was deeply moved to have been made an honorary life member.)

Ted and Rita's idyllic existence was interrupted on at least two occasions: once when their house was broken into, and once it was set on fire. On the first occasion, Ted was in the house at the time and simply told the burglars that there was nothing in his home worth stealing. They seemed to take his word for it and slipped away. On the second, Ted had a chip pan on the stove which suddenly exploded with an almighty whoosh and set fire to the kitchen. Ted's first priority was to get Rita out of the house (she was by then a little unsteady on her feet) and call for help. Fast-thinking neighbours came to his assistance and helped to put the fire out before it set the whole house ablaze. With wood-panelled ceilings it was a very real possibility. While structurally the building was sound, there was a considerable amount of smoke damage, and it was a full six months before Ted and Rita could move back into their home.

For the last six years of his life, Ted was on his own, Rita having predeceased him. Notwithstanding the loss of his wife, Ted remained stoic and fully active. He took a close interest in the return to the air of a Bristol Blenheim, serving for a time as vice chairman of the Blenheim Society where his counsel and advice proved invaluable in helping the society deliver on its objectives of promoting the history of the aircraft and its crews to a new audience.[191]

Ted was never one to boast of his wartime service though he did enjoy meeting aviation enthusiasts at various signing events lending his autograph to dramatic prints by the likes of the late Robert Taylor and Philip West depicting his various Mosquito exploits. His 'fame', if that is not too strong a word, was not a modern phenomenon, however. During the war, his photograph was often to be seen in the press, such that he came to the attention of the Germans. He remembers:

> "We had one navigator who was shot down and rather badly injured who was repatriated through Switzerland on a scheme where aircrew were exchanged between the UK and Germany. He came back having been assessed by a Swiss doctor and, fortunately, recovered rather better than he should. When he got back, he came to see me and told me that during his interrogation by the Luftwaffe [intelligence officer] they threw a folder on the table and told him to take a look. He said: 'I picked it up and it was you!' He then told me: 'Don't get shot down because they know all about you,' which was all a bit frightening. The fact they had taken the trouble to get to have a file on me, I suppose, made me think."

Meeting other wartime aircrew at events, Ted considered writing his own memoirs but was convinced that no-one would be interested and that in his words 'it has all been written about before'. He may also have been influenced by two other factors. When Reg Reynolds had submitted a copy of a proposed story about his wartime experiences in the 1960s, it had been returned to him as being 'of insufficient interest'.[192] That may have played a part in Ted's decision. But it may also have been that the loss of so many children in the attack on Copenhagen still disturbed him, and he felt uncomfortable in committing those memories to paper or being seen to benefit from them.

Ted died on March 22, 2012 at the age of 90 after a short illness. A large number of friends and family gathered to say their farewells, alongside many ex-servicemen, golfing buddies, and everyday tradesmen and women who remembered that he always had a kind word for everyone. Reg Reynolds, who for some inexplicable reason had been declined a permanent commission, died five years later on November 25, 2017. Released from the RAF on January 31, 1946, he had emigrated to Canada to pursue a highly successful career in civil aviation, accumulating more than 22,000 hours of flying on 60 different types of aircraft.

When Ted started on operations, it was well known that most Blenheim aircrew had little chance of surviving for very long. The statistics were that they stood a 25 per cent chance of surviving their first tour of operations, but such figures were never released. Ted like many of his contemporaries was endowed with such supreme optimism of youth it never occurred to him that he might one day add to these mournful statistics.[193] As it happens, he went through the war without a scratch, a classic combination of skill and luck in equal quantities and which he attributed largely to flying with some of the RAF's very best pilots. It might also have had something to do with the fact that he was one of the RAF's very best navigators.

SOURCES

ARTICLES AND JOURNALS

Air Clues, Vol. 20 No. 10, July 1966

Cape Times, May 2, 1947

Flypast – Doug Gordon – January 2024

Flypast – Tom Docherty – October 2017 (https://www.key.aero/article/flying-javelin)

The Guardian, 'How the great storm of 1953 caused Britain's worst peacetime disaster' (January 31, 2013) https://www.theguardian.com/environment/interactive/2013/jan/31/uk-great-storm-flood-1953-interactive last accessed 11 July 2024

Imperial War Museum, 'A Short History of the Aden Emergency', https://www.iwm.org.uk/history/a-short-history-of-the-aden-emergency accessed July, 11 2024

KentOnline, 'The night in 1953 when the North Sea flooded Sheerness, Whitstable, Herne Bay, Margate, Deal and many others' (January 31, 2023) https://www.kentonline.co.uk/kent/news/the-perfect-storm-that-left-kent-under-water-281328/ last accessed 11 July 2024

Royal Air Force in Germany 1945–1993, RAF Historical Society

RAF Historical Society Journal 18

RAF Transport Command Review No. 13, September 1946

BOOKS

Beamont, Roland, *Phoenix into Ashes* (William Kimber, 1968)
Bond, Steve, *Javelin Boys* (Grub Street, 2014)
Bowman, Martin W., *RAF Marham: Bomber Station* (The History Press, 2008)
Bowyer, Chaz, *History of the RAF* (Hamlyn, 1977)
Bowyer, Chaz, *Mosquito at War* (Ian Allan Publishing, 1973)
Bowyer, Michael J. F., *2 Group RAF: A Complete History, 1936–1945* (Faber and Faber, 1974)
Embry, Sir Basil, *Mission Completed* (Methuen, 1957)
Eyton-Jones, Arthur, *Day Bomber* (Sutton, 1998)
Feast, Sean, and Mitchell, John, *Churchill's Navigator* (Grub Street, 2010)
Fishman, Jack, *And the Walls Came Tumbling Down* (Souvenir, 1982)
Gillman, R. E., *The Shiphunters* (John Murray, 1976)
Goulding, James, and Moyes, Philip, *RAF Bomber Command and its aircraft, 1936–1940* (Ian Allan, 1975)
Gunston, Bill, *The Illustrated Encyclopaedia of Combat Aircraft of World War II* (Salamander Books, 1978)
Harris, MRAF Sir Arthur, *Bomber Offensive* (Collins, 1947)
Jefford, Wg Cdr C. G., *Observers and Navigators* (Grub Street, 2014)
Lloyd, Hugh Pughe Sir, K.C.B., *Briefed to Attack* (Hodder & Stoughton, 1949)
Lucas, Laddie, *Wings of War: Airmen of all nations tell their stories 1939–1945* (Grafton, 1985)
Middlebrook, Martin, and Everitt, Chris, *The Bomber Command War Diaries: An Operational Reference Book, 1939–1945* (Midland, 1996)
Passmore, Richard, *Blenheim Boy* (Thomas Harmsworth, 1981)
Pudney, John Sleigh, *Pride of Unicorns: Richard and David Atcherley of the RAF* (Oldbourne, 1960)
Reilly, Robin, *The Sixth Floor* (Frewin, 1969)
Remy, *The Gates Burst Open* (Arco Publishers, 1955)
Roskill, Captain S. W., *The War at Sea Volume I The Defensive* (HMSO, 1954)
Saward, Dudley, *The Bombers' Eye* (Cassell, 1959)
Shaw, Michael, *Twice Vertical: The History of No. 1 Squadron RAF* (Macdonald and Co., 1971)
Shores, Christopher, *2nd Tactical Air Force* (Osprey, 1970)
Shores, Christopher, Williams, Clive, *Aces High* (Grub Street, 1994)

Sniders, Edward, *Flying In, Walking Out: Memories of War and Escape, 1939–1945* (Leo Cooper, 1999)

Spooner, Tony, *Clean Sweep: The Life of Air Marshal Sir Ivor Broom* (Crécy, 2001)

Thetford, Owen, *Aircraft of the Royal Air Force since 1918* (Putnam, 1962)

Turner, Michael, *Royal Air Force: The Aircraft in Service since 1918* (Hamlyn, 1981)

Vielle, E. E., *Almost a boffin: The memoirs of Group Captain E. E. Vielle, OBE, RAF (Rtd)* (Dolman Scott 2013)

Waterton, William Arthur, *The Quick and the Dead* (Grub Street, 2012)

White, Rowland, *Harrier 809* (Bantam Press, 2000)

Wooldridge, John de L., *Low Attack: The Story of Two Mosquito Squadrons in World War Two* (Sampson Low, Marston & Co., 1946)

Wynn, Humphrey, *The Bomber Role 1945–1970* (Air Historical Branch, 1984)

PRIMARY SOURCES

Author interview with Al Greethurst, former 8 Squadron navigator in Aden, September 26, 2018

Kinloss Mountain Rescue Team Incident Report: https://rafmountainrescue.com/wp-content/uploads/19660202-KMRT-REPORT-A-2-Feb-66-Canberra-crash.pdf, accessed July 11, 2024

Letter to Martin Sismore April 12, 2012

Letter to Martin Sismore from Graham Warner April 14, 2012

Letter from Reg Reynolds dated October 20, 1995 in The RAF Pathfinders Archive

Ted's logbook in the Hendon Archive MF10073/1-5

The Higgs/Vigar Tapes (HVT)

The National Archives (TNA), AIR 2/4974 – DECORATIONS, MEDALS, HONOURS AND AWARDS (Code B, 30): Immediate awards: operational

TNA, AIR 27/827 – No. 105 Squadron Operations Record Book (January 1943–December 1944)

TNA, AIR 27/960 – No. 139 Squadron Operations Record Book (June 1942–December 1943)

TNA, AIR 27/1935 – No. 487 Squadron (RNZAF): Operations Record Book

TNA, AIR 27/2606 – No. 29 Squadron Operations Record Book (January 1, 1951–December 31, 1955)

TNA, AIR 27/2704 – No. 85 Squadron Operations Record Book (January 1, 1951–December 31, 1955)

TNA, AIR 29/668/1 – No. 24 OTU Operations Record Book

TNA, AIR 29/2809 – Operational Conversion Unit: No. 228 OCU, Leeming

TNA, AIR 29/4052 – Central Reconnaissance Establishment RAF Wyton. With appendices

TNA, DEFE 71/1065 – Surface Wave Over the Horizon Radar for the Falkland Islands

War Cabinet weekly resumé No. 90.

WEBSITES

Aviation Safety Network, https://asn.flightsafety.org/wikibase/152443, accessed July 11, 2024

Furnerama – reminiscences of Jack Furner, last AOC of the CRE, http://www.furnerama.com/jack-furner/, accessed July 11, 2024

Marconi Radar, https://marconiradarhistory.pbworks.com/w/page/29024389/MARCONI%20RADAR, accessed July 11, 2024

Men of 24 Operational Training Unit, Honeybourne, https://www.aviationarchaeology.org.uk/marg/men_of_24otu.htm, accessed July 11, 2024

Spink Online Catalogue, https://spink.com/lot/19001000583, accessed July 11, 2024

MUSEUMS

Calgary Mosquito Society

The Civil Aviation Historical Society and Airways Museum

ENDNOTES

CHAPTER ONE

1. Letter to Martin Sismore April 12, 2012
2. The Higgs/Vigar Tapes (HVT). (See explanation in the Acknowledgements.)
3. Wg Cdr C. G. Jefford, *Observers and Navigators* (Grub Street, 2014), p.130
4. Owen Thetford, *Aircraft of the Royal Air Force since 1918* (Putnam, 1962), p.407
5. Jefford, *Observers and Navigators*, p.150
6. John Mitchell and Sean Feast, *Churchill's Navigator* (Grub Street, 2010), pp.7–8
7. R. E. Gillman, *The Shiphunters* (John Murray, 1976), p.37
8. After William was killed, later in the war, 'Dee' married John Yeomans, another airman, before leaving Yeomans for Tom Dalton-Morgan DSO DFC, a very well-known Battle of Britain pilot.
9. Tony Spooner, *Clean Sweep: The Life of Air Marshal Sir Ivor Broom* (Crécy, 2001), p.13
10. James Goulding and Philip Moyes, *RAF Bomber Command and its aircraft, 1936–1940* (Ian Allan, 1975), p.71
11. Bill Gunston, *The Illustrated Encyclopaedia of Combat Aircraft of World War II* (Salamander Books, 1978), p.91
12. Gillman, *The Shiphunters*, p.38
13. Spooner, *Clean Sweep*, p.17
14. Ibid. p.26
15. Spink Online Catalogue, https://spink.com/lot/19001000583, accessed July 11, 2024
16. Having joined the RAF in 1930 and passing out from Cranwell the following year, Philip flew Torpedo bombers from the deck of HMS *Furious*, similarly achieving the rare feat of an above average rating for his deck landings. He survived a number of hair-raising incidents in his early flying days, including a ditching and striking a ship's funnel

while carrying out a low-level dummy attack. With Coastal Command just before the outbreak of war he gained his first experience on Blenheims, and after a short spell with 101 Squadron at Raynham he was posted to 82 Squadron as a flight commander. He proved his mettle early, being awarded the Distinguished Flying Cross (DFC) in March 1940 for a dangerous low-level reconnaissance of Sylt Island to assess the results of a raid on the Luftwaffe seaplane base at Hornum on the night of 19/20th. Churchill had been told the attack had been magnificent, and the damage extensive, and the media had been informed accordingly. Philip's photographs were to prove otherwise, so much so that the press story was quashed, and the true details of the raid not released until ten years after the war. For his part, Philip had to avoid fighters and intense flak, at one point his aircraft being rocked by a violent explosion that put a hole through his wing and nearly cut short his flying career and his life. His period in France with 82 Squadron soon after typifies the futility of the RAF's attempts to stem the German tide. On one terrible day, 11 out of 12 Blenheims from B Flight 82 Squadron were shot down, victims of flak and fighters, and nine officers lost. Somehow Philip survived, and after a spell instructing, returned for a second tour, this time with 110 Squadron. He took part in many of the squadron's night-time raids over Germany, and was nearly shot down by his own side one night over Ipswich.

17 Richard Passmore, *Blenheim Boy* (Thomas Harmsworth, 1981), p.208
18 Mitchell and Feast, *Churchill's Navigator*, p.22
19 Michael J. F. Bowyer, *2 Group RAF: A Complete History, 1936–1945* (Faber and Faber, 1974), p.139
20 Ibid. p.140
21 Actually, Gericke had survived being shot down by the ship's flak and ditched a kilometre from the Dutch coast. He lived but his two crew members were killed. Gericke spent the rest of the war as a prisoner, initially in Oflag IX, Spangenberg. He resumed a career in the services on his return from Germany, being awarded the Queen's Commendation for Valuable Service in the Air in 1958. He later returned to his home country where he died in 1965.
22 Captain S. W. Roskill, *The War at Sea Volume I The Defensive* (HMSO, 1954)
23 Sir Hugh Pughe Lloyd KCB, *Briefed to Attack* (Hodder & Stoughton, 1949), p.18
24 Whenever a compass has been subjected to a shock, even something as simple as a hard landing, the aircraft is swung through the various magnetic directions to reflect the true position of the aircraft when flying.
25 Ian Spencer retired as an air vice-marshal.
26 War Cabinet weekly resumé No. 90
27 Tudor Beattie was a fifth-year medical student from Northern Ireland.

CHAPTER TWO

28 Lloyd, *Briefed to Attack*, p.28
29 Bowyer, *2 Group RAF*, p.207
30 Adrian Warburton was one of the war's most accomplished reconnaissance pilots, later disappearing in mysterious circumstances. Sir Arthur Tedder believed him to be the most important pilot in the RAF.

31   Lloyd, *Briefed to Attack*, p.48

32   'Bish' later qualified as a pilot and flew Hampdens with 162 Squadron. He was shot down in January 1942, spending the remainder of the war as a POW.

33   Gillman, *The Shiphunters*, p.61

34   The Condor was a four-engined long-range aircraft that had originally been designed as an airliner but converted to a military role. Its ability to stay in the air for anything up to 14 hours made it a much feared and respected adversary.

35   In the official Italian bulletin, only two Blenheims were shot down by fighters and the other two by flak. Buvoli had fought in the Spanish Civil War under a *nom de guerre*, Aldo Briotti. He was shot down on June 23, 1942, becoming a POW.

36   Flight Sergeants Bertie Mulford and William McDougall.

37   Sergeants Ronald Baird and Harold Lummus.

38   Michael's brother suggests that the 21-year-old had volunteered to fly in first to draw the flak away from the other aircraft, and as such had been shot down, but not before ordering his crew to bale out. He then targeted the fatally hit bomber at the bridge of one of the vessels they were attacking. It is difficult to either verify or dispute this version of events. The missing crew members were Pilot Officer Theodore Griffith-Jones and Sergeant D. H. Wythe.

39   Lloyd, *Briefed to Attack*, p.53

40   This is the date on the CWGC site. On the ORB he is recorded as being killed in the attack on the 22nd.

41   Believed to be Sergente Maggiore Vincenzo Graffeo of the 367^a Squadriglia.

42   The citation for Ware's DFM reads: *'This NCO, whilst detached at Malta, carried out a most determined and successful operation on the 22nd July 1941. He participated in an attack on four merchant ships and five escorting destroyers, and in spite of intense opposition, succeeded in hitting a 6,000-ton ship, which eventually sank. A minute or so before dropping his bombs, Sergeant Ware was hit in the thigh and right shoulder by fragments from a shell which exploded in the front cockpit, killing his observer.'* Ware died in Egypt on September 28, 1942. The citation for Forsythe's DFC reads: *'In July 1941 this officer participated in an attack on an enemy convoy consisting of five merchant ships with five escorting destroyers. As a result, one merchant ship of 7,000 tons, with ammunition on board, blew up, and another 6,000-ton ship was so severely damaged that, about an hour later, only the stern was above water. A third ship was so badly hit that the speed of the convoy was reduced in consequence. This enabled Swordfish aircraft to complete the destruction of the disabled vessel and also to destroy another one. By his splendid leadership and skill, Squadron Leader Forsythe contributed materially to the brilliant success of this operation.'*

CHAPTER THREE

43   Martin Middlebrook and Chris Everitt, *The Bomber Command War Diaries: An Operational Reference Book, 1939–1945* (Midland, 1996), p.241

44   MRAF Sir Arthur Harris, *Bomber Offensive* (Collins, 1947), p.109

45   TNA, AIR 29/668/1 – No. 24 OTU Operations Record Book

46 Mason later went on to win the DFC with 70 Squadron in 1944.

47 Ted's crew for this trip included Sergeants Graver and Whicher as wireless operator and air gunner respectively.

48 Men of 24 Operational Training Unit, Honeybourne, https://www.aviationarchaeology.org.uk/marg/men_of_24otu.htm

49 Thetford, *Aircraft of the Royal Air Force since 1918*, p.192

50 Lord Beaverbrook, Minister of Aircraft Production, dismissively referred to the Mosquito as 'Freeman's Folly'.

51 Ken later wrote in his diary: 'Very shaky do. Three shells in the nose. One got Polly, blew half his head away. Port wing smashed, tail and elevators riddled. Big shell hole in the fin. Bomb doors shot away. Electrical systems shot away. Cockpit, belly and both engines riddled with holes. Saw Bob (Sgt Ratcliffe) go down with engine on fire. Made mess of the island. Bags of smoke, dust and flames. Hell of a lot of flak ships.'

52 Edward Sniders, *Flying In, Walking Out: Memories of War and Escape, 1939–1945* (Leo Cooper, 1999), pp.22–23

53 Dodwell later flew with 1409 Meteorological Flight and 571 Squadron, before being killed in action in the summer of 1944. He baled out of his stricken Mosquito with his navigator, George Cash, but only Cash survived.

54 Peter Channer had won the DFC with 18 Squadron in August 1941 and went on to earn the DSO with 105 Squadron in the autumn of 1944 by which time he had notched up more than 80 sorties.

55 RAF Pathfinders Archive

56 John de L. Wooldridge, *Low Attack: The Story of Two Mosquito Squadrons in World War Two* (Sampson Low, Marston & Co., 1946), p. 30

57 Ibid. p.29

58 Letter from Reg Reynolds dated October 20, 1995 in The RAF Pathfinders Archive.

CHAPTER FOUR

59 Von Paulus and his troops surrendered the next day.

60 Laddie Lucas, *Wings of War: Airmen of all nations tell their stories 1939–1945* (Grafton, 1985), p.230

61 Ibid. p.231

62 Bowyer, *2 Group RAF*, p.288

63 Lucas, *Wings of War*, p.231

64 Ibid.

65 Wooldridge, *Low Attack*, pp.40–41

66 A Belgium iron, steel and manufacturing company that could trace its roots back to an Englishman, John Cockerill, whose family had been established in the region for almost 150 years. From its inception in 1817, the complex in Liège had expanded to include a coke-fired blast furnace and facilities for steam engines, railway locomotives, steam-powered blowers for blast furnaces and traction engines.

67 Wooldridge, *Low Attack*, pp.88–91

68   Ted's logbook in the Hendon Archive MF10073/1-5

69   Operation Oyster led to the loss of nine Venturas, four Bostons and a Mosquito. More than 50 other aircraft were damaged, requiring the group to stand down for ten days. Tragically, 135 Dutch citizens were also killed.

70   The pilot (Flying Officer Onslow Thompson) and his navigator (Flying Officer Wallace Horne) had both been decorated. 'Tommy' Thompson is remembered in Edward Sniders' book *Flying In, Walking Out* as 'a tall and sweet-natured boy from his father's great sheep farm in New Zealand who sang lovely haunting Māori songs to his friends which we pressed him to sing over and over again'.

71   TNA, AIR 27/827 – No. 105 Squadron Operations Record Book (January 1943–December 1944)

CHAPTER FIVE

72   Martin W. Bowman, *RAF Marham: Bomber Station* (The History Press, 2008), p.117

73   TNA, AIR 27/960 – No. 139 Squadron Operations Record Book (June 1942–December 1943)

74   Wooldridge, *Low Attack*, pp.22–23

75   TNA, AIR 2/4974 – DECORATIONS, MEDALS, HONOURS AND AWARDS (Code B, 30): Immediate awards: operational

CHAPTER SIX

76   TNA, AIR 27/960

77   Sniders, *Flying In, Walking Out*, p.25

78   Letter in RAF Pathfinders Archive

79   Sir Basil Embry, *Mission Completed* (Methuen, 1957), p.242

80   John Sleigh Pudney, *Pride of Unicorns: Richard and David Atcherley of the RAF* (Oldbourne, 1960), p.184

81   Arthur Eyton-Jones, *Day Bomber* (Sutton, 1998), p.108

82   Christopher Shores, *2nd Tactical Air Force* (Osprey, 1970), p.1

83   Originally built for Edward Beevor, the MP for Arundel, the building was remarkable as being one of the first in the world to use steel girders in the supporting structure.

84   Eyton-Jones, *Day Bomber*, p.109

85   TNA, AIR 27/1935 – No. 487 Squadron (RNZAF): Operations Record Book

86   Eyton-Jones, *Day Bomber*, p.109

CHAPTER SEVEN

87   Jack Fishman, *And the Walls Came Tumbling Down* (Souvenir, 1982), p.95

88   Embry, *Mission Completed*, p.264

89   Maxwell Sparks in Chaz Bowyer's *Mosquito at War* (Ian Allan Publishing, 1973), pp.132–133

90   Remy, *The Gates Burst Open* (Arco Publishers, 1955), p.179

91   Embry, *Mission Completed*, p.264

CHAPTER EIGHT

92 Dudley Saward, *The Bombers' Eye* (Cassell, 1959), p.216

93 Remy, *The Gates Burst Open*. Philippe Livry-Level had fought in the First World War and became a resistance leader in the second before escaping to Britain via Spain. He flew with Coastal Command and the Moonshine squadrons, dropping agents and supplies into France. His time in the RAF in recorded in his book *Missions dans le RAF*, published in 1946.

CHAPTER NINE

94 Letter in The RAF Pathfinders Archive
95 Embry, *Mission Completed*, p.273
96 Letter in The RAF Pathfinders Archive
97 Embry, *Mission Completed*, p.276
98 Remy, *The Gates Burst Open*, p.95
99 Robin Reilly, *The Sixth Floor* (Frewin, 1969), p.91
100 Ibid. p.155
101 Embry, *Mission Completed*, p.277
102 Reilly, *The Sixth Floor*, p.159
103 Embry, *Mission Completed*, p. 277
104 He had himself taken over from Wing Commander Victor Oats who was lost a month after taking command.
105 Embry, *Mission Completed*, p.277
106 Embry, *Mission Completed*, p.279
107 Calgary Mosquito Society

CHAPTER TEN

108 *Cape Times* May 2, 1947
109 Ibid.
110 This was to be flown by Flight Lieutenants G. A. Hanson and A. E. Woods.
111 The letter is in the Hendon Archive. MF10073/1-5. Ulic Young Shannon, a Kiwi, won the DFC in 1945 with 10 Squadron when he was nearly 40. He'd commanded 30 Squadron in Iraq, Egypt and Greece between 1938 to 1941.
112 Frank Griffiths spent some of the war with a special duties squadron where he was engaged in parachuting agents and supplies for SOE to resistance units in the occupied territories of Europe. Of his nine months with the squadron five were spent flying and four walking home via the Pyrenees after being shot down in eastern France.
113 Tubby Vielle was a long-range navigation specialist who lived to the age of 101.
114 *RAF Transport Command Review* No. 13, September 1946
115 The Civil Aviation Historical Society and Airways Museum
116 Thetford, *Aircraft of the Royal Air Force since 1918*, p.429

117 The last pilots to qualify for their wings on Harvards completed their course at 3FTS in March 1955.
118 Burnett, like Frank Griffiths, flew special duties operations after two tours in Main Force.
119 Thetford, *Aircraft of the Royal Air Force since 1918*, p.271
120 *The Guardian*, 'How the great storm of 1953 caused Britain's worst peacetime disaster' (January 31, 2013) https://www.theguardian.com/environment/interactive/2013/jan/31/uk-great-storm-flood-1953-interactive last accessed 11 July 2024
121 KentOnline, 'The night in 1953 when the North Sea flooded Sheerness, Whitstable, Herne Bay, Margate, Deal and many others' (January 31, 2023) https://www.kentonline.co.uk/kent/news/the-perfect-storm-that-left-kent-under-water-281328/ last accessed 11 July 2024
122 TNA, AIR 27/2704 – No. 85 Squadron Operations Record Book (January 1, 1951–December 31, 1955)
123 Ibid.
124 Horsley later retired as an air marshal.
125 As recounted in *Flypast* (January 2024) by Doug Gordon
126 The record was held for only three weeks; on September 26, a Supermarine Swift F4 flown by Mike Lithgow flew five mph faster.
127 TNA, AIR 27/2606 – No. 29 Squadron Operations Record Book (January 1, 1951–December 31, 1955)
128 Mike Shaw, *Twice Vertical: The History of No. 1 Squadron RAF* (Macdonald and Co., 1971), p.208
129 Aiken had served with 611 Squadron in North-West Europe and later with 548 Squadron in the Far East. Prior to taking up his post he was Personal Staff Officer to the AOC at Fighter Command.
130 William Arthur Waterton, *The Quick and the Dead* (Grub Street, 2012), p.212
131 Ibid.
132 The DH110 did later enter service as the Sea Vixen.
133 John Gard'ner was a New Zealander who had flown Defiants in the Battle of Britain and who survived being shot down in the Channel.
134 Street, a former Fleet Air Arm officer who had won the Distinguished Service Cross in the Pacific, would receive the Queen's Commendation for Valuable Services in the Air for his work with the JMTU, and later the AFC.
135 Nos. 23, 25, 33, 64, 87, 89, 141, 151, 235 Squadrons were all visited by the JMTU during Ted's time in charge.
136 TNA, AIR 29/2809 – Operational Conversion Unit: No. 228 OCU, Leeming
137 Christopher Shores and Clive Williams, *Aces High* (Grub Street, 1994), p.585
138 *Flypast* (October 2017) Tom Docherty, (https://www.key.aero/article/flying-javelin)
139 The T3 had first flown on August 10, 1956.
140 Richard Martin OBE, DFC & Bar, AFC.
141 The Higgs/Vigar Tapes. Peter Varley had learned to fly in America and fought in the Far East with 89 Squadron on night-fighter Beaufighters and Mosquitoes. He joined Glosters

in 1955 as assistant to the chief test pilot Dickie Martin who had been his commander when he was with the aero flight at the Royal Aircraft Establishment in Farnborough.

142   Steve Bond, *Javelin Boys* (Grub Street, 2014), pp.69–70
143   Bond, *Javelin Boys,* p.83
144   It is now a De Vere luxury hotel.
145   E. E. Vielle, *Almost a boffin: The memoirs of Group Captain E. E. Vielle, OBE, RAF (Rtd)* (Dolman Scott 2013), p.286
146   Imperial War Museum, 'A Short History of the Aden Emergency', https://www.iwm.org.uk/history/a-short-history-of-the-aden-emergency accessed July, 11 2024
147   Air Chief Marshal Sir David Lee – quoted in *RAF Historical Society Journal 18*
148   The first British Unified Command came into being in October 1959 as British Forces Arabian Peninsula.
149   Author interview with Al Greethurst, former 8 Squadron navigator in Aden, September 26, 2018
150   Sir Hubert Patch was in office between September 1959 and August 1960 and was superseded by Sir Charles Elworthy.
151   As described by Group Captain Min Larkin.
152   Mitchell and Feast, *Churchill's Navigator.* John Mitchell was assistant air attaché in Washington.

CHAPTER ELEVEN

153   Chaz Bowyer, *History of the RAF* (Hamlyn, 1977), p.201
154   *Royal Air Force in Germany 1945–1993*, RAF Historical Society, p.33
155   Roland Beamont, *Phoenix into Ashes* (William Kimber, 1968), p.104
156   Michael Turner, *Royal Air Force: The Aircraft in Service since 1918* (Hamlyn, 1981)
157   *The Royal Air Force in Germany 1945 – 1993*, RAF Historical Society, p.33
158   Spooner, *Clean Sweep*, p.201
159   Aviation Safety Network, https://asn.flightsafety.org/wikibase/152443, accessed July 11, 2024
160   Ibid.
161   Kinloss Mountain Rescue Team Incident Report: https://rafmountainrescue.com/wp-content/uploads/19660202-KMRT-REPORT-A-2-Feb-66-Canberra-crash.pdf, accessed July 11, 2024
162   A category of instrument approach.
163   Kinloss Mountain Rescue Team Incident Report
164   Later air commodore
165   Furnerama – reminiscences of Jack Furner, last AOC of the CRE, , http://www.furnerama.com/jack-furner/, accessed July 11, 2024
166   Young, a South African, had fought with the Air Component of the British Expeditionary Force in France and was shot down on May 16, 1940 while flying a Hurricane with 615 Squadron. He bailed out, badly burned, and was shot up by his own side, adding insult

to painful injury. He didn't return to flying for almost two years. Since the war he'd held a number of senior positions, including OC of 232 OCU at RAF Gaydon converting crews to Valiants.

167   Science Museum Group website and *Air Clues*, Vol. 20 No. 10, July 1966

168   Furnerama – reminiscences of Jack Furner, last AOC of the CRE

169   Humphrey Wynn, *The Bomber Role 1945–1970* (Air Historical Branch, 1984)

170   Report on Operation Web by E. B. Sismore in TNA, AIR 29/4052 – Central Reconnaissance Establishment RAF Wyton. With appendices

171   Ibid.

172   Furnerama – reminiscences of Jack Furner, last AOC of the CRE

173   The establishment was disbanded on October 1, 1970.

174   Orrock had flown Beaufighters in the Mediterranean and North Africa before converting to the Mosquito. He was shot down leading a strike force to Norway in March 1945, spending the remainder of the war as a PoW.

CHAPTER TWELVE

175   Marconi Radar, https://marconiradarhistory.pbworks.com/w/page/29024389/MARCONI%20RADAR, accessed July 11, 2024

176   Ian Gillis. Ian was the Display Console Requirement Authority for UKADGE.

177   Marconi Radar

178   Ibid.

179   Ibid.

180   Ibid.

181   Ibid.

182   Ibid.

183   A full account of Operation Fingent is given in Rowland White's *Harrier 809* (Bantam Press, 2000).

184   Barnes retired in 2021 after 16 years as CEO of the Farnborough Aerospace Consortium.

185   Later Air Chief Marshal Sir David Harcourt-Smith.

186   As detailed in TNA, DEFE 71/1065 – Surface Wave Over the Horizon Radar for the Falkland Islands

187   Ibid.

188   Letter April 3, 2012

189   Letter April 11, 2012

190   Correspondence with author March 2024.

191   Letter to Martin Sismore from Graham Warner April 14, 2012.

192   Letter in The RAF Pathfinders Archive

193   Spooner, *Clean Sweep*, p13.

INDEX

Aarhus, Denmark 115–16, 122, 126
Addis Ababa, Ethiopia 162
Aden 161–2
Aeroplane and Armament Experimental Establishment (A&AEE) 158
Armstrong Whitworth Whitley 48, 50–2
Atcherley, David 89–91

Bateson, Bob 'Pinpoint' 125, 128–31, 133–4
Battle of the Atlantic 25
Beamont, Roland 166
Bennett, Donald 86–7, 90, 91
Bennike, Vagn 117
Berlin 48, 54, 63, 76
1943 raid 64–71, 84
Boeing B-17 Flying Fortress 93, 138, 177
Bomber Command 19, 20, 23, 25, 37, 48–9, 51, 71, 83, 85, 87, 90, 147, 164, 172, 173, 175
  changes in aircraft 49
  raids 19, 50, 64
  tactics 49
Bremen 50, 51, 55, 60, 69, 88
Bristol Blenheim 16–22, 24, 26, 27–33, 37–44, 47, 54, 56, 59, 60, 91, 189, 197 n16, 198 n35
Britannia Trophy 137, 142

Broom, Ivor 165, 188–9

Cape Town, South Africa 137, 138, 141–2
Central Reconnaissance Establishment (CRE) 171–7
Clapham, Peter 91, 126, 129
Coningham, Arthur 'Mary' 93, 97, 99, 102, 123
Copenhagen, Denmark 115, 126–8
Crew, Edward 175

Dale, Ivor 'Daddy' 101, 119, 125–6
De Havilland aircraft:
  DH9 18–19
  DH110 153–4, 202 n132
  Mosquito 52–4, 55, 58–60, 66, 71, 73, 82, 87, 91, 93, 100–1, 105, 110, 112, 138–9, 199 n50
Derry, John 154
Dimbleby, Richard 110
Duke, Neville 149
Düsseldorf, Germany 23, 51, 87, 108

Edwards, Hughie 55, 60, 72
El Adem, Libya 138–40, 142
Embry, Basil 90–1, 94–7, 99–103, 105, 111, 113, 117–19, 123, 127–31, 133, 136
  command of 2 Group 90, 93

'Wing Commander Smith' alias 91, 96, 118, 133
English Electric Canberra 147, 150, 165–6, 168, 174
   accidents in RAF service 169–70
   B.2 165
   B(I)6 165, 166
   PR.7 165, 166–7
   T.4 165
Exercises:
   Ardent 146
   Dividend 150
   Howler 174–5
   Mick/Mickey Finn 174–5
   Momentum 149
   Mop Up 174
   Wicked Lady 173
   Window Box 149
Eyton-Jones, Arthur 96–7

Gayford, Oswald 30
GEC Marconi 172, 179, 184–7, 189
   Marconi Radar Systems Limited (MRSL) 180–3
   reorganisation 187
Gee-H 108
Gericke, Donovan 'Don' 21, 22, 24–6, 197 n21
Giddings, Michael 174–5
Gillis, Ian 180, 204 n176
Gloster Javelin 153–61
   Air Ministry Specification F.4/48 153
   entering RAF service 155, 157
   FAW5 156–7
   FAW7 157
   prototypes:
      WD804 153
      WD808 154
   T3 158–9, 202 n139
Gloster Meteor 145–9, 151, 152, 163
   F3 145
   NF11 146, 148
   T7 145–6

Gravesend, Kent 109
Griffiths, Frank 143, 201 n112

Hamburg, Germany 20, 25, 51, 54, 66, 87, 88
Handley Page Victor 164–5, 172, 173–4, 176
   B/SRIII 173
Harris, Sir Arthur 49–50, 54, 65, 85–8, 90
Henry, Cyril 15–18, 21, 29

Iredale, 'Bob' 101, 126, 129, 132

Jena, Germany 76, 82, 83, 84, 90
Joint Air Reconnaissance Intelligence Centre (JARIC) 171–2

Kisumu, Kenya 138, 140, 142
Kyle, Wallace 'Digger' 47–8, 55, 60, 64–6, 69, 70, 108, 172, 175

Latham, Colin 182, 187
Light Night Striking Force (LNSF) 87–9
Livry-Level, Philippe 110, 125, 201 n93
Lloyd, Hugh Pughe 30, 36–7, 42, 43

Malta 34, 35–7, 40, 42, 44, 45, 156, 172, 173
   shipping operations 37, 40–4
Martin, Mick 138, 143, 152, 161
   London to Cape Town flight 139–42
Matthews, Alan 'Matty' 181–2
Miles Magister 11
Mitchell, John 13–14, 23, 203 n152

Navigation:
   introduction of Gee 49, 110, 118
   introduction of Oboe 86–7, 110
   LORAN 126
North Sea flood of 1953 147

Odense, Denmark 126, 132–5
Operations:
   Bulbasket 111
   Carthage 129–31
   Circus 30–4
      losses 32
   Floodlight 147

Gomorrah 88
Jericho 102, 106

Parry, George 55
Passmore, Richard 22
Pathfinder Force (PFF) 85–90
Patterson, Charles 94, 96, 97
Pattinson, William 15–16, 18, 21
Perry, Ken 183, 188
Pickard, Percy 'Pick' 91–2, 96–7, 101, 104–6
Pollard, A. M. 146, 148

radar systems:
  Skywave 183–4, 186
  Surface Wave 183–6, 188
RAF squadrons and units:
  1 Air Observers Navigation School (1AONS) 12
  1 Squadron 152
  2 Group 19, 22, 25, 27, 30, 37, 53, 55, 72, 74, 85, 87, 90–1, 93, 94, 97, 99, 104, 108, 111
    aircraft 90–1
    losses during raids 27
    raids on German targets 30
  8 Group 85–7, 89, 90
    aircraft 90
  9 Bombing and Gunnery School 12
  13 OTU 46, 47
  17 OTU 14–15, 18
  21 Squadron 33, 37, 92, 96, 97, 100, 101, 107, 111–12, 113, 119, 129, 133
  24 OTU 48
  29 Squadron 148, 150, 152–3, 165
  34 Squadron 152
  47 Group 138
  80 Squadron 165, 169
  82 Squadron 31, 37, 64, 197 n16
  85 Squadron 146–7
  105 Squadron 33, 53, 56, 58, 60, 64, 71, 75, 77, 82, 85, 87, 107, 199 n54
  107 Squadron 18, 19, 32, 56, 90, 119
  109 Squadron 86, 87
  110 (Hyderabad) Squadron 18–20, 24, 27, 31–3, 37, 38, 55, 197 n16
  114 Squadron 16, 18, 27
  139 Squadron 47, 53, 58, 59, 60, 62, 64, 65, 69, 70–1, 75, 77, 83, 85, 87, 89
  140 Wing 92, 95, 100, 106, 107, 109, 110–12, 114, 118, 119, 125, 126, 128, 133, 148
  206 Advanced Flying School 144
  213 Squadron 165, 167, 168, 169
  228 OCU 146, 155
  231 OCU 165
  1655 Mosquito Training Unit 57–8
  Javelin Mobile Training Unit (JMTU) 155–6, 202 n134–5
RAF stations:
  Acklington 146, 149
  Bassingbourn 56, 139, 142, 165, 171, 172
  Brampton 171–2
  Brüggen 175, 165, 167–70
  Honeybourne 48, 51, 53
  Horsham St Faith 21
  Leeming 146, 153, 156, 157–61, 164
  Marham 53–5, 61, 64, 66, 69, 70, 73, 87, 94, 175
  Sculthorpe 92–5
  Steamer Point 162
  Swanton Morley 32, 53, 107, 118–19, 122
  Thorney Island 109, 112, 119
  Upwood 14–15
  Wattisham 18, 19, 21, 29, 30, 31, 34, 38, 46, 56, 164
  Wyton 87, 89, 171, 173, 176
Ralston, Roy 55–6, 114
Republic P-47 Thunderbolt 93
Resistance movement 98, 201 n112
  Danish Resistance 116–17, 126, 132
  French Resistance 99–100, 103
Reynolds, Reg 53–62, 74, 76, 107, 117–19
  conversion onto Mosquito 57–8
  DSO award 70
    bar to DSO 84

DFC award 54
operations with Ted Sismore 60–2, 64–8, 71, 74, 77–82, 88–9, 109, 111, 113, 120–2, 124–5, 190
posting to 10 OTU 89
promotion to wing commander 75
rejection of wartime memoir 190
Rosières-en-Santerre, France 132
Royal Air Force Volunteer Reserve (RAFVR) 10
Royal Observer Corps (ROC) 177–8

Second Tactical Air Force 90, 93
Selassie, Haile 162
Shell House 126–8, 133, 136
Shipley, Eric 89
Sismore, Edward 'Ted':
attendance of the Day Fighter Leader School (DFLS) 151
attendance of RAF Staff College 152
award of Air Force Cross 153
award of DFC 70, 76
receiving bar to DFC 124
award of DSO 84
award of flying badge 144
becoming a pilot 144–6
command of 29 Squadron 148–53
death 190
decision to join RAF 10
early life 8–10
final appointment in the RAF 178
flying with Bob Bateson 129–31
flying with Basil Embry 94–5, 96–7
introduction to Mosquito aircraft 52, 57–8
learning to fly Meteor aircraft 145–6
life after the RAF 179–90
London to Cape Town flight 138–41
meeting Reg Reynolds 53
missing D-Day 110

operations against the Gestapo 115–35
operations with Reg Reynolds 60–2, 64–8, 71, 74, 77–82, 88–9, 109, 111, 113, 120–2, 124–5, 190
passion for golf 168, 188–9
posted overseas 37–46, 161–3, 165–71
promotion to air commodore 177
promotion to squadron navigation officer 75
qualifying as air observer/navigator 12–18
role as air attaché 162
role as SASO 171–7
role as station commander 165, 169–71
time at Air Ministry 143–4
time at GEC Marconi 179–88
time in Malta 40–5
Sismore family:
Fiona 153
Martin 152–3, 168
Rita 152, 188–9
SS *Torrey Canyon* 174
Staton Air Cdre Bill 'Crack'em' 141–2
Stevenson, Donald 25, 27
Sutcliffe, Philip 20, 31, 196–7 n16

Thomas, Lew 121–2
Thompson, John 'Tommy' 156
Tonkin, John 111, 113
Transport Command 138, 143

Vielle, Eugene 'Tubby' 143, 201 n113

Waterton, William Arthur 153–4
Weinstock, Arnold 186–7
Window (weapon) 88
Woodham Walter, Essex 188
Wooldridge, John 'Dim' 72, 83
Wykeham-Barnes, Peter 112, 114, 117, 121–2, 123, 125

Young, Brian 171, 172, 174, 204 n166